Bible Stories Revisited

Bible Stories Revisited

Discover Your Story in the
Old Testament

MACRINA SCOTT, O.S.F.

ST. ANTHONY MESSENGER PRESS
Cincinnati, Ohio

Nihil Obstat: Rev. Timothy P. Schehr
Rev. Hilarion Kistner, O.F.M.

Imprimi Potest: Rev. John Bok, O.F.M.
Minister Provincial
Archdiocese of Cincinnati

Imprimatur: † Most Rev. Carl K. Moeddel, V.G.
Archdiocese of Cincinnati
June 24, 1999

The *nihil obstat* and *imprimatur* are a declaration that a book or pamphlet is considered to be free from doctrinal or moral error. It is not implied that those who have granted the *nihil obstat* and *imprimatur* agree with the contents, opinions or statements expressed.

Scripture citations are taken from the *New Revised Standard Version Bible,* copyright ©1989 by the Division of Christian Education of the National Council of Churches of Christ in the U.S.A., and used by permission.

Cover and book design by Constance Wolfer
Electronic format and pagination by Sandy L. Digman

ISBN 0-86716-314-3

Published by St. Anthony Messenger Press
Printed in the U.S.A.

Acknowledgments

THIS BOOK WOULD NEVER HAVE BEEN STARTED without the help of many friends: Rev. Gerard P. Weber, who encouraged me to pursue my vision of a book about the Bible for mature Catholics; Lisa Biedenbach of St. Anthony Messenger Press, who accepted my proposal and supported me throughout the writing process; my community, the Sisters of St. Francis of Marycrest in Denver, who permitted me to take a five-month sabbatical to write the book; and the staff of the Catholic Biblical School of the Archdiocese of Denver, who encouraged me by their confidence and covered for me during my absence.

The Sisters of St. Benedict of St. Joseph, Minnesota, provided an ideal place for writing, Studium. While I worked there, Madeleine Beaumont, Nancy McDarby and Sister Katherine Howard, O.S.B., read the manuscript and provided many helpful suggestions.

When I returned to Denver, 110 wonderful seniors gathered to participate in a pilot program. Their warm response reassured me, and their suggestions led to many improvements, especially in the discussion questions. They composed the prayers found at the end of each chapter.

Graduates of the Catholic Biblical School assisted me in teaching and evaluating the pilot program. Angeline Hubert carefully edited the revised version.

Contents

1   Introduction

4   Hints for Facilitators

7   CHAPTER ONE:
Abraham, Father of Our Faith

15   CHAPTER TWO:
Family and Friends of Abraham

25   CHAPTER THREE:
Hagar and Sarah

37   CHAPTER FOUR:
Near-Death and Death

47   CHAPTER FIVE:
Rebekah and the Twins

59   CHAPTER SIX:
The Young Joseph

71   CHAPTER SEVEN:
The Mature Joseph and His Father

83   CHAPTER EIGHT:
Moses: The First Eighty Years

95   CHAPTER NINE:
Liberation

107   CHAPTER TEN:
Education in the Desert

119   CHAPTER ELEVEN:
The End of Moses' Journey

131   CHAPTER TWELVE:
The Book of Naomi

143   CHAPTER THIRTEEN:
Hannah and Her Son

155   CHAPTER FOURTEEN:
Samuel the Kingmaker

167   CHAPTER FIFTEEN:
David the Outlaw

179   CHAPTER SIXTEEN:
David the King

191   CHAPTER SEVENTEEN:
The Decline of David

203   CHAPTER EIGHTEEN:
King Solomon

215   CHAPTER NINETEEN:
Jeremiah: A Prophet Who Failed

227   CHAPTER TWENTY:
The Widow Judith

239   CHAPTER TWENTY-ONE:
Tobit: Touched by an Angel

253   CHAPTER TWENTY-TWO:
The Patience of Job?

265   CHAPTER TWENTY-THREE:
The Agony of Job

277   CHAPTER TWENTY-FOUR:
God Speaks to Job

291   Suggestions for Further Reading

Introduction

MANY OF US LEARNED BIBLE STORIES as children. When we revisit them later in life we bring a rich treasure of experience that gives a depth and meaning to the stories far beyond what we could have imagined as children. At the same time, the biblical stories help us to appreciate and share stories from our own lives.

I was motivated to write this book by my excitement over one of the new phenomena of our times: large numbers of people who live many healthy years after completing their responsibilities to children and careers. These "extra" years, so rare in the past, now provide new opportunities for learning and spiritual growth. Retired people are free to pursue the inner journey in a way that was not possible while they were burdened with the demands of the earlier phases of life. However, because the pressures of the previous years often prevented them from acquiring the tools needed for inner work, this rich opportunity may be lost. This book aims to provide one of these tools: the ability to use the Scriptures as a way of reflecting on one's life.

What This Book Includes

— Old Testament stories, with reflections based on both modern scholarship and my own experiences. The reflections aim to prime the pump of each participant's experience.

— Questions to enable the reader to reflect on the stories in the light of her or his own experience. These are not questions with right or wrong answers. It has been said that the way human beings learn is by taking two stories and placing them one on top of the other. When we place our story on top of the biblical story, we learn more about both.

1

— Prayers written by seniors who participated in a pilot program. These can serve as guides to praying with the Scriptures.

What This Book Does **Not** Include

— Clear, simple answers to life's problems. In these Bible stories, God gives us help to reflect on life, not clear-cut answers.

— The information discovered by scholars about who wrote these stories and when, the cultural background of the stories, why translations sometimes differ and to what extent the stories are based on historical facts. These questions require a much bigger book than this one.

— The entire story of any biblical character. Only highlights have been selected. Other passages are suggested for further reading for those motivated to go beyond what is in the lesson.

Who Can Use This Book?

Bible Stories Revisited is suitable for those with or without biblical background. It bypasses the issues dealt with in academic biblical study to focus on practical applications of the biblical stories to the events and insights of ordinary experience.

Aging is one of the key issues explored in this book. People of any age who are willing to reflect on the aging process will find this book helpful and enlightening. Individuals of any age who choose to avoid reflection on aging will not be comfortable with this book.

Ways to Use This Book

1. In a group, ideally of four to eight persons. This could be a group of friends, a parish group, a group in a senior cen-

ter or a bridge club that wants to do something different for a while.

The questions provide an opportunity for participants to share their own experiences, which enriches all participants and brings the stories to life even for those who have not personally experienced anything like what happened in a particular story.

The chapter can be read aloud if there are good readers in the group. One person should read the commentary and another the Scripture quotations in order to emphasize the distinction between the two. It is important for readers to prepare, as the quality of the reading can make or break the session. A group may choose several readers for a Scripture passage, each taking a different part. If the members prefer, or if no skilled readers are available, the meeting can begin with quiet time during which each one reads the chapter silently.

The opening prayer (found on page 6) is best read by all together. The concluding prayer (found at the end of each chapter) can be read at the end of the discussion either by one reader or by all together. Some groups may want to add prayers for particular intentions or a hymn such as "Come, Holy Spirit."

It is important to name a facilitator. The role of the facilitator is not to teach but to encourage all participants to share experiences related to the biblical story. If the facilitator has biblical training, he or she may also answer any questions members raise about the scriptural story, but this should not take more than a few minutes. "Hints for Facilitators" can be found on page 4.

Each session will probably take about seventy-five minutes: thirty-five for reading aloud and forty for discussion and prayer. Some groups may want a longer discussion, but it is important to set the schedule in advance and stick to it. Other groups may want a shorter session, perhaps in connection with another activity. They can use half a chapter, stopping both reading and discussion at the point marked ⎯⎯.

2. As a couple. Two friends or a married couple can read and discuss together, in much the same way as a group.

3. Alone. The book can simply be read through, but will have greater value if the reader pauses to reflect on the questions or uses them for journaling.

Miscellaneous Items

The first chapter is shorter, to allow time for the group to get acquainted and tend to any organizational matters that need to be addressed.

Each chapter can stand alone. A group might use a single chapter as part of a meeting, or do a series of four, six, eight, twelve or twenty-four chapters.

I am indebted to authors and teachers of Scripture who have cast light on God's word for me over the past fifty years. Their insights have become so much part of me that I can no longer trace my ideas to their sources, nor does the format of this book permit it.

The translation used here is the *New Revised Standard Version*. It capitalizes the word LORD whenever this translates the Hebrew proper name for God, Yahweh.

Hints for Facilitators

1. Start and end the discussion on time. Expect resistance on this from some in the group, but know that others will not return if you allow talkers to keep you from the subject at the beginning or keep you overtime at the end.

2. Ask participants to introduce themselves at the beginning and make a point of calling each one by name.

3. Keep the discussion focused on the discussion questions or on the lecture just heard. Gently lead it back when necessary by repeating or rewording the question and asking if any who have not spoken would like to respond to it.

4. Move the discussion to the next question when the group

seems to have done what it can with the present question. Do not feel pressured to complete all the questions.

5. Be a model of courteous listening. Keep eye contact with the person speaking and never allow yourself to be pulled into a side conversation.

6. Take responsibility for making your group as physically comfortable as possible. See that participants are seated in the way that makes it easiest to hear each other. If some are hard of hearing, ask others to speak distinctly.

7. Encourage those who find it difficult to talk, but do not force them. Do not allow others to interrupt them when they do try to speak. The person interrupting may not have heard the person speaking. You might say gently but firmly, "Excuse me, but Alice was saying something and I want to hear the rest of it."

8. Avoid making any lengthy contribution of your own unless it is the only way to get the group started. Your role is to empower others to share.

9. Do not allow anyone to belittle the contribution of another. Affirm the diversity of experience and opinion in your group.

10. Do not fear silence. The introverts in your group need silent spaces to prepare to make their contributions.

Prayer

O loving God, you plant your word like seed in our hearts. Send your Holy Spirit to nourish this precious seed and make it bear fruit for your glory. This we ask through Jesus your Word Made Flesh. Amen.

CHAPTER ONE

Abraham,
Father of Our Faith

The Call of Abraham

ALL JEWS, CHRISTIANS AND MUSLIMS look to Abraham as the "father of our faith." This is well over two billion people today, more than half of the population of the world. Probably no one in history has fathered such a vast spiritual family.

We know about Abraham and his wife Sarah only from the Bible. Their story is told in chapters twelve through twenty-five of the Book of Genesis, the first book of the Bible. It is important to understand what kind of literature this is.

The story of Abraham is quite different from the first eleven chapters of the Bible, which told a story of cosmic beginnings: how the universe and human beings came to be. Chapter twelve tells the story of the beginnings of the Hebrew people. For the author, this was family history: the story of very-great-grandfather Abraham and grandmother Sarah, their son Isaac and his wife Rebekah, their sons Esau and Jacob, and the four wives and twelve sons of Jacob. This part of Scripture reminds me of a family scrapbook: much about weddings, births, funerals, family moves; some interesting tidbits about family members' eccentricities and moral lapses; emphasis on the manliness of the grandfathers and the beauty of the grandmothers.

These are family stories that have been lovingly retold and embellished in various versions for so many generations that a scientific historian would have a hard time figuring out exactly what happened. For example, the modern reader often wonders if the patriarchs actually lived to the extraordinary ages ascribed to them. Probably not, but we have to read the story as we have it and try to find its meaning for us. These chapters are not written to satisfy the curiosity of historians, but to give joy and a sense of continuity to members of the family.

This is very different from other books of the Bible that deal with the usual stuff of history: kings and wars and great empires. The focus here is on one rather ordinary man, Abraham, and his family. It is not a family that would ever make it into the history books of the times. But it is an important family for us who read the Bible because it is our family.

Abraham and Sarah were nomads. They lived much as Bedouin in the Middle East live today: in tents, surrounded by flocks that were their livelihood. Each time the flocks had eaten everything they could find in an area, Sarah took down the tent and they moved on. It is interesting that all Christians, Jews and Muslims look back to a nomad as a model for their spiritual journey. Though few of us live in tents, deep in our hearts we all sense that if we are faithful to God, our life will be a journey; we will not be allowed to settle down and build a house of concrete that will give us security. The call of God is always onward.

The first time we hear of God calling a particular person to a particular path is in Genesis 12, the famous story of the call of Abraham. We are told, with no preparation, that God spoke to Abraham. It is an amazing thing that the great God should speak to anyone. Why did God choose this elderly nomad? We are not told that Abraham was particularly virtuous or courageous or intelligent. We are not told that he was a prayerful person, a seeker of God. We are given no clue as to why God chose to speak to this one person out of all humanity. Perhaps the message is that we cannot know how God chooses friends. God may speak to any one of us, or to any one of our acquaintances!

What we do know about Abraham is that he was seventy-five years old at the time God first spoke to him. This is an important point to keep in mind as we read the story. Abraham and Sarah were not teenagers, with a natural yearning to seek new worlds to conquer. They were at a stage of life where they had put down roots. Nomads in their day did not move about at random, but according to a pattern that assured periodic contact with family and business connections that were important to them. The very way the call is given emphasizes how much they are leaving. "Go from your country *and* your kindred *and* your father's house" (Genesis 12:1). All three refer to the same thing, the extended support system that provided essential security and assistance. The repetition just emphasizes that at age seventy-five Abraham and Sarah were to leave everything behind.

We can compare them to a couple today leaving their own home, friends and neighbors, the familiar church and bank and grocery store and senior center, to move to a totally strange part of the country. Abraham and Sarah left everything behind to begin the great adventure of their lives. Perhaps we today are in a position to identify with them as generations before us could not. Today, for the first time in human history, large numbers of people reach seventy-five in good mental and physical health. These are not old folks who need to be taken care of, but vital people, rich in experience, ready to hear God's call to set out on the adventure of conscious aging, pioneering the way for future generations who, we hope, will have the same opportunity. Even today, people may awaken only in their later years to spiritual experience, to hearing the voice of God.

Abraham and Sarah had no children. They started on their journey accompanied only by their nephew and servants. In their society, unlike ours, grown sons would normally stay with their parents through their old age. There were no Social Security checks or IRA funds. In fact, the responsibility of the younger generation for the older was the only form of social security the society knew. To be childless was a disaster for the elderly.

Even from a spiritual point of view, childlessness was tragic. At the time of Abraham and Sarah, God had not yet revealed that human life continues after death, so people believed that they lived on only in their children. To die childless was to die absolutely, and ancient people dreaded this. So Abraham and Sarah, despite their wealth in flocks and gold, were objects of pity to all who knew them, even to their own servants.

Perhaps Abraham gained courage for the move from the memory of his own father Terah, who had led his family and flocks six hundred miles from Ur (in what is now Iraq) to Haran (near what is now the border between Turkey and Syria). Perhaps he remembered, or imagined, that his father's real goal had been far-off Canaan. Terah had been content to settle in the region of Haran, but Abraham was called to break away from Haran to continue the journey another five hundred miles to Canaan.

If he thought of his journey as a continuation of his father's, that was not much practical help. He and Sarah had no map, no Triptik, no hotel reservations for the journey. In a violent world where strangers were not always welcomed, they had no certainty that the Canaanites would allow them to live in their land.

Abraham's greatness is that, in spite of all his fears, he obeyed the call of God. God told him to leave everything and go to "a land that I *will* show you" (Genesis 12:1). He journeyed in blind faith, trusting God to show him the way and the place to settle.

Abraham is so great a figure in Christian spirituality because his call is the model of every call from God. We are called again and again to leave what is known, familiar, safe; to move into the unknown, strange and frightening. It is the call to the infant to leave the safe home of the womb to begin life in this world, and the call to the dying to leave this familiar world for a better, but unknown one. In between we experience the same kind of call so often: to leave home for the first day at school, to leave school for the world of work, to leave work for retirement, to leave our own home for other living arrangements, to leave old ideas for new, untried ones. We are children of Abraham, called by God. Though his story is set almost four thousand years ago, we recognize ourselves in it.

Read the story as the biblical writer tells it.

Terah took his son Abram and his grandson Lot son of Haran, and his daughter-in-law Sarai, his son Abram's wife, and they went out together from Ur of the Chaldeans to go into the land of Canaan; but when they came to Haran, they settled there. The days of Terah were two hundred five years; and Terah died in Haran.

Now the LORD said to Abram, "Go from your country and your kindred and your father's house to the land that I will show you. I will make of you a great nation, and I will bless you, and make your name great, so that you will be a blessing. I will bless those who bless you, and the one who curses you I will curse; and in you all the families of the earth shall be blessed."

So Abram went, as the LORD had told him; and Lot went with him. Abram was seventy-five years old when he departed from Haran. Abram took his wife Sarai and his brother's son Lot, and all the possessions that they had gathered, and the persons whom they had acquired in Haran; and they set forth to go to the land of Canaan. When they had come to the land of Canaan, Abram passed through the land to the place at Shechem, to the oak of Moreh. At that time the Canaanites were in the land. Then the LORD appeared to Abram, and said, "To your offspring I will give this land." So he built there an altar to the LORD, who had appeared to him. From there he moved on to the hill country on the east of Bethel, and pitched his tent, with Bethel on the west and Ai on the east; and there he built an altar to the LORD and invoked the name of the LORD.

Genesis 11:31—12:8

The Frailty of Abraham

WHEN ABRAHAM AND SARAH ARRIVED at Shechem in Canaan, God finally became more specific about the promise of land. "*This is the land*," said God. Abraham knew then that he was in the promised land, so he built an altar and thanked God for bringing him to it. He then began what seems to have been the chief occupation of the rest of his life, walking back and forth over this land that was to be his children's, checking it out.

The land was owned by the Canaanites; Abraham and Sarah could travel with their flocks only through the hilly area that was not good enough for farming, always keeping on friendly terms with the residents so that they would not be put out. If the natives had known with what possessive eyes he looked on their land, they would surely have done away with him. Abraham was discreet, but he knew he was home.

This "home" looked wonderful to the nomads Abraham and Sarah, but if you travel it today you may wonder why anyone would value it so much. It is a hilly, rocky land. When rain comes it is briefly green and beautiful. But rain is not to be taken for granted. Today Jews throughout the world in their official prayers pray for rain for Israel. When rain fails, famine quickly sets in.

No sooner do we read that Abraham and Sarah had found the promised land than we read that it was struck by famine. There was no longer grass in the uncultivated areas for their flocks. Eventually even their store of gold could not buy grain from the farmers, for their crops had failed. Then, like many others in their day and in ours, Abraham and Sarah crossed the border into the neighboring country. They moved to Egypt, where crops were irrigated from the Nile, so the people lived in abundance.

Egypt was one of the great nations of the ancient world, well organized under a powerful Pharaoh. Poor immigrants fleeing problems in their own lands were not always welcome. Abraham was an old man, and felt vulnerable in the strange and mighty land of Egypt.

He had an odd idea about how to protect himself. He felt that his wife Sarah was so beautiful that every man who saw her would desire her. Since she was over sixty-five at the time, we see that it is not only young women who are attractive to men! In a hierarchical society like Egypt, of course, it would be Pharaoh who would get such a beauty. No one could prevent Pharaoh from killing Abraham and taking his wife into the royal harem. On the other hand, if Abraham pretended that Sarah was his sister, Pharaoh would enter into marriage negotiations with him. In either case, Sarah would end up in Pharaoh's harem. But in the first, Abraham would end up dead. In the second, he would be not only alive, but rich, a favored brother-in-law of Pharaoh.

Abraham thought he could see clearly where his interests lay. He used his wife to buy his own safety and prosperity. The man of faith, in whom all the families of the earth are to be blessed, was not always a model of moral behavior. He was not even a model of good judgment. Fear made him imagine powerful Pharaoh as a thoroughly evil man. The story shows, to the contrary, that Pharaoh was a man of conscience and goodwill. Abraham was the cad. The aged nomad felt so vulnerable as he traveled into mighty Egypt that he fell into paranoia.

Read the Bible's account of the human weakness of our father Abraham.

> Now there was a famine in the land. So Abram went down to Egypt to reside there as an alien, for the famine was severe in the land. When he was about to enter Egypt, he said to his wife Sarai, "I know well that you are a woman beautiful in appearance; and when the Egyptians see you, they will say, 'This is his wife'; then they will kill me, but they will let you live. Say you are my sister, so that it may go well with me because of you, and that my life may be spared on your account." When Abram entered Egypt the Egyptians saw that the woman was very beautiful. When the officials of Pharaoh saw her, they praised her to Pharaoh. And the woman was taken into Pharaoh's house. And for her sake he dealt well with Abram; and he had sheep, oxen, male donkeys, male and female slaves, female donkeys, and camels.
>
> But the LORD afflicted Pharaoh and his house with great plagues because of Sarai, Abram's wife. So Pharaoh called Abram, and said, "What is this you have done to me? Why did you not tell me that she was your wife? Why did you say, 'She is my sister,' so that I took her for my wife? Now then, here is your wife, take her, and be gone."

Genesis 12:10-19

Questions for Reflection

1. The biblical author has collected stories from his family history that he wants preserved for future generations. What events from your family history would you like preserved for younger members of your family?

2. When have you felt called as Abraham did?

3. What is God calling you to leave now? To what new place are you being called?

4. When have you drawn strength for your journey from the memory of your parents' journey?

—◊—

5. What person of our times started a new venture in later life, as Abraham did?

6. Have you ever had the experience of being a stranger in a foreign land? How do you feel about immigrants like Abraham and Sarah who come to our country because of poverty in their own? Do you think they have reason to be frightened as Abraham was?

Suggestions for Further Reading

Genesis 15
Sirach 44:19-23
Psalm 105:1-15
Romans 4

Prayer

God of Abraham and Sarah and our God, too, thank you for calling us to walk with you and with all the companions you have given us for our journey. Continue to bless us with faith to hear you and confidence that your loving kindness supports us every step of the way. In Jesus' name we pray. Amen.

Jeanne M. Griffiths, 50, Denver, Colorado

CHAPTER TWO

Family and Friends of Abraham

Abraham and His Nephew

ABRAHAM HAD HAD A BROTHER NAMED HARAN who had died as a young man. Haran's son Lot lived with Abraham and Sarah, and came with them on the great adventure. However, in Genesis 13 we find that Lot had outgrown his dependent relationship with his uncle. His flocks and herds were so large that the sparse land of Canaan could not support both them and Abraham's flocks. Quarrels broke out between employees of Lot and employees of Abraham.

There may also be an unspoken issue here. Perhaps Lot was feeling a normal need for independence, to be his own person, free of the dominance of the older generation. Whatever the reasons, the time for separation had come. There are few families today that do not know the mixture of sadness and relief that comes at that moment.

Abraham, always a man of peace, took the initiative. He saw that the way to peace was separation. His terms were generous. He told Lot to go in whatever direction he pleased. The old man would take whatever the young man did not choose. Young people may need to have their hearts' desire, but mature people tend to be wiser and better able to adapt. Lot chose the lush plain around the Jordan river, leaving Abraham the dry hilly land of Canaan.

When Lot had left, God repeated to Abraham the promises of land and of a multitude of descendants. Perhaps the old man needed such encouragement as he prepared to live without the support of his young nephew. He and Sarah must have felt more painfully than ever the lack of a son of their own. It must have become increasingly hard to believe in the promise of a multitude of descendants.

Read the biblical author's account of the relationship between Abraham and his nephew Lot.

> Now Lot, who went with Abram, also had flocks and herds and tents, so that the land could not support both of them living together; for their possessions were so great that they could not live together, and there was strife between the herders of Abram's livestock and the herders of Lot's livestock....
>
> Then Abram said to Lot, "Let there be no strife between you and me, and between your herders and my herders; for we are kindred. Is not the whole land before you? Separate yourself from me. If you take the left hand, then I will go to the right; or if you take the right hand, then I will go to the left." Lot looked about him, and saw that the plain of the Jordan was well watered everywhere like the garden of the LORD, like the land of Egypt, in the direction of Zoar; this was before the LORD had destroyed Sodom and Gomorrah. So Lot chose for himself all the plain of the Jordan, and Lot journeyed eastward; thus they separated from each other. Abram settled in the land of Canaan, while Lot settled among the cities of the Plain and moved his tent as far as Sodom. Now the people of Sodom were wicked, great sinners against the LORD.
>
> The LORD said to Abram, after Lot had separated from him, "Raise your eyes now, and look from the place where you are, northward and southward and eastward and westward; for all the land that you see I will give to you and to your offspring forever. I will make your offspring like the dust of the earth; so that if one can count the dust of the earth, your offspring also can be counted. Rise up, walk through the length and the breadth of the land, for I will give it to you."
>
> *Genesis 13:5-17*

Abraham Rescues Lot

IN GENESIS 14 WE SEE THAT ABRAHAM DID NOT CEASE feeling responsible for his nephew who had moved away. He reminds me of parents today who take on all kinds of difficult responsibilities when their grown children, long gone from home, have problems.

Lot had moved to the city of Sodom. A great war arose in the area, with many kings lined up against each other. Reading this chapter reminds me of reading the newspapers in time of war. They are full of unpronounceable names of places I had never dreamed existed, but which have suddenly become important battlegrounds. The war was no business of Lot's, but, like so many helpless people, he became its victim. Abraham received a message that Lot had been taken prisoner and carried off by one of the armies.

This is a surprising chapter, in which the otherwise peaceful Abraham suddenly turns into a warrior. Many peaceful people can do the same to protect their own flesh and blood. Abraham, whom his family remembers as successful in all he does, wins a great victory, and rescues Lot and his family.

Read about Abraham the warrior.

In the days of King Amraphel of Shinar, King Arioch of Ellasar, King Chedorlaomer of Elam, and King Tidal of Goiim, these kings made war with King Bera of Sodom, King Birsha of Gomorrah, King Shinab of Admah, King Shemeber of Zeboiim, and the king of Bela (that is, Zoar). All these joined forces in the Valley of Siddim (that is, the Dead Sea). Twelve years they had served Chedorlaomer, but in the thirteenth year they rebelled. In the fourteenth year Chedorlaomer and the kings who were with him came and subdued the Rephaim in Ashteroth-karnaim, the Zuzim in Ham, the Emim in Shaveh-kiriathaim, and the Horites in the hill country of Seir.... Then the king of Sodom, the king of Gomorrah, the king of Admah, the king of Zeboiim, and the king of Bela (that is, Zoar) went out, and they joined battle in the Valley of Siddim with King Chedorlaomer of Elam, King Tidal of Goiim, King Amraphel of Shinar, and King Arioch of Ellasar, four kings against five. Now the Valley of Siddim was full of bitumen pits; and as the kings of Sodom and Gomorrah fled, some fell into them, and the rest fled to the hill country. So the enemy took all the goods of Sodom and Gomorrah, and all their provisions, and went their way; they also took Lot, the son of Abram's brother, who lived in Sodom, and his goods, and departed.

Then one who had escaped came and told Abram the Hebrew, who was living by the oaks of Mamre.... When Abram heard that his nephew had been taken captive, he led forth his trained men, born in his house, three hundred eighteen of them, and went in pursuit as far as Dan. He divided his forces against them by night, he and his servants, and routed them and pursued them to Hobah, north of Damascus. Then he brought back all the goods, and also brought back his nephew Lot with his goods, and the women and the people.

Genesis 14:1-16

Abraham's Hospitality

HOSPITALITY IS A HIGHLY VALUED VIRTUE among desert nomads, even today. In a land without roads or police or hotels, no traveler could survive in the desert without the help of those who live there. Generally, nomads take little interest in the wider world. Even today in Israel, they pay no taxes, and they ignore national borders. Their way of being open to the wider world is through hospitality. Real hospitality is universal. It is not offered only to those who are like us or to those we like, but to anyone who happens to arrive at our doorway. It is a sign of a heart open to all humanity.

In Genesis 18, Abraham is pictured as the perfect host. At midday the desert heat sends everyone to rest in the shade of the tent. It is then that Abraham, drowsing at the entrance of his tent, suddenly opens his eyes to see three strangers standing nearby. To one familiar with the slow, easy pace of the desert, the scene surprises by its jump into high speed. The aged Abraham runs to meet the strangers, bows down to the ground in reverence to them, and urgently begs them to accept his hospitality.

When they agree, he rushes into the tent, tells Sarah to hurry to make half a bushel of flour into bread, runs on to the herd, selects a fine tender calf and orders his servant to prepare it quickly. Nomads live mostly from the milk and wool their flocks produce; only on very special occasions do they kill one of their animals for meat. Abraham is a host of extraordinary generosity.

All this time Sarah, the proper Bedouin woman, remains hidden in the tent. We may think of tent living as informal, with the whole family crowded together. Actually, perhaps because they have no walls or locks to protect their women, in Bedouin encampments the sexes are strictly separated. Typically, a heavy curtain divides the tent into men's quarters and women's quarters, and men and women keep strictly to their sides. On the other hand, the curtain is no barrier to sound, so there is no such thing as a private conversation. Sarah does not appear before the male guests, but she hears all that they say.

After Abraham has served his guests with the banquet, one of them repeats the old promise of offspring for Abraham. This time the promise is more specific: At this season next year, in springtime, your wife Sarah will have a son. We are not surprised that ninety-year-old Sarah, listening from within the tent, laughs.

Read the story of the hospitality of Abraham and Sarah.

> The LORD appeared to Abraham by the oaks of Mamre, as he sat at the entrance of his tent in the heat of the day. He looked up and saw three men standing near him. When he saw them, he ran from the tent entrance to meet them, and bowed down to the ground. He said, "My lord, if I find favor with you, do not pass by your servant. Let a little water be brought, and wash your feet, and rest yourselves under the tree. Let me bring a little bread, that you may refresh yourselves, and after that you may pass on—since you have come to your servant." So they said, "Do as you

have said." And Abraham hastened into the tent to Sarah, and said, "Make ready quickly three measures of choice flour, knead it, and make cakes." Abraham ran to the herd, and took a calf, tender and good, and gave it to the servant, who hastened to prepare it. Then he took curds and milk and the calf that he had prepared, and set it before them; and he stood by them under the tree while they ate.

They said to him, "Where is your wife Sarah?" And he said, "There, in the tent." Then one said, "I will surely return to you in due season, and your wife Sarah shall have a son." And Sarah was listening at the tent entrance behind him. Now Abraham and Sarah were old, advanced in age; it had ceased to be with Sarah after the manner of women. So Sarah laughed to herself, saying, "After I have grown old, and my husband is old, shall I have pleasure?" The LORD said to Abraham, "Why did Sarah laugh, and say, 'Shall I indeed bear a child, now that I am old?' Is anything too wonderful for the LORD? At the set time I will return to you, in due season, and Sarah shall have a son." But Sarah denied, saying, "I did not laugh"; for she was afraid. He said, "Oh yes, you did laugh."

Genesis 18:1-15

Abraham's Prayer for Sodom

WHEN HIS GUESTS LEAVE, Abraham, still the model of hospitality, walks with them the first part of their journey. Only at this point in the conversation does it become clear that one of the guests is God. God, reflecting on his intimate relationship with Abraham, decides to reveal to Abraham the purpose of this journey. God has heard complaints about the wickedness of the city of Sodom, and has come down to investigate.

Abraham probably knows all about the wickedness of Sodom; he does not try to deny it. But he tries mightily to save the city from the destruction it deserves. Why is he so concerned? Surely he is concerned because his nephew Lot now lives in Sodom. But he does not pray only for Lot; he prays for the whole sinful city. Perhaps this story is suggesting to us that the elderly, who have experienced their own sinfulness and have outgrown the judgmental attitudes of youth, are the ones to intercede for sinners. They may have a role especially in situations of violence and addiction, which seem about to bring about wholesale destruction, like that of Sodom.

Abraham's method of prayer is delightful, and difficult to understand if you have no experience of the bargaining that is part of social life in the Middle East even today. Not having the knack of bargaining or the enthusiasm for it, when I travel in Israel I find shopping an ordeal. But the shopkeepers clearly expect and enjoy the customary haggling. The descendants of Abraham who wrote this story respected the skillful bargainer, and they were proud to say that their ancestor had bargained with God, and come out very well.

Abraham began, like every shopkeeper in Israel today, with flattery. God has such a reputation for justice; surely he will not endanger it by punishing the good with the bad. Only after the compliment comes the crucial step, the mention of a proposed number. Surely God would not destroy the whole city if fifty just people could be found in it? God agrees to the figure. So Abraham pushes further and further, until finally he has God down to ten. The rabbis comment that Abraham's mistake was to stop too soon. If he had had the courage to push God yet further, he could have saved the city for a single just person! (Christians know the rabbis were right. God has saved us all because of the one perfectly righteous person, Jesus.)

Abraham in this story is a great model for the prayer of intercession. It springs out of a great heart, concerned for all of humanity, even the least deserving. It also springs from a relationship with God so strong that one can even argue with God. It is a kind of argument that God loves.

Today the number of retired people in our society is becoming so great that there is danger that the young will come to resent the old as a burden too great to be supported. All people need to find appropriate ways in which they can contribute, can be givers and not just takers. We can get some ideas about ways in which seniors can contribute today from the hospitality of the aged Abraham and from his prayerful concern for his world.

Read the story of Abraham's prayer for Sodom.

Then the men set out from there, and they looked toward Sodom; and Abraham went with them to set them on their way. The Lord said, "Shall I hide from Abraham what I am about to do, seeing that Abraham shall become a great and mighty nation, and all the nations of the earth shall be blessed in him? No, for I have chosen him, that he may charge his children and his household after him to keep the way of the Lord by doing righteousness and justice; so that the Lord may bring about for Abraham what he has promised him." Then the Lord said, "How great is the outcry against Sodom and Gomorrah and how very grave their sin! I must go down and see whether they have done altogether according to the outcry that has come to me; and if not, I will know."

So the men turned from there, and went toward Sodom, while Abraham remained standing before the Lord. Then Abraham came near and said, "Will you indeed sweep away the righteous with the wicked? Suppose there are fifty righteous within the city; will you then sweep away the place and not forgive it for the fifty righteous who are in it? Far be it from you to do such a thing, to slay the righteous with the wicked, so that the righteous fare as the wicked! Far be that from you! Shall not the Judge of all the earth do what is just?" And the Lord said, "If I find at Sodom fifty righteous in the city, I will forgive the whole place for their sake." Abraham answered, "Let me take it upon myself to speak to the Lord, I who am but dust and ashes. Suppose five of the fifty righteous are lacking? Will you destroy the whole city for lack of five?" And he said, "I will not destroy it if I find forty-five there." Again he spoke to him, "Suppose forty are found there." He answered, "For the sake of forty I will not do it." Then he said, "Oh do not let the Lord be angry if I speak. Suppose thirty are found there." He answered, "I will not do it, if I find thirty there." He said, "Let me take it upon myself to speak to the Lord. Suppose twenty are found there." He answered, "For the sake of twenty I will not destroy it." Then he said, "Oh do not let the Lord be angry if I speak just once more. Suppose ten are found there." He answered, "For the sake of ten I will not destroy it." And the LORD went his way, when he had finished speaking to Abraham; and Abraham returned to his place.

Genesis 18:16-33

Questions for Reflection

1. What feelings surface when young adults, like Lot, move away from home?
2. Was Abraham right in going to war to rescue his nephew Lot? When, if ever, do you think war is justified?
3. Where in the world today are there people who, like Lot, are torn from their homes by war?
4. Do you think the loneliness of those who have no children grows greater or less as they age? How can others be of help to those who are alone in their old age?

—∿∿—

5. In what ways can older people today follow the example of Abraham's hospitality?
6. For whom do you think God wants you to pray as Abraham prayed for Sodom?

Suggestions for Further Reading

Genesis 13
Genesis 14
Genesis 17
Genesis 18
Genesis 19

Prayer

Lord, we thank you for the many gifts you give us and praise you for your knowledge and compassion concerning our needs. We ask that you grant us the wisdom shown by Abraham to recognize when our families and friends need their independence from us. May we also know when we are needed and be able to respond with Abraham's courage.

Lord, in Abraham you have given us a model of hospitality, a model of great faith and a wonderful model for prayer, especially in intercession. We know that you are able to do anything. We ask you to enter our hearts and fill them with the faith and compassion we need to be a people with the good qualities of Abraham.

We ask this of you through Jesus Christ, our Lord. Amen.

Sandra L. Durand, 57, Elbert, Colorado

CHAPTER THREE

Hagar and Sarah

Slave Girl and Mistress

THIS CHAPTER CONCERNS THE RELATIONSHIP between an old woman and a young woman, and includes a kind of preview of the relationship between their sons. This is women's business, and the mighty patriarch Abraham remains in the background, taking orders meekly from his wife.

To understand the story it is helpful to know that in biblical times the role of women was very different from what it is today. We easily say that women in these ancient cultures were oppressed because they had no place in public life. Biblical women and men themselves probably did not see it quite that way. They thought of life as divided into two spheres: the public and the private. The public was the domain of men; the private, the home, was the domain of women. The home was extremely important in this family-centered culture, so the power of the woman in her domain was not to be taken lightly.

Once when travelling through the desert area of Israel, I wanted to visit one of the Bedouin tents we occasionally passed. We stopped the bus and our guide, an Arab, went up to talk with the Bedouin to see if they would welcome us. He returned, saying, "There are only two people there now: a man and a woman. He does not want us to come, but she does." I did not want to go under such circumstances, but the guide assured me it was quite all right, as long as we did not take pictures outside the tent. We walked up, rather nervously. The man glowered at us, but said nothing. A wrinkled old woman welcomed us with a broad toothless smile. She held open the flap of her tent and gestured politely for us to enter. There was no furniture in the tent, but, with the graciousness of a queen, she spread mats on the floor and invited us to sit on them. She then danced for our entertainment, accompanying herself with her own singing. When we asked if we might take pictures, she agreed enthusiastically, and she brought in her two lovely young daughters to pose for us also. When we left, the three of them waved us off like old friends. The man was nowhere to be seen.

I did not understand this incident until long after when I heard from someone learned in the cultural approach to Scripture that everything inside the tent is the domain of the woman. She does not have to ask her husband's permission to have guests in her tent. But once outside the tent, we could not take pictures without his consent. This incident has provided me with background for understanding the story of Sarah and Hagar, and other stories of women in Genesis.

Sarah is an old woman who has been trying all her life to bear a child, but is unable to do so. Childlessness is a great suffering for many couples today, but it was immeasurably worse in Sarah's time. Children were the only way a couple could expect to be provided for in their old age, and the only way they expected to live on after death. For a woman, bearing children was her whole reason for being. To fail at this was to fail completely. So Sarah, even though wealthy and happily married, was a tragic figure.

God had promised Abraham a multitude of descendants. But it seemed to Sarah that God needed some help to bring this about. So, in desperation, she took advantage of a custom of the times. When a wife was unable to produce offspring for her husband, she sometimes designated one of her maidservants to take her place to bear a child for her husband. In fact, one ancient law code makes this the legal responsibility of the barren wife. Sarah sent Hagar to Abraham for this purpose, thinking that if Hagar bore a child it would belong to Sarah. Abraham did as Sarah asked, as he does throughout this story. His feelings are irrelevant. Sarah is the active character.

Not a word is said about Hagar's feelings either. No one speaks to her. No one calls her by name. Throughout the story, she is only "Sarah's servant."

The Egyptian slave Hagar becomes pregnant with Abraham's child. Suddenly everything changes. Up till now the old woman Sarah had all the power. She was a wealthy freewoman; the young Hagar was a slave, totally dependent on her mistress's whims. Now the young woman realizes that she has power of a different kind. The thing her mistress has yearned to do and been unable to do throughout her life Hagar has power to do: give Abraham an heir.

When the young first have the heady experience of power, they do not yet have the wisdom of age. It is only natural for them to look with contempt on the old who have ruled them for so long, but whom they now see not to be all-powerful. It is a rebellion that happens in every generation, but in the case of Hagar and Sarah it was particularly tragic.

Sarah, already humiliated by her long barrenness, smarted under the thinly disguised contempt of Hagar. She complained angrily to Abraham, perversely blaming him for doing precisely what she had asked him to do. This was women's business, and Abraham refused to be involved. Life within the tent was not his domain. He said, "She is your servant. Do what you like with her." Sarah then became the nasty old woman, making life so unbearable for Hagar that she ran away.

Read the story of young Hagar and her elderly mistress.

Now Sarai, Abram's wife, bore him no children. She had an Egyptian slave-girl whose name was Hagar, and Sarai said to Abram, "You see that the LORD has prevented me from bearing children; go in to my slave-girl; it may be that I shall obtain children by her." And Abram listened to the voice of Sarai. So, after Abram had lived ten years in the land of Canaan, Sarai, Abram's wife, took Hagar the Egyptian, her slave-girl, and gave her to her husband Abram as a wife. He went in to Hagar, and she conceived; and when she saw that she had conceived, she looked with contempt on her mistress. Then Sarai said to Abram, "May the wrong done to me be on you! I gave my slave-girl to your embrace, and when she saw that she had conceived, she looked on me with contempt. May the LORD judge

between you and me!" But Abram said to Sarai, "Your slave-
girl is in your power; do to her as you please." Then Sarai
dealt harshly with her, and she ran away from her.

Genesis 16:1-6

Hagar's Encounter with God

I HAVE TRAVELLED THROUGH THE STARK DESERT into which Hagar
ran. I am amazed at the courage of a pregnant teenager who
would try to walk through it alone. She stood little chance of
survival. But she set out in the direction of Egypt, dreaming
some impossible dream of finding a place in her homeland.

Unlike many runaway girls, she was fortunate. When she
stopped by a well to rest, an angel of God came to speak to
her. He was the first being in the story who spoke to her, and
the first who used her name. To Abraham and Sarah, she had
been simply a slave, not a person in her own right. Clearly, to
God she was someone special, because she is the first person
in the Bible to whom an angel is sent.

First, the angel listened to Hagar's tale of abuse. Up to this
point in the story, no one had given her the opportunity to
speak. Only after she had received the healing that comes
from being truly listened to did he give her advice. He told
her sternly to return to the abuse of Sarah. He did not suggest
that the situation would grow easier. But he changed the situation in a different way. He told her that God had heard her
story, an amazing message to a slave girl whose story so far
had been of interest to no one. He then made an extraordinary promise to this poor girl. He promised her a great son,
from whom a strong nation would be descended.

We are reminded of God's promise to Abraham. But in the
case of Abraham, the promise was made to the father. In the
case of this slave, used and abused by Abraham and Sarah, the
promise was made to the mother. She was to be the matri-
arch, powerful ancestor of a great nation. This is one of the
many parts of Scripture that show God's special love for the
poorest and most helpless.

The angel did not promise Hagar that life with nasty Sarah would be any easier. But he gave her a motive for endurance. He assured her that in the end her son would be worth all she would suffer. Motivation is everything in life. We can bear almost anything if we believe it is leading us to a goal we value enough. Hagar retraced her steps, no doubt to face a still more angry Sarah.

But the encounter with the angel by the well seems to have lifted this oppressed girl to another spiritual level. She does something no one else in the Bible dares to do; she gives God a name. She calls God "The God of Seeing." God has noticed her, and she is clearly full of awe at this unexpected grace. Hagar reminds us that intense experience of God can come to those who seem most unlikely because of their age, gender or place in society.

Read about Hagar's meeting with God's angel.

The angel of the LORD found her by a spring of water in the wilderness, the spring on the way to Shur. And he said, "Hagar, slave-girl of Sarai, where have you come from and where are you going?" She said, "I am running away from my mistress Sarai." The angel of the LORD said to her, "Return to your mistress, and submit to her." The angel of the LORD also said to her, "I will so greatly multiply your offspring that they cannot be counted for multitude." And the angel of the LORD said to her,

> "Now you have conceived and shall bear a son;
>   you shall call him Ishmael,
>   for the LORD has given heed to your affliction.
> He shall be a wild ass of a man,
> with his hand against everyone,
>   and everyone's hand against him;
> and he shall live at odds with all his kin."

So she named the LORD who spoke to her, "You are El-roi"; for she said, "Have I really seen God and remained alive after seeing him?" Therefore the well was called Beer-lahai-roi; it lies between Kadesh and Bered.

Hagar bore Abram a son; and Abram named his son,

whom Hagar bore, Ishmael. Abram was eighty-six years old when Hagar bore him Ishmael.

Genesis 16:7-16

—⁓—

Sarah the Matriarch

IN GENESIS 12 WE SAW THE WEAKNESS of our father Abraham, who gave his beautiful wife Sarah to Pharaoh to save his own skin. In chapters sixteen and eighteen we see the weakness of our mother Sarah, so jealous of Hagar she tried to kill her. The biblical authors do not turn our spiritual ancestors into plastic statues. They want us to see ourselves in them: chosen by God, yet sinful.

God's promise in chapter eighteen, when he visited Abraham and Sarah's tent, was that ninety-year-old Sarah would have a child in the coming springtime. Sarah laughed, but she soon ceased to laugh as she felt her miraculous pregnancy beginning. It is hard to imagine the astonishment and joy of this old couple who are finally receiving the gift for which they yearned for so many years, and for which they had long ago given up hope.

This is one of the high points of Scripture. In the New Testament, when Mary sings her song of wonder at her own miraculous pregnancy she remembers the promises made to her father Abraham and fulfilled contrary to all human possibility. The story of Sarah's giving birth to Isaac at ninety is a strong statement that the really important things are accomplished by God, and for God nothing is impossible. If Sarah can give birth at ninety, no one of us can claim that we are too old or poor or disabled to be God's instrument in accomplishing great things.

There was joy at the birth of Isaac, but infant death was so frequent in ancient times, that people often did not celebrate a birth till the child was weaned, a few years after birth. If it survived that long, its chances of living to adulthood were considered good. So at the weaning of Isaac, Abraham put on a great feast.

At this time of relief because the precious child seemed likely to survive, we see Sarah at her very worst. She had given Hagar to Abraham so that Hagar might bear a child that would build up Sarah. But things had turned out very differently.

At the weaning feast, when Sarah sees Ishmael playing with little Isaac she orders Abraham curtly, "Cast out this slave woman with *her* son; for the son of this slave woman will not inherit along with *my* son Isaac" (Genesis 21:10). She speaks as if she did not even know the names of Hagar or Ishmael. For her, they are now only a threat to the inheritance of her precious son Isaac.

As when he slept with Hagar to beget Ishmael, Abraham meekly obeys Sarah. Domestic arrangements, everything concerning household slaves and children, are in her domain. However, this time we do hear how Abraham feels about Sarah's decision. "The matter was very distressing to Abraham on account of his son" (Genesis 21:11). He could not save his son and Hagar from almost certain death. He knew that no one could survive long in the desert except in a caravan with tents, flocks and supplies. The poor best that Abraham could do was to give Hagar a leather container of water and some bread, and send her off early in the morning, before the sun was at its height.

Read the story of the birth of Isaac and its effect on Hagar and Ishmael.

> The LORD dealt with Sarah as he had said, and the LORD did for Sarah as he had promised. Sarah conceived and bore Abraham a son in his old age, at the time of which God had spoken to him. Abraham gave the name Isaac to his son whom Sarah bore him. And Abraham circumcised his son Isaac when he was eight days old, as God had commanded him. Abraham was a hundred years old when his son Isaac was born to him. Now Sarah said, "God has brought laughter for me; everyone who hears will laugh with me." And she said, "Who would ever have said to

Abraham that Sarah would nurse children? Yet I have borne him a son in his old age."

The child grew, and was weaned; and Abraham made a great feast on the day that Isaac was weaned. But Sarah saw the son of Hagar the Egyptian, whom she had borne to Abraham, playing with her son Isaac. So she said to Abraham, "Cast out this slave woman with her son; for the son of this slave woman shall not inherit along with my son Isaac." The matter was very distressing to Abraham on account of his son. But God said to Abraham, "Do not be distressed because of the boy and because of your slave woman; whatever Sarah says to you, do as she tells you, for it is through Isaac that offspring shall be named for you. As for the son of the slave woman, I will make a nation of him also, because he is your offspring." So Abraham rose early in the morning, and took bread and a skin of water, and gave it to Hagar, putting it on her shoulder, along with the child, and sent her away. And she departed, and wandered about in the wilderness of Beer-sheba.

Genesis 21:1-14

Survivors

HAGAR WAS NO LONGER A NAIVE TEENAGER trying to flee through the desert to a better place. She knew there was no way for her and her son to survive. When their water had run out, she left Ishmael in the "shade" of one of those sparse bushes that can only slightly lessen the awful power of the desert sun and walked on a short distance. She could not bear to watch the death of this son for whom she had already sacrificed so much. She wept. At this, the lowest point in her life, an angel again spoke to her.

Under the circumstances, the angel's words seem heartless and out of place. "What troubles you, Hagar? " (Genesis 21:17). Then God opens Hagar's eyes, and she sees a well of water. The well had probably been dug by nomads and then covered with a stone. It could easily be overlooked by anyone except those who had dug it. But it was there at her feet as she wept in despair. In the desert, water is life. This well is a sign that, contrary to all human expectations, this abandoned single mother and her child will survive in the desert. It will be a rough, hard life, and it will make them strong.

I think we can have experiences like Hagar's. We feel we are dying for lack of something we need. But the thing or person we need is there; we have not noticed them. We need God to open our eyes.

Through all the adventures of her life, Hagar never forgot her native land. She no longer imagined that there was a place for her in Egypt, but she obtained a wife for her grown son from there. In a society where the daughter-in-law moved into the tent of her mother-in-law, Hagar in her old age would finally have the company of a woman of her own land.

The author who wrote this story knew the descendants of Ishmael, the Ishmaelites, as enemies. It is interesting that he tells the story of their origins with respect. He shows God's tender care for Hagar and Ishmael. He is reminding his readers that their enemies are also their relatives, descendants of their great-uncle Ishmael.

One of the most moving experiences I had in Israel was near the tomb of Abraham in Hebron. Our Arab guide, a lively storyteller, was telling the story of Isaac and Ishmael from the point of view of the Arabs, traditional descendants of Ishmael. "Our father Abraham had two sons: an older son Ishmael and a younger son Isaac. The two of them together buried their father here in Hebron. Ishmael had twelve sons, from whom the Arabs are descended, and Isaac had twelve grandsons, from whom the Jews are descended. All of Abraham's children should live together in peace in this land." He knew, as we did, that in reality the bitter strife between Sarah and Hagar continued between their sons and down to our day.

The conflict among Abraham, Sarah and Hagar is a complex one, like most family conflicts. There are no heroes or villains, just three people with imperfect vision and mixed motives, struggling with a difficult family situation.

God is active in the story, but does not take sides for one woman against the other. Both women, in different ways, are poor, and God cares lovingly for both.

Read the conclusion of the story of Hagar and Ishmael.

> When the water in the skin was gone, she cast the child under one of the bushes. Then she went and sat down opposite him a good way off, about the distance of a bowshot; for she said, "Do not let me look on the death of the child." And as she sat opposite him, she lifted up her voice and wept. And God heard the voice of the boy; and the angel of God called to Hagar from heaven, and said to her, "What troubles you, Hagar? Do not be afraid; for God has heard the voice of the boy where he is. Come, lift up the boy and hold him fast with your hand, for I will make a great nation of him." Then God opened her eyes and she saw a well of water. She went, and filled the skin with water, and gave the boy a drink.
>
> God was with the boy, and he grew up; he lived in the wilderness, and became an expert with the bow. He lived in the wilderness of Paran; and his mother got a wife for him from the land of Egypt.
>
> *Genesis 21:15-21*

Questions for Reflection

1. Who are some women today who find themselves in situations like Sarah's or Hagar's?

2. Sarah felt like a failure because she had not borne a child. In what way do you feel like a failure?

3. Do you know of any parent or employer who mistreated an employee or a child so badly that they quit a job or fled, like Hagar?

4. Have you had an experience of God that turned you around as Hagar was turned around by her first experience of God in the desert?

5. Has God ever "opened your eyes" like Hagar's, to see that what you painfully thirst for is actually very near you?

6. For Sarah, the birth of Isaac was a completely unexpected gift. Have you or anyone you know ever received a completely unexpected gift?

Suggestions for Further Reading
Genesis 20
Genesis 21
Galatians 4:21-31.

Prayer

Heavenly Father, it is through you that we receive all things. We ask that you help us to be understanding and forgiving of the young who often look upon us with contempt and disgust. Help us to look at each person with love, for everyone is a special child to you, especially the poor and helpless. When we feel hopeless, and as though we can't go on, fill our hearts with your love and open our eyes to see the wonders that you have placed in our midst. In our weakness help us endure, for we know that nothing is impossible for you. With your guidance we, too, can become strong and accomplish wondrous things. We ask you this through Christ, our Lord. Amen.

Sandra L. Durand, 57, Elbert, Colorado

CHAPTER FOUR

Near-Death and Death

The Sacrifice of the Child

WHEN YOU WANT TO GIVE A GIFT to someone very special you may put a great deal of thought into choosing the gift. You may not be quite sure what the person really wants. You may want to spend a lot of money on the gift because that is a way of showing how much you value the person.

Most ancient peoples thought this way about their gods. All the peoples Abraham knew offered sacrifices to their gods, sometimes animals, sometimes children. One of the sad things often found by archaeologists in the Ancient Near East is a little box with the bones of an infant buried beneath the threshold of a house. The owner of the house sacrificed a newborn child to obtain a god's blessing on the house.

The practice seems barbaric to us. Yet is it so different from what every modern nation does when it declares war: sacrifices the lives of its young men and women for some value which it holds in high esteem?

The people of Israel believed that their God was the greatest of all gods. It seemed natural, then, that they should offer him the greatest of all gifts. The most valuable thing they knew was a firstborn son. So some Israelites sacrificed their sons to God. The biblical writers try to explain to the people that, while love for God is a good thing, this is not the kind of gift God wants. The story of Abraham's sacrifice of his son Isaac, which sounds so strange to us, was probably originally part of this attempt to discourage the practice of child sacrifice.

Ishmael and Hagar have been sent off into the desert. Abraham and Sarah probably presume they are dead. So, in their extreme old age, they have only one child, Isaac, whom they love beyond measure. All the labor of their lives, and all God's promises for their future, are centered in this precious son, God's gift. But Abraham hears the voice of God asking him to sacrifice Isaac. It is as if God wanted Abraham, and all his descendants, to be clear about Abraham's relationship to God. Was his a religion of practicality, serving God only in order to obtain God's gifts? Or was it true religion, devotion not based on self-interest? It is a question we often ask ourselves, but we rarely have as dramatic a way as Abraham did to find the answer.

Yet it can happen in our lives, too, that God seems to take away the very thing God gave us in answer to the prayers of a lifetime. When this happens in extreme old age, it is particularly agonizing because it seems that there is no time to try again; what one has is all one can expect to have.

The aged Abraham agreed to sacrifice all of his life's hopes by sacrificing Isaac. It does not seem to have occurred to him that Sarah or Isaac should have any part in his decision making. The story is only about Abraham, and aims to show in the most vivid way possible how totally obedient to God he was. We have to value the story for the point it is making and not get distracted by questions that are irrelevant to the storyteller's intent.

The story of father and son walking together to the place of sacrifice is one of the most poignant in Scripture. The puzzled boy asks, "The fire and the wood are here, but where is the lamb for a burnt offering?" (Genesis 22:7). In his anguish, the father answers with pious words, "God himself will provide the lamb" (Genesis 22:8). He does not yet know how truly he speaks.

When they come to the place appointed for the sacrifice and Abraham has actually lifted his hand to kill his well-loved son, God intervenes and shows Abraham how mistaken he had been to think that God wanted this terrible sacrifice.

Abraham had misunderstood God's message the first time, but the important thing is that he did not stop listening. People who are convinced that they know God's will can be dangerous unless they always have an ear cocked for some new message from God that may be different from what they heard yesterday. If Abraham had stood stubbornly on what he heard from God in the past, Isaac would have died and the story would have ended.

After the intense drama, God does provide and sends a ram for the sacrifice. It is a reminder that God always provides, though in ways and on a schedule that is not what we would choose. Abraham's call is to let God be in control, completely.

Incidentally, Muslims tell this same story about the obedience of Father Abraham. But in their version, it is his firstborn son, Ishmael, whom Abraham almost sacrifices.

God is pleased with Abraham's attempt at obedience, as God must often be pleased with us when we try to do what is right, even if we later realize that we badly misunderstood the will of God. God repeats the wonderful promises of multitudes of descendants and of a blessing to come upon all nations through the descendants of Abraham. As the story comes to its conclusion, we look forward to Jesus, in whom these promises will be fulfilled in a way far beyond Abraham's imaginings.

Read the story of the "sacrifice of Isaac."

After these things God tested Abraham. He said to him, "Abraham!" And he said, "Here I am." He said, "Take your son, your only son Isaac, whom you love, and go to the land of Moriah, and offer him there as a burnt offering on one of the mountains that I shall show you." So Abraham rose early in the morning, saddled his donkey, and took two of his young men with him, and his son Isaac; he cut the wood for the burnt offering, and set out and went to the place in the distance that God had shown him. On the third day Abraham looked up and saw the place far away. Then Abraham said to his young men, "Stay here with the donkey; the boy and I will go over there; we will worship, and then we will come back to you." Abraham took the wood of the burnt offering and laid it on his son Isaac, and he himself carried the fire and the knife. So the two of them walked on together. Isaac said to his father Abraham, "Father!" And he said, "Here I am, my son." He said, "The fire and the wood are here, but where is the lamb for a burnt offering?" Abraham said, "God himself will provide the lamb for a burnt offering, my son." So the two of them walked on together.

When they came to the place that God had shown him, Abraham built an altar there and laid the wood in order. He bound his son Isaac, and laid him on the altar, on top of the wood. Then Abraham reached out his hand and took the knife to kill his son. But the angel of the LORD called to him from heaven, and said, "Abraham, Abraham!" And he said, "Here I am." He said, "Do not lay your hand on the boy or do anything to him; for now I know that you fear God, since you have not withheld your son, your only son, from me." And Abraham looked up and saw a ram, caught in a thicket by its horns. Abraham went and took the ram and offered it up as a burnt offering instead of his son. So Abraham called that place "The LORD will provide"; as it is said to this day, "On the mount of the LORD it shall be provided."

The angel of the LORD called to Abraham a second time from heaven, and said, "By myself I have sworn, says the LORD: Because you have done this, and have not withheld your son, your only son, I will indeed bless you, and I will make your offspring as numerous as the stars of heaven and as the sand that is on the seashore. And your offspring shall possess the gate of their enemies, and by your offspring shall all the nations of the earth gain blessing for themselves, because you have obeyed my voice." So Abraham returned to his young men, and they arose and went together to Beer-sheba; and Abraham lived at Beer-sheba.

Genesis 22:1-19

Family News

FROM THIS MOMENT OF HIGH DRAMA, Genesis goes on to a newsy bit about word that Abraham received from his brother Nahor's family. In days before telephone or postal service, receiving such news must have been a rare event. The death of Sarah and Abraham is approaching. Perhaps by placing this information here the author is reminding us that even if we distance ourselves from our family of origin during our active years, toward the end it becomes important to rebuild those relationships. Abraham will do this by sending for a bride for Isaac from among his relatives back in Haran. Rebekah is specially mentioned here because she is to be Isaac's wife.

Read this bit of family news.

> Now after these things it was told Abraham, "Milcah also has borne children, to your brother Nahor: Uz the first-born, Buz his brother, Kemuel the father of Aram, Chesed, Hazo, Pildash, Jidlaph, and Bethuel." Bethuel became the father of Rebekah. These eight Milcah bore to Nahor, Abraham's brother.
>
> *Genesis 22:20-23*

The Death of Sarah

ABRAHAM ALMOST LOST HIS SON in a terrible and extraordinary way. Next he loses his spouse, an experience he shares with about half the married people of the earth. In this story we see Abraham as an ordinary human being. He mourns for Sarah, even though she is 127 years old at her death. Suddenly it seems important to him that this woman, with whom he has shared so much of life, should not be forgotten, that her death should have meaning for future generations. He reminds me of bereaved families who want a memorial window in a church or a memorial donation to some charity to bear the name of their loved one.

In the face of the death of a loved one, we want to make clear the meaning of that person's life. The meaning of the life of Sarah and Abraham came from the promises of God to them. For Abraham, the death of Sarah was an opportunity for a strong expression of faith in those promises. Sarah died before the promise of land was fulfilled, but her death precipitated the first step in the fulfillment of that promise.

41

So far, Abraham and Sarah had lived as immigrants in the land. They were not citizens. They did not own one square foot of the promised land. When Sarah died Abraham could endure this situation no longer. He entered into negotiations with the natives to purchase a burial ground. He was not content to accept a burial plot as a gift, which would leave him indebted to them. He must purchase this precious bit of land so it would be his with no strings attached. The negotiations were difficult and the price exorbitant. The natives did not part willingly with their land. The haggling was in the style of middle eastern bargaining today; a hard business deal is hidden under an abundance of flowery phrases.

Abraham was willing to pay any price to gain a foothold in the promised land. By purchasing this field and burying Sarah there, he was affirming in the strongest way he knew his faith in God's promise that one day the land of Canaan would belong to his descendants. He himself, his son and grandson and their wives would be buried in this same cave in Hebron. It is as if even with their dead bodies they wanted to proclaim that their family belonged in this land.

Today the cave at Hebron is covered with a shrine where both Jews and Arabs, descendants of Abraham through Isaac and through Ishmael, pray. I have prayed there, and found it a strange experience, with many soldiers with big guns on guard while Arabs and Jews pray intently above the grave of Abraham, but never look at each other. The peaceful Abraham, who was willing to wait for God to give the land to him, never imagined what violence would swirl about his tomb in later days.

His concern was to affirm at any price the value of the life of Sarah and to give expression to his undying faith in God's promise that his descendants would own this land.

Read the story of the purchase of Sarah's burial plot at Hebron.

Sarah lived one hundred twenty-seven years; this was the length of Sarah's life. And Sarah died at Kiriath-arba (that is, Hebron) in the land of Canaan; and Abraham went in to mourn for Sarah and to weep for her. Abraham rose up from beside his dead, and said to the Hittites, "I am a stranger and an alien residing among you; give me property among you for a burying place, so that I may bury my dead out of my sight." The Hittites answered Abraham, "Hear us, my lord; you are a mighty prince among us. Bury your dead in the choicest of our burial places; none of us will withhold from you any burial ground for burying your dead." Abraham rose and bowed to the Hittites, the people of the land. He said to them, "If you are willing that I should bury my dead out of my sight, hear me, and entreat for me Ephron son of Zohar, so that he may give me the cave of Machpelah, which he owns; it is at the end of his field. For the full price let him give it to me in your presence as a possession for a burying place." Now Ephron was sitting among the Hittites; and Ephron the Hittite answered Abraham in the hearing of the Hittites, of all who went in at the gate of his city, "No, my lord, hear me; I give you the field, and I give you the cave that is in it; in the presence of my people I give it to you; bury your dead." Then Abraham bowed down before the people of the land. He said to Ephron in the hearing of the people of the land, "If you only will listen to me! I will give the price of the field; accept it from me, so that I may bury my dead there." Ephron answered Abraham, "My lord, listen to me; a piece of land worth four hundred shekels of silver—what is that between you and me? Bury your dead." Abraham agreed with Ephron; and Abraham weighed out for Ephron the silver that he had named in the hearing of the Hittites, four hundred shekels of silver, according to the weights current among the merchants.

So the field of Ephron in Machpelah, which was to the east of Mamre, the field with the cave that was in it and all the trees that were in the field, throughout its whole area, passed to Abraham as a possession in the presence of the Hittites, in the presence of all who went in at the gate of his city. After this, Abraham buried Sarah his wife in the cave of the field of Machpelah facing Mamre (that is, Hebron) in the land of Canaan. The field and the cave that is in it passed from the Hittites into Abraham's possession as a burying place.

Genesis 23:1-20

The Death of Abraham

ABRAHAM MOURNED THE DEATH OF SARAH, but even at 137 years of age he could not live without a wife. He married Keturah, who bore him more children! He would provide for these children, but they would not inherit the promise because they were not the children of Sarah.

Finally, at the age of one hundred seventy-five, Abraham dies. Suddenly, Ishmael reappears, and Isaac and Ishmael together bury their father beside Sarah at Hebron. Death sometimes has power to bring together long estranged family members.

Read about the death of Abraham.

Abraham took another wife, whose name was Keturah. She bore him Zimran, Jokshan, Medan, Midian, Ishbak, and Shuah.... All these were the children of Keturah. Abraham gave all he had to Isaac. But to the sons of his concubines Abraham gave gifts, while he was still living, and he sent them away from his son Isaac, eastward to the east country.

This is the length of Abraham's life, one hundred seventy-five years. Abraham breathed his last and died in a good old age, an old man and full of years, and was gathered to his people. His sons Isaac and Ishmael buried him in the cave of Machpelah, in the field of Ephron son of Zohar the Hittite, east of Mamre, the field that Abraham purchased from the Hittites. There Abraham was buried, with his wife Sarah.

Genesis 25:1-2; 4-10

Questions for Reflection

1. Have you ever been called on to let go of something or someone as precious to you as Isaac was to Abraham? What was it?

2. Do you know of any person or group that believed, like Abraham, that God wanted some particular sacrifice, but later came to think differently?

3. Do you think that the sacrifice of young men and women in war is ever justified?

—⁓—

4. To Abraham, funeral arrangements for Sarah were important. How do you feel about funerals and all that goes with them?

5. How do you feel about widows and widowers who, like Abraham, remarry in their old age? Would you be open to remarriage if you were widowed?

6. What would you like to leave to your children when you die? to other people?

7. Do you know any case of estranged family members who came together, like Isaac and Ishmael, at the time of a death?

Suggestions for Further Reading

Genesis 22
Genesis 23
Genesis 24
Hebrews 11:1-12
Isaiah 51:1, 2

Prayer

Beloved Father, thank you for the story of Abraham. We reflect on Abraham's willingness to sacrifice his son Isaac, out of faith and obedience to you. His ability to surrender the great gift of the life of his son prompts me to look at my willingness to surrender my will to yours.

Strengthen me to surrender my attachments to material possessions and those things which distract me from you and my spiritual journey with you. Help me to be an obedient and trusting servant remembering that you always provide for me. It is you who are in control, not me.

Abraham listened and heard your words of reprieve for his beloved son. Show me ways of listening more attentively for your words spoken to me. Help me to make moments of silence a regular part of my prayer practice so I can hear you in the intimate quiet of silence.

As Abraham grieved for Sarah, then began a new phase of his life and remarried, provide comfort to me through my grieving over the loss of spouse and loved ones. Enable me to let go and be open to new beginnings.

I ask you this through Christ Jesus, our Lord. Amen.

Dorothy Liston, 59, Denver, Colorado

CHAPTER FIVE

Rebekah and the Twins

The Birth of Twins

WHEN ISAAC, THE CHILD OF PROMISE, was forty years old his father, Abraham, sent a servant back to the area around Haran, where his own journey had begun, to find a wife for his son. The servant prayed for a sign by which he could recognize the woman God had chosen as Isaac's wife. He was quite specific about the sign. When he came to a well and a girl approached to draw water, he would say, "Please offer your jar that I may drink." The girl God had chosen would reply, "Drink, and I will water your camels" (Genesis 24:14). This was an extraordinarily generous reply, since a camel can drink twenty gallons of water. This girl volunteered to do a long, heavy job for a total stranger.

Beautiful young Rebekah gives exactly this sign, and also invites the servant to her home. Her brother Laban is willing to send her as a bride for Isaac, and Rebekah shows herself eager for this adventure in a strange land. She becomes a strong woman, just the wife a rather weak Isaac needs.

For twenty years she is childless, like Sarah. But Isaac prays for her, and she becomes pregnant. The barrenness of the matriarchs is a recurring theme in Genesis and always highlights the fact that children are a gift of God, not attainable by merely human effort.

Rebekah's pregnancy is difficult. Frantic, she prays. God replies by explaining why she is suffering so much. There are two sons struggling in her womb, from whom two nations will be descended. The one who comes out of the womb last will rule over the one who comes out first. It is interesting that this prophecy, which is the key to the rest of the story of Esau and Jacob, is given to Rebekah, not to Isaac. God seems to have known on whom he could rely in this family.

This was an extraordinary prophecy in the culture of Rebekah's time. The law of primogeniture, the special rights of the firstborn, was fundamental to the order of ancient society. As we take it for granted that American citizenship confers many privileges, people in the Ancient Near East took it for granted that being the firstborn son entitled one to the favor of one's parents and to the bulk of the inheritance. At the death of the father, the firstborn inherited the dominant position of the father in the extended family. Anything else would turn the whole structure of society upside down. Yet God's plan here, and in many other places in the Bible, goes completely against this established order.

This fundamental law of primogeniture applied even to twins, so it was extremely important for the midwife to mark the first child to emerge from the womb in such a way that there could be no confusion later.

Rebekah's twins struggled at their birth to get out first. Esau was the firstborn, but as he came out Jacob was clutching his heel, trying to supplant him. Jacob will continue as he grows up to struggle against the order society imposed that put him under his brother. Life will never be easy for Jacob, or for those around him.

Read about the struggle between Esau and Jacob that began in the womb.

Isaac was forty years old when he married Rebekah, daughter of Bethuel the Aramean of Paddan-aram, sister of Laban the Aramean. Isaac prayed to the LORD for his wife, because she was barren; and the LORD granted his prayer, and his wife Rebekah conceived. The children struggled together within her; and she said, "If it is to be this way, why do I live?" So she went to inquire of the LORD. And the LORD said to her,

"Two nations are in your womb,
    and two peoples born of you shall be divided;
the one shall be stronger than the other,
    the elder shall serve the younger."

When her time to give birth was at hand, there were twins in her womb. The first came out red, all his body like a hairy mantle; so they named him Esau. Afterward his brother came out, with his hand gripping Esau's heel; so he was named Jacob. Isaac was sixty years old when she bore them.

When the boys grew up, Esau was a skillful hunter, a man of the field, while Jacob was a quiet man, living in tents. Isaac loved Esau, because he was fond of game; but Rebekah loved Jacob.

Genesis 25:20-28

A Family Divided

THE STRUGGLE FOR POWER CONTINUED between these twins, so different in temperament. Rebekah, to whom God had revealed that Jacob was the specially chosen one, favored Jacob, who liked to remain around the tent. Isaac, who liked the taste of game, preferred Esau the hunter. The biblical narrator speaks of Jacob as Rebekah's son, and Esau as Isaac's son: the little family of four was divided into two camps.

Isaac always appears as a rather weak character, overshadowed by his great father Abraham, by his assertive wife Rebekah, and eventually by his clever son Jacob. In his old age, his weakness is pathetic. In total contrast to his father Abraham who was a tower of strength at 175, Isaac is blind and senile, and his main interest seems to be in his food. Feeling that death is approaching, he sends Esau out to get him the meat he craves, promising his blessing when the food is brought to him.

The blessing, or curse, of a father has tremendous power in the biblical story. It determines the whole future life of the son. Once spoken, even by a senile father who does not know to whom he is speaking, it cannot be changed. This may seem strange to us, but if you listen carefully to adult children today, you may be surprised at how sensitive they are to words of affirmation or criticism, of love or dislike, from even the most disoriented parents. In some ways we never out-grow our dependence on our parents.

In spite of his deterioration in old age, Isaac as father still has all the power in the family. In theory the woman had no power in such issues as who was to inherit the blessing given by God to Abraham. In the Bible, as in our world, those who are deprived of power by the established social structures often use their wits to deceive the powerful.

This is frequently the method used by women in the Bible, since women were seen as having no power outside their homes. Rebekah organizes a scheme to trick Isaac into giving his blessing to Jacob instead of Esau. We see the same thing we noticed when Abraham gave his wife to Pharaoh. Our biblical ancestors were not always models for ethical behavior. God loved them in spite of their sins and used them to carry out the divine plan. Why God chose them, or us, rather than someone else is a mystery.

Read the story of the trick played on Isaac as the Bible tells it.

When Isaac was old and his eyes were dim so that he could not see, he called his elder son Esau and said to him, "My son"; and he answered, "Here I am." He said, "See, I am old; I do not know the day of my death. Now then, take your weapons, your quiver and your bow, and go out to the field, and hunt game for me. Then prepare for me savory food, such as I like, and bring it to me to eat, so that I may bless you before I die."

Now Rebekah was listening when Isaac spoke to his son Esau. So when Esau went to the field to hunt for game and bring it, Rebekah said to her son Jacob, "I heard your father say to your brother Esau, 'Bring me game, and pre-pare for me savory food to eat, that I may bless you before the LORD before I die.' Now therefore, my son, obey my word as I command you. Go to the flock, and get me two choice kids, so that I may prepare from them savory food for your father, such as he likes; and you shall take it to your father to eat, so that he may bless you before he dies."

But Jacob said to his mother Rebekah, "Look, my brother Esau is a hairy man, and I am a man of smooth skin. Perhaps my father will feel me, and I shall seem to be mocking him, and bring a curse on myself and not a blessing." His mother said to him, "Let your curse be on me, my son; only obey my word, and go, get them for me." So he went and got them and brought them to his mother; and his mother prepared savory food, such as his father loved. Then Rebekah took the best garments of her elder son Esau, which were with her in the house, and put them on her younger son Jacob; and she put the skins of the kids on his hands and on the smooth part of his neck. Then she handed the savory food, and the bread that she had prepared, to her son Jacob.

So he went in to his father, and said, "My father"; and he said, "Here I am; who are you, my son?" Jacob said to his father, "I am Esau your firstborn. I have done as you told me; now sit up and eat of my game, so that you may bless me." But Isaac said to his son, "How is it that you have found it so quickly, my son?" He answered, "Because the LORD your God granted me success." Then Isaac said to Jacob, "Come near, that I may feel you, my son, to know whether you are really my son Esau or not." So Jacob went up to his father Isaac, who felt him and said, "The voice is Jacob's voice, but the hands are the hands of Esau." He did not recognize him, because his hands were hairy like his brother Esau's hands; so he blessed him. He said, "Are you really my son Esau?" He answered, "I am." Then he said, "Bring it to me, that I may eat of my son's game and bless you." So he brought it to him, and he ate; and he brought him wine, and he drank. Then his father Isaac said to him, "Come near and kiss me, my son." So he came near and kissed him; and he smelled the smell of his garments, and blessed him, and said,

> "Ah, the smell of my son
>   is like the smell of a field that the Lord
>   has blessed.
> May God give you of the dew of heaven,
>   and of the fatness of the earth,

and plenty of grain and wine.
Let peoples serve you,
   and nations bow down to you.
Be lord over your brothers,
   and may your mother's sons bow down to you.
Cursed be everyone who curses you,
   and blessed be everyone who blesses you!"

Now Esau hated Jacob because of the blessing with which his father had blessed him, and Esau said to himself, "The days of mourning for my father are approaching; then I will kill my brother Jacob." But the words of her elder son Esau were told to Rebekah; so she sent and called her younger son Jacob and said to him, "Your brother Esau is consoling himself by planning to kill you. Now therefore, my son, obey my voice; flee at once to my brother Laban in Haran, and stay with him a while...until your brother's anger against you turns away, and he forgets what you have done to him; then I will send, and bring you back from there. Why should I lose both of you in one day?"

Genesis 27:1-29; 41-45

Flight and Return

JACOB FLEES FROM HIS BROTHER'S RIGHTEOUS WRATH to his mother's brother Laban. At the beginning of the journey he has an experience of God in which he sees angels climbing up and down a ladder to heaven, and God promises to bring him back to Canaan and to fulfill for him the promises made to Abraham. Only at this point does the God of Abraham and Isaac become in a real way his God. Young people, then and now, often need to get away from the parental home before making the parental values really theirs.

God does help Jacob through many adventures. He acquires two wives, eleven sons and vast herds while working for his uncle Laban. But after many years he remembers the promise God made to him at the beginning of his journey.

To receive that promise, he would have to leave his adopted land and return to the land of his birth and to his brother Esau.

Jacob was terrified at the idea of returning to the brother he had cheated and run away from so many years before. But the need for reconciliation with his family and God's call to claim the promises combined to impel him to make the long journey back, with his family and flocks.

Jacob is a model of a person who in later life receives the grace to heal relationships broken in youth. This usually costs enormous effort and pain. Sometimes it happens, as in Jacob's case, that all dread of the former enemy is quite pointless. The other has long ago forgiven and forgotten. But one never knows this until one braves the encounter. In his life of adventure, probably the hardest thing Jacob ever did was to return to face his brother Esau. The storyteller depicts vividly his nervousness as the dreaded moment approaches.

At the height of tension, when Jacob has sent all his family ahead across the Jabbok river, he remains alone overnight by the river. At this point one of the most crucial events in the Old Testament occurs. A strange being appears, perhaps an angel, perhaps God himself. Jacob wrestles with this mysterious being until daybreak.

The stranger tells Jacob that his name will no longer be Jacob but Israel, "one who struggles with God." The people of Israel are named after their ancestor Jacob—not the foolish young Jacob who cheated his brother and fled in fear, but the mature Jacob who overcame his fears to return to face his brother, and then struggled through the night with his God. A change of name in the Bible shows that God has led the person to a new level and a new role in salvation history.

Read the Bible's story of Jacob's adventures.

> Jacob sent messengers before him to his brother Esau in the land of Seir, the country of Edom, instructing them, "Thus you shall say to my lord Esau: Thus says your servant Jacob, 'I have lived with Laban as an alien, and stayed until now; and I have oxen, donkeys, flocks, male and female

slaves; and I have sent to tell my lord, in order that I may find favor in your sight.'"

The messengers returned to Jacob, saying, "We came to your brother Esau, and he is coming to meet you, and four hundred men are with him." Then Jacob was greatly afraid and distressed; and he divided the people that were with him, and the flocks and herds and camels, into two companies, thinking, "If Esau comes to the one company and destroys it, then the company that is left will escape."

And Jacob said, "O God of my father Abraham and God of my father Isaac, O LORD who said to me, 'Return to your country and to your kindred, and I will do you good,' I am not worthy of the least of all the steadfast love and all the faithfulness that you have shown to your servant, for with only my staff I crossed this Jordan; and now I have become two companies. Deliver me, please, from the hand of my brother, from the hand of Esau, for I am afraid of him; he may come and kill us all, the mothers with the children. Yet you have said, 'I will surely do you good, and make your offspring as the sand of the sea, which cannot be counted because of their number.'"

So he spent that night there, and from what he had with him he took a present for his brother Esau, two hundred female goats and twenty male goats, two hundred ewes and twenty rams, thirty milch camels and their colts, forty cows and ten bulls, twenty female donkeys and ten male donkeys. These he delivered into the hand of his servants, every drove by itself, and said to his servants, "Pass on ahead of me, and put a space between drove and drove." He instructed the foremost, "When Esau my brother meets you, and asks you, 'To whom do you belong? Where are you going? And whose are these ahead of you?' then you shall say, 'They belong to your servant Jacob; they are a present sent to my lord Esau; and moreover he is behind us.'" He likewise instructed the second and the third and all who followed the droves, "You shall say the same thing to Esau when you meet him, and you shall say, 'Moreover your servant Jacob is behind us.'" For he thought, "I may appease him with the present that goes ahead of me, and afterwards I shall see his face; perhaps he will accept me." So the present passed on ahead of him; and he himself spent that night in the camp.

The same night he got up and took his two wives, his two maids, and his eleven children, and crossed the ford of the Jabbok. He took them and sent them across the stream, and likewise everything that he had. Jacob was left alone; and a man wrestled with him until daybreak. When the man saw that he did not prevail against Jacob, he struck him on the hip socket; and Jacob's hip was put out of joint as he wrestled with him. Then he said, "Let me go, for the day is breaking." But Jacob said, "I will not let you go, unless you bless me." So he said to him, "What is your name?" And he said, "Jacob." Then the man said, "You shall no longer be called Jacob, but Israel, for you have striven with God and with humans, and have prevailed." Then Jacob asked him, "Please tell me your name." But he said, "Why is it that you ask my name?" And there he blessed him. So Jacob called the place Peniel, saying, "For I have seen God face to face, and yet my life is preserved." The sun rose upon him as he passed Penuel, limping because of his hip.

Genesis 32:3-31

Reconciliation

JACOB'S STRUGGLE WITH THE DIVINE was successful, but it left him with a limp. Great struggles can have similar effects in our lives. Only after this intense experience of God, which made him into a new man, does Jacob/Israel actually meet Esau. Then, in the face of this brother he has hated and feared for so long he sees the face of the God he had met the night before.

Read about the encounter between the brothers.

Now Jacob looked up and saw Esau coming, and four hundred men with him. So he divided the children among Leah and Rachel and the two maids. He put the maids with their children in front, then Leah with her children, and Rachel and Joseph last of all. He himself went on ahead of them, bowing himself to the ground seven times, until he came near his brother.

But Esau ran to meet him, and embraced him, and fell on his neck and kissed him, and they wept. When Esau looked up and saw the women and children, he said, "Who are these with you?" Jacob said, "The children whom God has graciously given your servant." Then the maids drew near, they and their children, and bowed down; Leah likewise and her children drew near and bowed down; and finally Joseph and Rachel drew near, and they bowed down. Esau said, "What do you mean by all this company that I met?" Jacob answered, "To find favor with my lord." But Esau said, "I have enough, my brother; keep what you have for yourself." Jacob said, "No, please; if I find favor with you, then accept my present from my hand; for truly to see your face is like seeing the face of God—since you have received me with such favor. Please accept my gift that is brought to you, because God has dealt graciously with me, and because I have everything I want." So he urged him, and he took it.

Genesis 33:1-11

Questions for Reflection

1. Have you ever known a family, like Isaac's, torn apart because of favoritism on the part of parents?

2. Both Esau and Jacob desperately wanted their father's blessing. Do you think adults today care whether their elderly parents show approval or disapproval of them?

3. Have you known people, like Rebekah and Jacob, who took advantage of the handicaps of an elderly person? How do you think such abuses can be avoided?

—⁓—

4. Do you think that it is important for adult brothers and sisters to be reconciled as Esau and Jacob were? Do you have a relative with whom you need reconciliation?

5. Do you know any family where brothers and sisters have temperaments as different as Esau and Jacob? How do these relationships work?

6. What "rules" in our society give some people more privileges than others, as the "rule" of primogeniture gave special privileges to the firstborn?

Suggestions for Further Reading
Genesis 26—33
Romans 9:6-16

Prayer

Dear God, many are the times we need your help in closing canyons that divide us one from another as Jacob and Esau were divided. Help us to find ways to peace and understanding. Help us to be diligent in seeking reunions.

Please open our eyes to see the ways that we have failed to see and to be aware of the suffering that we have caused each other, for each of us in our own way may be at fault. Teach us to be humble as we seek reunions with those from whom we have been parted. Make us aware of how short life really is and how we need to unite our hearts without delay. Inspire us to see that separation can serve to bring opponents closer together after a reconciliation as it did with Jacob and Esau.

So, Lord of pardon and forgiveness, be with us as we seek to be reunited through reconciliation, after times of separation from our families, our friends or our peers. We ask this in your name, O Lord. Amen.

Joan Lennon, 62, Littleton, Colorado

CHAPTER SIX

The Young Joseph

Joseph the Dreamer

JOSEPH WAS ONE OF THE TWELVE SONS OF JACOB. His story, which occupies a quarter of the Book of Genesis, is different from the stories of Abraham, Isaac and Jacob. Unlike the family album of snapshots and sometimes unedifying tidbits about the patriarchs which seems to have been put together a bit haphazardly, the story of Joseph appears to have been carefully composed by an author who wanted to give us a model for living properly.

God walked with Abraham, Isaac and Jacob, and spoke directly to them, telling them what to do and giving them promises. The presence of God in the story of Joseph, as often in our lives, is much more hidden. God does not speak to Joseph, nor does Joseph speak to God. There are no visions, no miracles. Joseph's feet are firmly planted on this earth; there is nothing of the mystic about him.

Yet God is present. Joseph refuses to sin because he does not want to offend God. Joseph does not become proud in the time of his success because he recognizes his abilities as God's gifts. Above all, we feel the quiet working of God's providence through the apparently secular adventures of Joseph's life. It surely illustrates that "All things work together for good for those who love God" (Romans 8:28).

This part of Scripture has been described as "The Ups and Downs of Joseph." It is an adventure story that modern writers have successfully turned into a novel, a movie and a musical.

Jacob, who is also called Israel, had a "blended family" even more complicated than those to which we are accustomed today. He had two wives, who spent their lives competing to see who could give Jacob more children. Each of them at different times gave her servant woman to Jacob to obtain more offspring on her side. It is like the story of Sarah and Hagar expanded. Through years of this competition, the four women bore Jacob twelve sons. (The number of daughters is not even mentioned. They do not figure in the story except that they join the sons in trying to comfort Jacob for the loss of Joseph.)

Jacob's favorite son was young Joseph, the long-awaited son of the one woman he really loved, Rachel. Just before our story begins, Rachel had died giving birth to her second son, Benjamin, who is probably an infant as the story starts. Jacob never got over his grief at the loss of Rachel, so Joseph and baby Benjamin were especially precious to him as reminders of her.

Jacob had grown up in a family that was torn in two because he was his mother's favorite and Esau was his father's. But he does not seem to have learned from his experience. Like so many parents, he made his children suffer from the same poor child-raising patterns from which he himself had suffered. He spoiled Joseph shamelessly.

Not surprisingly, the older brothers hated the younger brother who was so cocky because he knew he had his father's favor. They would not even say good morning to him. The story is a warning of how serious the refusal of common courtesy within a family is, and how far it can lead. It is our first clue that the brothers will try to murder Joseph.

It is significant that the first story about Joseph is a story about his dreams. The major events in his later life will concern the interpretation of dreams. These dreams of his are a prelude that summarizes the whole story.

Read the story of Joseph's dreams.

Now Israel loved Joseph more than any other of his children, because he was the son of his old age; and he had made him a long robe with sleeves. But when his brothers saw that their father loved him more than all his brothers, they hated him, and could not speak peaceably to him.

Once Joseph had a dream, and when he told it to his brothers, they hated him even more. He said to them,

"Listen to this dream that I dreamed. There we were, binding sheaves in the field. Suddenly my sheaf rose and stood upright; then your sheaves gathered around it, and bowed down to my sheaf." His brothers said to him, "Are you indeed to reign over us? Are you indeed to have dominion over us?" So they hated him even more because of his dreams and his words.

He had another dream, and told it to his brothers, saying, "Look, I have had another dream: the sun, the moon, and eleven stars were bowing down to me." But when he told it to his father and to his brothers, his father rebuked him, and said to him, "What kind of dream is this that you have had? Shall we indeed come, I and your mother and your brothers, and bow to the ground before you?" So his brothers were jealous of him, but his father kept the matter in mind.

Genesis 37:3-11

Jealousy Erupts

JACOB AS FATHER HAS POWER TO PROTECT his favorite Joseph against the jealous brothers while they are all together. But one day, when the brothers have taken some flocks a distance away to find better grazing, Jacob makes the mistake of sending Joseph as a messenger to the brothers. How little he understands what is going on in his family!

The brothers seize Joseph angrily and throw him into one of the pits, or cisterns, which nomads dig in the desert to collect water from the rare rainfalls. It happens to be dry, so they can leave him there while they debate whether to kill him outright or sell him as a slave. They decide to take advantage of a passing caravan of traders descended from their great-uncle Ishmael to sell Joseph as a slave. It was more profitable than killing him, and also avoided the guilt of shedding blood.

The brothers told Jacob that Joseph had been killed by a wild beast. Jacob grieved and all of his sons and daughters together were unable to comfort him. Jacob's is not just a normal period of grief. He gets stuck in his grief for Rachel and Joseph for the rest of his life, treating the remaining part of the family as of no interest to him. He is a terrible example of a father who misuses his power by putting down the living members of his family and honoring only the dead. It is a temptation every bereaved parent must experience.

Read the story of the jealous brothers.

Now his brothers went to pasture their father's flock near Shechem. And Israel said to Joseph, "Are not your brothers pasturing the flock at Shechem? Come, I will send you to them." He answered, "Here I am." So he said to him, "Go now, see if it is well with your brothers and with the flock; and bring word back to me."...

So Joseph went after his brothers, and found them at Dothan. They saw him from a distance, and before he came near to them, they conspired to kill him. They said to one another, "Here comes this dreamer. Come now, let us kill him and throw him into one of the pits; then we shall say that a wild animal has devoured him, and we shall see what will become of his dreams." But when Reuben heard it, he delivered him out of their hands, saying, "Let us not take his life." Reuben said to them, "Shed no blood; throw him into this pit here in the wilderness, but lay no hand on him"— that he might rescue him out of their hand and restore him to his father. So when Joseph came to his brothers, they stripped him of his robe, the long robe with sleeves that he wore; and they took him and threw him into a pit. The pit was empty; there was no water in it.

Then they sat down to eat; and looking up they saw a caravan of Ishmaelites coming from Gilead, with their camels carrying gum, balm, and resin, on their way to carry it down to Egypt. Then Judah said to his brothers, "What profit is it if we kill our brother and conceal his blood? Come, let us sell him to the Ishmaelites, and not lay our hands on him, for he is our brother, our own flesh." And his brothers agreed.... [T]hey drew Joseph up, lifting him out of the pit, and sold him to the Ishmaelites for twenty pieces of silver. And they took Joseph to Egypt....

Then [the brothers] took Joseph's robe, slaughtered a goat, and dipped the robe in the blood. They had the long robe with sleeves taken to their father, and they said, "This we have found; see now whether it is your son's robe or not." He recognized it, and said, "It is my son's robe! A wild animal has devoured him; Joseph is without doubt torn to pieces." Then Jacob tore his garments, and put sackcloth on his loins, and mourned for his son many days. All his sons and all his daughters sought to comfort him; but he refused to be comforted, and said, "No, I shall go down to Sheol to my son, mourning." Thus his father bewailed him.

Genesis 37:12-35

Joseph in Prison

IN SLAVERY, FAR FROM HIS FATHER'S PROTECTION, the spoiled boy grows into a man of integrity. His competence and reliability win him a position of trust in the house of his master, Potiphar. However, Potiphar's wife tries to seduce the handsome young man. He refuses, with the predictable result that she denounces him to her husband, who puts him in prison.

Even in prison, Joseph's competence is so manifest that he becomes the right hand man of the chief jailer. Joseph is a person of integrity, but also one intent on climbing up the corporate ladder and quick to seize every opportunity God's providence offers.

His opportunity comes when two important officials are put in prison with him. One morning, they are sad-faced. Courteously, Joseph asks what troubles them. They have a serious problem indeed. They have each had a dream the previous night, but there is no one to interpret for them. Dream interpreters were a highly respected class in ancient Egypt; every person of the upper class had one. But in prison these officials had no access to their usual dream interpreters.

Joseph solves their problem by interpreting their dreams

for them. Events show he did it very accurately. But the official who was returned to favor forgot the imprisoned slave who had rendered him this great service.

Read the next installment of the "ups and downs" of Joseph.

Joseph's master took him and put him into the prison, the place where the king's prisoners were confined; he remained there in prison. But the LORD was with Joseph and showed him steadfast love; he gave him favor in the sight of the chief jailer. The chief jailer committed to Joseph's care all the prisoners who were in the prison, and whatever was done there, he was the one who did it. The chief jailer paid no heed to anything that was in Joseph's care, because the LORD was with him; and whatever he did, the LORD made it prosper.

Some time after this, the cupbearer of the king of Egypt and his baker offended their lord the king of Egypt. Pharaoh was angry with his two officers, the chief cupbearer and the chief baker, and he put them in custody...in the prison where Joseph was confined. The captain of the guard charged Joseph with them, and he waited on them; and they continued for some time in custody. One night they both dreamed—the cupbearer and the baker of the king of Egypt, who were confined in the prison—each his own dream, and each dream with its own meaning. When Joseph came to them in the morning, he saw that they were troubled. So he asked Pharaoh's officers, who were with him in custody in his master's house, "Why are your faces downcast today?" They said to him, "We have had dreams, and there is no one to interpret them." And Joseph said to them, "Do not interpretations belong to God? Please tell them to me."

So the chief cupbearer told his dream to Joseph, and said to him, "In my dream there was a vine before me, and on the vine there were three branches. As soon as it budded, its blossoms came out and the clusters ripened into grapes. Pharaoh's cup was in my hand; and I took the grapes and pressed them into Pharaoh's cup, and placed the cup in Pharaoh's hand." Then Joseph said to him, "This is its interpretation: the three branches are three days; within three days Pharaoh will lift up your head and restore you to your office; and you shall place Pharaoh's cup in his hand, just as you used to do when you were his cupbearer. But remember me when it is well with you; please do me the kindness to make mention of me to Pharaoh, and so get me out of this place. For in fact I was stolen out of the land of the Hebrews; and here also I have done nothing that they should have put me into the dungeon."

When the chief baker saw that the interpretation was favorable, he said to Joseph, "I also had a dream: there were three cake baskets on my head, and in the uppermost basket there were all sorts of baked food for Pharaoh, but the birds were eating it out of the basket on my head." And Joseph answered, "This is its interpretation: the three baskets are three days; within three days Pharaoh will lift up your head—from you!—and hang you on a pole; and the birds will eat the flesh from you."

On the third day, which was Pharaoh's birthday, he made a feast for all his servants, and lifted up the head of the chief cupbearer and the head of the chief baker among his servants. He restored the chief cupbearer to his cupbearing, and he placed the cup in Pharaoh's hand; but the chief baker he hanged, just as Joseph had interpreted to them. Yet the chief cupbearer did not remember Joseph, but forgot him.

Genesis 39:20-23 and 40:1-23

Joseph Comes Out on Top

JOSEPH REMAINS IN PRISON OVER TWO YEARS. This spoiled boy grew through the suffering that life brought, and he was ready when his great opportunity came. Pharaoh had a pair of dreams that none of his skilled dream interpreters could explain! Ancient Egyptians took dreams seriously, so the unexplained dreams caused consternation in the court. At this point the official whom Joseph had helped long before remembered him and suggested that Pharaoh try him. This was Joseph's big chance.

So Joseph was taken out of prison, shaved and clothed in the formal Egyptian attire expected of one who appeared before Pharaoh. He succeeded in interpreting the dreams. Pharaoh was so impressed, he placed Joseph in the highest office in the kingdom.

In this powerful position, Joseph shows the same competence and reliability he showed in the house of Potiphar and in prison. He is now responsible for all of Egypt, and he institutes a massive economic plan to prepare for the coming years of famine. The little nomad boy has become thoroughly Egyptianized, as so many clever immigrants to our country became Americanized and politically or economically successful. In fact, he seems to prefigure the American dream of "the poor boy who makes good."

We know that immigrants coming to this country generally face a great culture shock. They have to learn not only a new language, but also a whole new way of doing everything, from high finance to table manners. The trauma they go through can be compared to that of Joseph, the boy from the simple life-style of nomads, suddenly thrust into the highly advanced, complex civilization of Egypt. Joseph grew through a challenge that might have destroyed others.

Read the story of Joseph's rise to power.

After two whole years, Pharaoh dreamed that he was standing by the Nile, and there came up out of the Nile seven sleek and fat cows, and they grazed in the reed grass. Then seven other cows, ugly and thin, came up out of the Nile after them, and stood by the other cows on the bank of the Nile. The ugly and thin cows ate up the seven sleek and fat cows. And Pharaoh awoke. Then he fell asleep and dreamed a second time; seven ears of grain, plump and good, were growing on one stalk. Then seven ears, thin and blighted by the east wind, sprouted after them. The thin ears swallowed up the seven plump and full ears. Pharaoh awoke, and it was a dream. In the morning his spirit was troubled; so he sent and called for all the magicians of Egypt and all its wise men. Pharaoh told them his dreams, but there was no one who could interpret them to Pharaoh.

Then the chief cupbearer said to Pharaoh, "I remember my faults today. Once Pharaoh was angry with his servants, and put me and the chief baker in custody in the house of the captain of the guard. We dreamed on the same night, he and I, each having a dream with its own meaning. A young Hebrew was there with us, a servant of the captain of the guard. When we told him, he interpreted our dreams to us, giving an interpretation to each according to his dream. As he interpreted to us, so it turned out; I was restored to my office, and the baker was hanged."

Then Pharaoh sent for Joseph, and he was hurriedly brought out of the dungeon. When he had shaved himself and changed his clothes, he came in before Pharaoh. And Pharaoh said to Joseph, "I have had a dream, and there is no one who can interpret it. I have heard it said of you that when you hear a dream you can interpret it." Joseph answered Pharaoh, "It is not I; God will give Pharaoh a favorable answer." Then Pharaoh said to Joseph, "In my dream I was standing on the banks of the Nile; and seven cows, fat and sleek, came up out of the Nile and fed in the reed grass. Then seven other cows came up after them, poor, very ugly, and thin. Never had I seen such ugly ones in all the land of Egypt. The thin and ugly cows ate up the first seven fat cows, but when they had eaten them no one would have known that they had done so, for they were still as ugly as before. Then I awoke. I fell asleep a second time and I saw in my dream seven ears of grain, full and good, growing on one stalk, and seven ears, withered, thin, and blighted by the east wind, sprouting after them; and the thin ears swallowed up the seven good ears. But when I told it to the magicians, there was no one who could explain it to me."

Then Joseph said to Pharaoh, "Pharaoh's dreams are one and the same; God has revealed to Pharaoh what he is about to do. The seven good cows are seven years, and the seven good ears are seven years; the dreams are one. The seven lean and ugly cows that came up after them are seven years, as are the seven empty ears blighted by the east wind. They are seven years of famine. It is as I told Pharaoh; God has shown to Pharaoh what he is about to do. There will come seven years of great plenty throughout all the land of Egypt. After them there will arise seven years of famine, and all the plenty will be forgotten in the land of Egypt; the famine will consume the land. The plenty will no longer be known in the land because of the famine that will follow, for it will be very grievous. And the doubling of Pharaoh's dream means that the thing is fixed by God, and God will shortly bring it about. Now therefore let Pharaoh select a man who is discerning and wise, and set him over the land of Egypt. Let Pharaoh proceed to appoint over-seers over the land, and take one-fifth of the produce of the land of Egypt during the seven plenteous years. Let them gather all the food of these good years that are com-ing, and lay up grain under the authority of Pharaoh for food in the cities, and let them keep it. That food shall be a reserve for the land against the seven years of famine that are to befall the land of Egypt, so that the land may not per-ish through the famine."

The proposal pleased Pharaoh and all his servants. Pharaoh said to his servants, "Can we find anyone else like this—one in whom is the spirit of God?" So Pharaoh said to Joseph, "Since God has shown you all this, there is no one so discerning and wise as you. You shall be over my house, and all my people shall order themselves as you command; only with regard to the throne will I be greater than you." And Pharaoh said to Joseph, "See, I have set you over all the land of Egypt." Removing his signet ring from his hand, Pharaoh put it on Joseph's hand; he arrayed him in garments of fine linen, and put a gold chain around his neck. He had him ride in the chariot of his second-in-com-mand; and they cried out in front of him, "Bow the knee!" Thus he set him over all the land of Egypt.

Genesis 41:1-45

Questions for Reflection

1. Has a dream ever been important in your life or the life of someone you know?

2. Jacob in his youth experienced favoritism from his parents. In his old age he showed favoritism to two of his sons. Do you know a case where adults use the same methods in raising their children that their parents used in raising them?

3. Do you know a family where hostility among brothers and sisters is strong? Is this a blended family, like Jacob's? Is it a family where parents have shown favoritism?

—◆◆◆—

4. Joseph's spiritual growth seems to have begun when he was taken away from the security of home and had to struggle for survival in a foreign land. When have you experienced being in a foreign land or an unfamiliar situation? Do you think the experience contributed to your spiritual growth?

5. Joseph taught Pharaoh to plan to avoid future disaster. Are there ways in which our society should be doing this?

6. Do you know any success story as remarkable as Joseph's? What causes some people to become such outstanding successes?

Suggestions for Further Reading
Genesis 37—41
Psalm 105:16-24

Prayer

Father, we praise you and thank you for choosing us and for sending Jesus to show us how to be faithful sons and daughters.

Forgive us the times when our favoritism divided others.

Forgive us our pettiness when we resented others' being favored.

May we, like Joseph, embrace and share the gifts you have given us and trust in your ever-present guidance in all the ups and downs of our lives.

This we ask in Jesus' name. Amen.

Jeanne M. Griffiths, 50, Denver, Colorado

CHAPTER SEVEN

The Mature Joseph and His Father

A Journey to Egypt

FOR TWENTY-TWO YEARS AFTER JOSEPH was sold to the Egyptians as a slave, his father Jacob, who is also called Israel, continued to live with his eleven remaining sons in the arid hill country of Canaan. Then famine came on the land, as it had in the time of his grandfather Abraham.

In his old age Jacob was not as venturesome as Abraham had been. He was also better supplied with sons. So he remained in Canaan, but sent ten of his sons to Egypt to obtain grain for the family. He kept Benjamin with him because Benjamin, the second son of his favorite wife Rachel and only full brother of the missing Joseph, had now become his favorite. He was still grieving the loss of Joseph, and would not risk losing Benjamin also. He seemed not at all concerned about the possible loss of his other ten sons. He was like the many parents who are not even aware of the severe damage their favoritism is doing to their families.

The ten brothers made the journey to Egypt. Since Joseph was in charge of all the grain of Egypt, the brothers had to come to him to obtain what they needed. These rough nomads were awestruck on entering the court of a mighty Egyptian official. They prostrated themselves before him in a gesture of humility. Joseph by now was dressed and shaved like an Egyptian, and they did not recognize him. He, however, recognized them, and immediately remembered his childhood dreams in which they had bowed down to him. This is the first of several times when the dreams will be literally fulfilled.

Strangers were not always welcomed in Egypt, any more than they are in the United States today. The ten brothers were much like immigrants from poor countries today, bewildered and terrified by the all-powerful bureaucracy they had to face in order to survive. They were helpless when the governor accused them of being spies and threw them into prison for three days.

The grace of God worked in the brothers during this terrible experience. They had tried to bury their guilt about Joseph, and they probably thought they had succeeded, but God had not given up on them. Perhaps their suffering in an Egyptian prison made real to the brothers for the first time what they had subjected their brother to. God can use suffering to shake us out of our complacency and open our hearts, though only if we allow it.

When they are called for a second hearing, we get our first glimpse of what is going on in their hearts. They tell one another that what is happening to them must be a punishment for the great wrong they did to their brother Joseph so long ago. These are words spoken among themselves in their own language; they never guess that the governor, who has used an interpreter to communicate with them, understands what they are saying.

But Joseph hears this first indication that his brothers are moving toward repentance, and he weeps. This is the first suggestion that he is moving toward forgiveness. It is part of the realism of the story that the reconciliation is not instant. The process of conversion takes time on both sides.

Read the story of the brother's first trip to Egypt.

When Jacob learned that there was grain in Egypt, he said to his sons, "Why do you keep looking at one another? I have heard," he said, "that there is grain in Egypt; go down and buy grain for us there, that we may live and not die." So ten of Joseph's brothers went down to buy grain in Egypt. But Jacob did not send Joseph's brother Benjamin with his brothers, for he feared that harm might come to him...

Now Joseph was governor over the land; it was he who sold to all the people of the land. And Joseph's brothers came and bowed themselves before him with their faces to the ground. When Joseph saw his brothers, he recognized them, but he treated them like strangers and spoke harshly to them. "Where do you come from?" he said. They said, "From the land of Canaan, to buy food." Although Joseph had recognized his brothers, they did not recognize him. Joseph also remembered the dreams that he had dreamed about them. He said to them, "You are spies; you have come to see the nakedness of the land!" They said to him, "No, my lord; your servants have come to buy food.... We, your servants, are twelve brothers, the sons of a certain man in the land of Canaan; the youngest, however, is now with our father, and one is no more." But Joseph said to them, "It is just as I have said to you; you are spies! Here is how you shall be tested: as Pharaoh lives, you shall not leave this place unless your youngest brother comes here! Let one of you go and bring your brother, while the rest of you remain in prison, in order that your words may be tested, whether there is truth in you; or else, as Pharaoh lives, surely you are spies." And he put them all together in prison for three days.

On the third day Joseph said to them, "Do this and you will live, for I fear God: if you are honest men, let one of your brothers stay here where you are imprisoned. The rest of you shall go and carry grain for the famine of your households, and bring your youngest brother to me. Thus your words will be verified, and you shall not die." And they agreed to do so. They said to one another, "Alas, we are paying the penalty for what we did to our brother; we saw his anguish when he pleaded with us, but we would not listen. That is why this anguish has come upon us." They did not know that Joseph understood them, since he spoke with them through an interpreter. He turned away from them and wept; then he returned and spoke to them. And he picked out Simeon and had him bound before their eyes. Joseph then gave orders to fill their bags with grain, to return every man's money to his sack, and to give them provisions for their journey. This was done for them.

They loaded their donkeys with their grain, and departed.

Genesis 42:1-26

—◊—

73

A Second Journey to Egypt

JACOB AND HIS FAMILY CONSUMED ALL THE GRAIN the brothers had brought back from Egypt, but the famine continued. Jacob, who has become a cranky old man, demands that the brothers return to Egypt to buy more grain. When they insist that they cannot return without Benjamin, Jacob is as unreasonable as he is domineering. He blames them bitterly for ever letting the Egyptian governor know about the existence of Benjamin.

He is finally forced to let young Benjamin go, as most parents have to let go of even their most favored children. When the eleven brothers come before Joseph they again bow to the ground, reminding us again of Joseph's dreams. We feel their nervousness in this alien and threatening environment.

Joseph, in contrast, is very much in control and arranges his meeting with his brothers carefully, not in his official hall but at a meal in his own home. We can imagine how puzzled and ill at ease these sheep herders are in the luxurious palace of Pharaoh's governor.

When Joseph enters the banquet hall, he greets the brothers cordially, and inquires about their aged father. When he sees Benjamin, his one full brother, he is so overcome with emotion that he has to leave the room.

The banquet continues, with a diplomatic seating arrangement in which the unwashed and uncouth nomads are not seated with the refined Egyptians. Significantly, Joseph sits alone. He does not identify completely with either Egyptians or nomads. However, he makes clear his special interest in Benjamin.

Read the next installment of the story of Joseph and his brothers.

Now the famine was severe in the land. And when they had eaten up the grain that they had brought from Egypt, their father said to them, "Go again, buy us a little more food." But Judah said to him, "The man solemnly warned us, saying, 'You shall not see my face unless your brother is with you.' If you will send our brother with us, we will go down and buy you food; but if you will not send him, we will not go down, for the man said to us, 'You shall not see my face, unless your brother is with you.'" Israel said, "Why did you treat me so badly as to tell the man that you had another brother?" They replied, "The man questioned us carefully about ourselves and our kindred, saying, 'Is your father still alive? Have you another brother?' What we told him was in answer to these questions. Could we in any way know that he would say, 'Bring your brother down'?"...

Then their father Israel said to them, "If it must be so, then do this: take some of the choice fruits of the land in your bags, and carry them down as a present to the man— a little balm and a little honey, gum, resin, pistachio nuts, and almonds. ...Take your brother also, and be on your way again to the man; may God Almighty grant you mercy before the man, so that he may send back your other brother and Benjamin. As for me, if I am bereaved of my children, I am bereaved." So the men took the present, and they took double the money with them, as well as Benjamin. Then they went on their way down to Egypt, and stood before Joseph.

When Joseph saw Benjamin with them, he said to the steward of his house, "Bring the men into the house, and slaughter an animal and make ready, for the men are to dine with me at noon." The man did as Joseph said, and brought the men to Joseph's house....

When Joseph came home, they brought him the present that they had carried into the house, and bowed to the ground before him. He inquired about their welfare, and said, "Is your father well, the old man of whom you spoke? Is he still alive?" They said, "Your servant our father is well; he is still alive." And they bowed their heads and did obeisance. Then he looked up and saw his brother Benjamin, his mother's son, and said, "Is this your youngest brother, of whom you spoke to me? God be gracious to you, my son!" With that, Joseph hurried out, because he was overcome with affection for his brother, and he was about to weep. So he went into a private room and wept there. Then he washed his face and came out; and controlling himself he said, "Serve the meal." They served him by himself, and them by themselves, and the Egyptians who ate with him by themselves, because the Egyptians could not eat with the Hebrews, for that is an abomination to the Egyptians. When they were seated before him, the firstborn according to his birthright and the youngest according to his youth, the men looked at one another in amazement. Portions were taken to them from Joseph's table, but Benjamin's portion was five times as much as any of theirs. So they drank and were merry with him.

Genesis 43:1-7, 11, 13-17, 24-34

Reconciliation

AT LAST, JOSEPH CAN ENDURE THE INCREASING TENSION no more. (Nor can we the readers.) As a last preparation for the grand climax, Joseph sends the Egyptians from the room. Then he weeps for the third time, now without restraint, so that the Egyptians in the other room hear him. He tells the astonished brothers, "I am Joseph."

Pope John XXIII, whose baptismal name was Angelo Guiseppe (Joseph), recalled this moving scene on one occasion when he met with a group of Jewish leaders. He, too, wept, recalling the centuries of alienation between Jews and Christians, and said, "I am your brother Joseph."

Joseph's brothers, understandably, are terrified. The same can happen to us when a sin committed long ago and more or less forgotten suddenly intrudes into our lives.

Joseph's response to the frightened brothers is the heart of the story. Their guilt and shame are so obvious he does not need to mention the matter. Instead, he shows them the larger story of which their sin was a small part.

From this broader point of view, it is not the brothers who caused Joseph to go down to Egypt, but God. The purpose was not to give vent to jealousy, but to give life by putting Joseph in a position from which he would be able to save the whole family during the long famine.

Joseph has a sense of timing. If he had revealed this bigger picture to the brothers before they had come to repentance for their crime, it might have prevented their conversion. They had to face their guilt first. Then they could receive forgiveness and see the good that the providence of God had drawn out of their sin.

This moment of enlightenment for the brothers is also a moment of enlightenment for the reader. Up to this point, this has been a fairly typical "rags-to-riches" adventure story about Joseph. If this was the point of the story, we would expect the brothers to be punished and disappear from the scene. However, the story is not only about Joseph but also about God's loving care for the descendants of Abraham. So the story is not complete until the entire family is saved.

Read the climax of the Joseph story.

> Then Joseph could no longer control himself before all those who stood by him, and he cried out, "Send everyone away from me." So no one stayed with him when Joseph made himself known to his brothers. And he wept so loudly that the Egyptians heard it, and the household of Pharaoh heard it. Joseph said to his brothers, "I am Joseph. Is my father still alive?" But his brothers could not answer him, so dismayed were they at his presence.
>
> Then Joseph said to his brothers, "Come closer to me." And they came closer. He said, "I am your brother, Joseph, whom you sold into Egypt. And now do not be distressed, or angry with yourselves, because you sold me here; for God sent me before you to preserve life. For the famine has been in the land these two years; and there are five more years in which there will be neither plowing nor harvest. God sent me before you to preserve for you a remnant on earth, and to keep alive for you many survivors. So it was not you who sent me here, but God; he has made me a father to Pharaoh, and lord of all his house and ruler over all the land of Egypt. Hurry and go up to my father and say to him, 'Thus says your son Joseph, God has made me lord of all Egypt; come down

to me, do not delay. You shall settle in the land of Goshen, and you shall be near me, you and your children and your children's children, as well as your flocks, your herds, and all that you have. I will provide for you there—since there are five more years of famine to come—so that you and your household, and all that you have, will not come to poverty.'... You must tell my father how greatly I am honored in Egypt, and all that you have seen. Hurry and bring my father down here." Then he fell upon his brother Benjamin's neck and wept, while Benjamin wept upon his neck. And he kissed all his brothers and wept upon them; and after that his brothers talked with him.

Genesis 45:1-15

The Family Journey to Egypt

WHEN THE AGED JACOB RECEIVES THE NEWS of Joseph's position in Egypt and his invitation to the family to come to Egypt, he decides to go. This must have been a difficult decision for one who had been born in the promised land of Canaan and returned to it after his youthful adventures, expecting to inherit it as part of the promise of God to Abraham and Isaac. He is like many people today who have to make major moves at an age when they are not physically or psychologically ready to disrupt their lives.

Jacob leaves, so frail he has to be carried by his sons. On this final journey God once more speaks to him. God had spoken to him once at the beginning of his adult life, as he fled from his brother Esau; again, at the major turning point when he returned from Haran with his family to face Esau. This last time God tells him not to be afraid to go into the strange land, because God will go with him, and the promises will be fulfilled in spite of this temporary move out of the promised land. God adds a new promise, perhaps the one that means most to this father who had mourned the death of his son Joseph for twenty-two years. The new promise was that Joseph would close Jacob's eyes in death.

Read the story of Jacob's move to Egypt.

When Israel set out on his journey with all that he had and came to Beer-sheba, he offered sacrifices to the God of his father Isaac. God spoke to Israel in visions of the night, and said, "Jacob, Jacob." And he said, "Here I am." Then he said, "I am God, the God of your father; do not be afraid to go down to Egypt, for I will make of you a great nation there. I myself will go down with you to Egypt, and I will also bring you up again; and Joseph's own hand shall close your eyes."

Then Jacob set out from Beer-sheba; and the sons of Israel carried their father Jacob, their little ones, and their wives, in the wagons that Pharaoh had sent to carry him....

Joseph made ready his chariot and went up to meet his father Israel in Goshen. He presented himself to him, fell on his neck, and wept on his neck a good while. Israel said to Joseph, "I can die now, having seen for myself that you are still alive."

Genesis 46:1-5; 46:29-30

Jacob in Egypt

WITH GREAT LOVE AND REVERENCE Joseph presents his 130-year-old father to Pharaoh. Pharaoh receives him graciously, and the old nomad blesses the great ruler. This blessing is amazing in a culture that considered Pharaoh a god and has no respect for poor immigrants. It is a sign of the extreme respect in which old age was held that such a blessing was not seen as presumptuous. For the reader, it is also a reminder of God's promise to Abraham that he would be a blessing for all peoples.

As Joseph had lived seventeen years under the protection of his father Jacob, Jacob now lived seventeen years in Egypt under the protection of his powerful son Joseph. Reversal of parent and child roles is not only a current phenomenon.

During these final years Jacob thought about his coming death, and he made an extraordinary request. He asked Joseph to bring his body all the way back to Canaan and bury it in the cave Abraham had purchased at Hebron. Jacob was the bearer of God's promise that Canaan would belong to the descendants of Abraham. He had accepted the sojourn in Egypt as a necessary thing, but he did not want his family assimilated into the dominant Egyptian culture. With his dead body he wanted to remind them that Canaan was where they really belonged, and they must return there one day.

As he faced his death, Jacob felt his oneness with the past of his family and with its future. Jacob's plans for his funeral remind me of many funerals I have attended, where the body of the aged parent seems to link the words spoken about the past with the voices of grandchildren and great-grandchildren whose presence speaks of the future. Like Jacob, each of us is a link between past and future.

Read the final installment of the story of Jacob.

Joseph brought in his father Jacob, and presented him before Pharaoh, and Jacob blessed Pharaoh. Pharaoh said to Jacob, "How many are the years of your life?" Jacob said to Pharaoh, "The years of my earthly sojourn are one hundred thirty; few and hard have been the years of my life. They do not compare with the years of the life of my ancestors during their long sojourn." Then Jacob blessed Pharaoh, and went out from the presence of Pharaoh. Joseph settled his father and his brothers, and granted them a holding in the land of Egypt, in the best part of the land, in the land of Rameses, as Pharaoh had instructed.

Thus Israel settled in the land of Egypt, in the region of Goshen; and they gained possessions in it, and were fruitful and multiplied exceedingly. Jacob lived in the land of Egypt seventeen years; so the days of Jacob, the years of his life, were one hundred forty-seven years.

When the time of Israel's death drew near, he called his son Joseph and said to him, "If I have found favor with you, put your hand under my thigh and promise to deal loyally and truly with me. Do not bury me in Egypt. When I lie down with my ancestors, carry me out of Egypt and bury me in their burial place." He answered, "I will do as you have said."

Genesis 47: 7-11; 27-30

Questions for Reflection

1. What do you know about the practical and psychological problems of poor immigrants who come to the United States today as the ten brothers came to Egypt? Do you think they feel as helpless in the presence of our government officials as the brothers did before the governor?

2. Do you know a case, like that of Joseph's brothers, where suffering led to new insight and perhaps repentance?

—∿∿—

3. Does the Joseph story remind you of any story you know of reconciliation in a family? Or of a family that needs reconciliation?

4. Do you know any case of a person who, like Joseph, suffered ill treatment but eventually benefitted from it and was able to help others?

5. Do you know anyone who, like Jacob, in old age had to leave her or his home territory? What feelings go with such a move?

6. By the instructions he gave about his burial, Jacob gave a message to his children and grandchildren that they would never forget. Do you know people today whose instructions about their funerals have given an important message? What instructions have you left for your funeral?

Suggestions for Further Reading
Genesis 42—50.

Prayer

Loving God, we give you thanks and praise for the loving providence that you have shown us throughout our lives. Guide us in our pilgrimage as you did Jacob. Lead us to reconciliation with family and friends as you did Joseph and his brothers. Feed our souls and bodies as you did the starving Israelites. Protect and guard us as we, too, face the unknown journeys of life. Be our hope and refuge in suffering and pain. Change the evil that surrounds us to good as you did for Joseph. Give us compassionate and sharing hearts for all we meet on life's journey. Comfort us at the moment of our death as you did Jacob. We place ourselves in your boundless providence knowing that you are always with us. Amen.

Rosemary Angelos, 76, Littleton, Colorado

CHAPTER EIGHT

Moses:
The First Eighty Years

A Conspiracy of Women

THE SECOND BOOK OF THE BIBLE, Exodus, is the story of Moses, who led the people out of slavery in Egypt. It begins with a brief glance back at Jacob and Joseph, who brought the people into Egypt in the first place. This context is important because it reminds us that, though Israel has been four hundred years in Egypt, they really belong elsewhere, in the promised land of Canaan.

The ruling dynasty that had been so supportive of Joseph and his family is overthrown by different leadership, so the Israelites find themselves in the situation of any loyal party member when a different party comes into power. They lose their privileges and become slaves of Pharaoh.

But these oppressed people multiply amazingly. After reading the stories of Abraham, Isaac and Jacob, we know that fruitfulness is a gift from God, so this great increase in numbers is something to marvel at, fulfillment of one of God's promises to Abraham. Pharaoh does not see it that way at all. The oppressor is always afraid of the oppressed, so Pharaoh fears that his many slaves, who had such good reason to hate him, would join with some foreign enemy to topple his regime.

He decided that national security required the gradual elimination of the threatening minority. His method was population control, aimed at drastically reducing the alarming birth rate. His ultimate goal was genocide. The story would seem farfetched if we had not seen so many examples in our time of those set on wiping out some race or tribe or type of people.

First, Pharaoh enlisted the help of the midwives who assisted the Hebrew women in giving birth. He instructed them to kill all the male children. The baby girls could be allowed to live, since he thought women were useful as servants, but not dangerous. The story will show how wrong he was.

We do not know whether the midwives worshipped the God of Abraham, Isaac and Jacob, but they believed in a god who was in favor of life, not death. Therefore, "insignificant" women though they were, they practiced civil disobedience against almighty Pharaoh. They refused to kill the babies. It is interesting that the Bible records the names of these women, but not the name of the Pharaoh. The people worth remembering are not always those in high places. So, thanks to God and to the midwives, the people of Israel continued to multiply.

The Egyptians' fear also escalated. So Pharaoh ordered that the baby boys should all be drowned in the Nile River. (He makes us think of King Herod, who was so afraid of a new king that he had all the baby boys in the area around Bethlehem slaughtered.)

Again, it was a woman who resisted the all-powerful Pharaoh. One of the slave women bore a son and refused to give him up to Pharaoh's decree of death. She hid him as long as she could. Then, in effect, she gave him up for adoption. She decided to risk everything on the hope that a woman, even the daughter of Pharaoh himself, would have pity on the beautiful child. A slave woman could not approach a woman of the royalty, but she placed Moses in a watertight basket among the reeds at the edge of the Nile, knowing Pharaoh's daughter would come there to bathe.

Moses' mother was wise. When Pharaoh's daughter saw the crying baby she took pity on it and risked her father's wrath by protecting the baby. A little girl, Moses' sister, was standing by, watching. She would be a good patroness for teenage baby-sitters. When she saw that the moment was right, the quick-witted child offered to find a nurse for the baby and brought her mother. She completed the circle of women, young and old, Egyptian and Israelite, who joined hands to protect the life of the baby Moses. By their collaboration they overcame the Pharaoh. It is a story about the power of those who seem to have no power.

Read the story of baby Moses.

> These are the names of the sons of Israel who came to Egypt with Jacob, each with his household: Reuben, Simeon, Levi, and Judah, Issachar, Zebulun, and Benjamin, Dan and Naphtali, Gad and Asher. The total number of people born to Jacob was seventy. Joseph was already in Egypt. Then Joseph died, and all his brothers, and that whole generation. But the Israelites were fruitful and prolific; they multiplied and grew exceedingly strong, so that the land was filled with them.
>
> Now a new king arose over Egypt, who did not know Joseph. He said to his people, "Look, the Israelite people are more numerous and more powerful than we. Come, let us deal shrewdly with them, or they will increase and, in the event of war, join our enemies and fight against us and escape from the land." Therefore they set taskmasters over them to oppress them with forced labor. They built supply cities, Pithom and Rameses, for Pharaoh. But the more they were oppressed, the more they multiplied and spread, so that the Egyptians came to dread the Israelites....
>
> The king of Egypt said to the Hebrew midwives, one of whom was named Shiphrah and the other Puah, "When you act as midwives to the Hebrew women, and see them on the birthstool, if it is a boy, kill him; but if it is a girl, she shall live." But the midwives feared God; they did not do as the king of Egypt commanded them, but they let the boys live. So the king of Egypt summoned the midwives and said to them, "Why have you done this, and allowed the boys to live?" The midwives said to Pharaoh, "Because the Hebrew women are not like the Egyptian women; for they are vigorous and give birth before the midwife comes to them." So God dealt well with the midwives; and the people multiplied and became very strong. And because the midwives feared God, he gave them families. Then Pharaoh commanded all his people, "Every boy that is born to the Hebrews you shall throw into the Nile, but you shall let every girl live."

Now a man from the house of Levi went and married a Levite woman. The woman conceived and bore a son; and when she saw that he was a fine baby, she hid him three months. When she could hide him no longer she got a papyrus basket for him, and plastered it with bitumen and pitch; she put the child in it and placed it among the reeds on the bank of the river. His sister stood at a distance, to see what would happen to him.

The daughter of Pharaoh came down to bathe at the river, while her attendants walked beside the river. She saw the basket among the reeds and sent her maid to bring it. When she opened it, she saw the child. He was crying, and she took pity on him, "This must be one of the Hebrews' children," she said. Then his sister said to Pharaoh's daughter, "Shall I go and get you a nurse from the Hebrew women to nurse the child for you?" Pharaoh's daughter said to her, "Yes." So the girl went and called the child's mother. Pharaoh's daughter said to her, "Take this child and nurse it for me, and I will give you your wages." So the woman took the child and nursed it. When the child grew up, she brought him to Pharaoh's daughter, and she took him as her son. She named him Moses, "because," she said, "I drew him out of the water."

Exodus 1:1—2:10

Activist and Exile

FOR FORTY YEARS MOSES LIVED in the luxury of Pharaoh's court. Eventually, like so many minority people who succeed in the majority culture, he became uncomfortable with his mixed heritage. He visited the Hebrew slaves and recognized them as his own people, even though their lives were so completely different from his. His anger at their oppression broke out into violence: He killed an Egyptian. This accomplished nothing for his people, and he had to flee the country to escape the police.

He is taken into the tent of Reuel, a desert nomad living in the style in which Abraham, Isaac and Jacob had lived, four hundred years earlier. The culture shock for Moses, product of the sophisticated Egyptian court, must have been comparable to what Joseph experienced long before when he made the same transition in reverse. Moses married Reuel's daughter and stayed with her family for forty years. Moses did not know that the skills of desert survival which he was learning would serve him well in the great work he would begin at the age of eighty.

Read the story of the angry young Moses.

One day, after Moses had grown up, he went out to his people and saw their forced labor. He saw an Egyptian beating a Hebrew, one of his kinsfolk. He looked this way and that, and seeing no one he killed the Egyptian and hid him in the sand. When he went out the next day, he saw two Hebrews fighting; and he said to the one who was in the wrong, "Why do you strike your fellow Hebrew?" He answered, "Who made you a ruler and judge over us? Do you mean to kill me as you killed the Egyptian?" Then Moses was afraid and thought, "Surely the thing is known." When Pharaoh heard of it, he sought to kill Moses.

But Moses fled from Pharaoh. He settled in the land of Midian, and sat down by a well. The priest of Midian had seven daughters. They came to draw water, and filled the troughs to water their father's flock. But some shepherds came and drove them away. Moses got up and came to their defense and watered their flock. When they returned to their father Reuel, he said, "How is it that you have come back so soon today?" They said, "An Egyptian helped us against the shepherds; he even drew water for us and watered the flock." He said to his daughters, "Where is he? Why did you leave the man? Invite him to break bread." Moses agreed to stay with the man, and he gave Moses his daughter Zipporah in marriage. She bore a son, and he named him Gershom; for he said, "I have been an alien residing in a foreign land."

Exodus 2:11-22

The Burning Bush

ONE DAY MOSES WAS GOING about his ordinary task of watching
the sheep of his father-in-law Reuel (who is also called
Jethro). You can see men and women at that same rather bor-
ing task in that part of the world today. Moses noticed something unusual, a bush that just kept burning. The whole
action of our story starts because an eighty-year-old shepherd
was curious enough to walk over to see this burning bush
more closely. When he did so he found that the bush not only
burned, it talked! God is skilled at using audiovisuals in religious education.

God introduced himself as "the God of your father." We
know nothing about Moses' father Amram, who took no part
in his wife's scheme to save Moses as an infant, but his faith
in God must have made a deep impression on Moses, because
it is the entry point by which God now makes himself known
to Moses. Many adults who have wandered far from their faith
are brought back to it by the grace of God using the memory
of a parent's faith.

God also identifies himself with a longer tradition, as "the
God of Abraham, of Isaac, and of Jacob." We, too, need to
receive faith from the witness of our parents, but also from
that of the wider, longer history of the people of God.

God then confided to Moses that he had heard the
laments of the Israelites, and wanted Moses to go to bring
them out of Egypt. This old shepherd, still wanted by the
police back in Egypt, was hardly a likely prospect to lead an
oppressed minority group out of a great nation that had
enslaved them. Nor did he have any interest in the job. He had
created a new and secure life for himself in the desert and
had nothing left of the youthful zeal that caused him to kill
the Egyptian so long ago.

Now comes a wonderful conversation between God and
Moses in which Moses is anything but a properly respectful
and instantly obedient servant. He raises one objection after
another against his assignment.

God tried to encourage him by offering him a sign. One

day he would bring the whole people back to this mountain to worship. It was a strange kind of sign, since it would take place only after Moses had gone through the laborious and risky work of bringing the people out of Egypt. Perhaps God is hinting to us that we often have to bumble along through difficult times, not really sure that what we are doing is God's will. Afterward, when we look back, we will see clearly that God was guiding us all along. This is the blessing of reviewing our lives as we grow older; God's presence is often so much more visible through hindsight than it was in the midst of things.

The name of God, Yahweh, had not yet been revealed to Israel. Moses complained that he could hardly be expected to convince the people, who lived in a land of many gods, that he was a messenger of God if he did not even know the name of the god who had sent him. Ancient peoples put great importance on names. It was felt that knowing someone's name gave a kind of power over that person. To call a person by name suggested a relationship, or at least the possibility of one. It is very significant when Jesus says that he calls each of his sheep by name. We do not acknowledge the power of names as readily as ancient people did, but in reality names are important to us, too. We feel affirmed when someone calls us by name. We show an unwillingness to enter into relationship with a person by refusing to take the trouble to learn his or her name. Not to give our name puts the other at a distance, makes clear that the relationship will be purely functional, not personal.

So it was important for Moses to know God's name. The name God gave was a strange one, *Yahweh*. Scholars argue about what it means—probably something like "I am who I am." It is a name that suggests the mystery of God's being. Among Jews, this name is considered so sacred that it is never pronounced. When it appears in the Bible the Jewish reader substitutes *Adonai* or *Lord*. Most English Bibles except the Jerusalem Bible follow this custom. When your Old Testament says "Lord," the original is probably *Yahweh*. When your Old

Testament says "God," the original is probably *El*, a more generic term for God, one also applied to pagan gods. At the burning bush God revealed to Moses God's personal name. This was the beginning of an intensely personal relationship between God and Moses.

Moses was to go to the Israelites enslaved in Egypt and give them hope for freedom. This is the first step in the process of change: The people cannot be motivated to the difficult process of liberating themselves from slavery unless they have hope. The same could be said of people enslaved to drugs or any bad habit. Without hope, nothing happens.

But Moses does not feel that he is the one to bring hope to the people. Notice the contrast to the forty-year-old Moses who, without any invitation from God, took on himself the role of saving an Israelite from the Egyptian who was beating him. At eighty, he is aware of his own inadequacy, and he argues that he is a poor choice because he is handicapped by a speech impediment. It is a bit difficult to imagine a person who stutters rallying an oppressed people, negotiating with the oppressive government officials and leading the people to freedom.

God assures Moses that he will have divine help with his speech problem. Moses is not impressed. He has run out of arguments, so he simply pleads, "Please, send someone else!" God is angry, but still determined to bring his chosen leader around. God offers him his brother Aaron to do the speaking for him. As a prophet is a mouth for God, giving God's message to the people, so Aaron will be a mouth for Moses, giving Moses' message to the people. It is interesting that in the end God's original plan seems to have been the best. God did overcome Moses' handicap so that he was able to speak to the people and to Pharaoh himself. But at the time of the burning bush he was not yet at the point where he could imagine that happening.

However, thanks to Moses' sense of his own inadequacy, Aaron did become part of the liberation of the people. Other work was found for him: that of a priest. Often our awareness of our inadequacies serves a good purpose. It motivates us to get others involved and that strengthens our ministry.

Read the story of Moses' call at the burning bush.

Moses was keeping the flock of his father-in-law Jethro, the priest of Midian; he led his flock beyond the wilderness, and came to Horeb, the mountain of God. There the angel of the LORD appeared to him in a flame of fire out of a bush; he looked, and the bush was blazing, yet it was not consumed. Then Moses said, "I must turn aside and look at this great sight, and see why the bush is not burned up." When the LORD saw that he had turned aside to see, God called to him out of the bush, "Moses, Moses!" And he said, "Here I am." Then he said, "Come no closer! Remove the sandals from your feet, for the place on which you are standing is holy ground." He said further, "I am the God of your father, the God of Abraham, the God of Isaac, and the God of Jacob." And Moses hid his face, for he was afraid to look at God.

Then the LORD said, "I have observed the misery of my people who are in Egypt; I have heard their cry on account of their taskmasters. Indeed, I know their sufferings, and I have come down to deliver them from the Egyptians, and to bring them up out of that land to a good and broad land, a land flowing with milk and honey, to the country of the Canaanites, the Hittites, the Amorites, the Perizzites, the Hivites, and the Jebusites.... So come, I will send you to Pharaoh to bring my people, the Israelites, out of Egypt." But Moses said to God, "Who am I that I should go to Pharaoh, and bring the Israelites out of Egypt?" He said, "I will be with you; and this shall be the sign for you that it is I who sent you: when you have brought the people out of Egypt, you shall worship God on this mountain."

But Moses said to God, "If I come to the Israelites and say to them, 'The God of your ancestors has sent me to you,' and they ask me, 'What is his name?' what shall I say to them?" God said to Moses, "I AM WHO I AM." He said further, "Thus you shall say to the Israelites, 'I AM has sent me to you.'" God also said to Moses, "Thus you shall say to the Israelites, 'The LORD, the God of your ancestors, the God of

Abraham, the God of Isaac, and the God of Jacob, has sent me to you':

> This is my name forever,
> and this my title for all generations.

Go and assemble the elders of Israel, and say to them, 'The LORD, the God of your ancestors, the God of Abraham, of Isaac, and of Jacob, has appeared to me, saying: I have given heed to you and to what has been done to you in Egypt. I declare that I will bring you up out of the misery of Egypt, to the land of the Canaanites, the Hittites, the Amorites, the Perizzites, the Hivites and the Jebusites, a land flowing with milk and honey.' They will listen to your voice; and you and the elders of Israel shall go to the king of Egypt and say to him, 'The LORD, the God of the Hebrews, has met with us; let us now go a three days' journey into the wilderness, so that we may sacrifice to the LORD our God.' I know, however, that the king of Egypt will not let you go unless compelled by a mighty hand. So I will stretch out my hand and strike Egypt with all my wonders that I will perform in it; after that he will let you go....

But Moses said to the LORD, "O my Lord, I have never been eloquent, neither in the past nor even now that you have spoken to your servant; but I am slow of speech and slow of tongue." Then the LORD said to him, "Who gives speech to mortals? Who makes them mute or deaf, seeing or blind? Is it not I, the LORD? Now go, and I will be with your mouth and teach you what you are to speak." But he said, "O my Lord, please send someone else." Then the anger of the LORD was kindled against Moses and he said, "What of your brother Aaron, the Levite? I know that he can speak fluently; even now he is coming out to meet you, and when he sees you his heart will be glad. You shall speak to him and put the words in his mouth; and I will be with your mouth and with his mouth, and will teach you what you shall do. He indeed shall speak for you to the people; he shall serve as a mouth for you, and you shall serve as God for him.

Exodus 3:1-20; 4:10-16

Questions for Reflection

1. Can you think of any things that have happened in your lifetime that are like Pharaoh's attempt to kill all the baby boys?

2. Do you know of anyone who, like the midwives, disobeyed a law, but did what was right?

3. Have you heard of anyone who, like young Moses who killed the Egyptian, is indignant in a just cause, but does more harm than good?

—᙭᙭—

4. Moses heard God's call from the burning bush. How have you heard God's call?

5. When have you felt you were standing on holy ground, like Moses at the burning bush?

6. Moses the stutterer did not seem to be a good candidate for the work to which he was called. Do you know any unlikely person called by God to a particular work?

Suggestions for Further Reading

Exodus 1—10
Hebrews 11:23-29

Prayer

Loving and powerful God, the God of Abraham, the God of Isaac, the God of Jacob, we praise you and love you as the "I Am" of all generations of all time.

We ask you to lead us, and protect us in the tasks and events of our daily lives as you did Moses and the Israelites. Make each of us a 'burning bush,' enflamed with your love and empowered to help all in our midst who seek freedom in their lives.

We give you thanks for the particular gifts you have given to each and every one of us. Help us to use these gifts wisely and most of all to know you will be with us as we speak in your name, as you were with Moses and Aaron. Amen.

Nancy M. Van Anne, 69, Greeley, Colorado

CHAPTER NINE

Liberation

Escape in the Night

NOW WE COME TO THE HEART of the story of how God liberated Israel from slavery in Egypt. Moses had argued vehemently with God in his attempts to get out of his assignment. Finally God won, as God has a way of doing. From that point on God's enthusiasm for the liberation of the people seems to take hold of Moses, and he gives the last forty years of his life with tremendous energy to this cause. In the process we see that this old shepherd has leadership qualities of which no one but God could have guessed.

He returns to Egypt and begins a long, drawn-out confrontation with Pharaoh. He demands in the name of Yahweh that Pharaoh allow the Hebrew slaves to go. Pharaoh is himself seen as a god by the Egyptians, and he is not at all impressed by a message from the god of one of his groups of slaves. Then begins a profoundly symbolic story of a struggle between God and the forces of this world which seem so powerful that humans would never even think to challenge them. (Some of us have faced such powers in our own small worlds.)

Moses works a series of wonders to convince Pharaoh of the power of this God of whom Pharaoh has never heard. First come harmless signs, like turning Moses' staff into a serpent and back again. When this does not work, one by one Moses unleashes the famous ten plagues. God turns the water of the Nile into blood, sends plagues of frogs, gnats, flies and locusts, sends a terrible storm and more terrible darkness. After each plague Moses tries again to negotiate with Pharaoh. Anyone with experience of negotiations between great powers will delight in the vivid tale of this struggle between the greatest human power on earth and an old shepherd who speaks for a power beyond this earth. Like most negotiations, it is long and drawn out. We will read only about the final, climactic plague.

God knows that this tenth plague will finally convince Pharaoh to let the people go, so he tells them to prepare themselves for the journey by collecting gold and silver from their Egyptian neighbors. We see here how integrated the Israelites must have been into Egyptian society if each woman could go to her Egyptian neighbor and each man to his to ask for the precious objects that would support them through the desert journey. We also see that the struggle was between Pharaoh and Yahweh; the Egyptian people show no hostility to the slaves who want to escape. It is not only in modern times that those in power fight one another, while ordinary people would prefer to live and let live.

This story also makes us think of all the long-oppressed people of the world who sometimes try, as the Israelites did, to get some kind of compensation for all the years during which they did not have equal opportunities or who demand the return of property taken from their ancestors many generations ago. These demands, like those of the Israelites, can contradict what is ordinarily thought of as property rights. The Egyptians seem to have had less trouble than the privileged class today with "compensatory justice."

The final plague is terrible, perhaps some deadly disease that strikes only children. And it strikes every home, from that of the poorest Egyptian to that of Pharaoh himself. In every family, the firstborn child is stricken and dies. Pharaoh, who killed so many Israelite babies, now suffers the death of his firstborn and those of all his people.

Read the story of the most dramatic night in Moses' life.

The LORD said to Moses, "I will bring one more plague upon Pharaoh and upon Egypt; afterwards he will let you go from here; indeed, when he lets you go, he will drive you away. Tell the people that every man is to ask his neighbor and every woman is to ask her neighbor for objects of silver and gold." The LORD gave the people favor in the sight of the Egyptians....

Moses said, "Thus says the LORD: About midnight I will go out through Egypt. Every firstborn in the land of Egypt shall die, from the firstborn of Pharaoh who sits on his throne to the firstborn of the female slave who is behind the handmill, and all the firstborn of the livestock. Then there will be a loud cry throughout the whole land of Egypt, such as has never been or will ever be again. But not a dog shall growl at any of the Israelites—not at people, not at animals—so that you may know that the LORD makes a distinction between Egypt and Israel. Then all these officials of yours shall come down to me, and bow low to me, saying, 'Leave us, you and all the people who follow you.' After that I will leave." And in hot anger he left Pharaoh....

At midnight the LORD struck down all the firstborn in the land of Egypt, from the firstborn of Pharaoh who sat on his throne to the firstborn of the prisoner who was in the dungeon, and all the firstborn of the livestock. Pharaoh arose in the night, he and all his officials and all the Egyptians; and there was a loud cry in Egypt, for there was not a house without someone dead. Then he summoned Moses and Aaron in the night, and said, "Rise up, go away from my people, both you and the Israelites! Go, worship the LORD, as you said. Take your flocks and your herds, as you said, and be gone. And bring a blessing on me too!"

The Egyptians urged the people to hasten their departure from the land, for they said, "We shall all be dead." So the people took their dough before it was leavened, with their kneading bowls wrapped up in their cloaks on their shoulders. The Israelites had done as Moses told them; they had asked the Egyptians for jewelry of silver and gold, and for clothing, and the LORD had given the people favor in the sight of the Egyptians, so that they let them have what they asked. And so they plundered the Egyptians.

Exodus 11:1-8; 12:29-36

The Passover Meal

DURING THE TRAUMATIC NIGHT when the angel of death visited every home except those of the Israelites, which were protected by the blood of a lamb smeared on the doorpost, the Israelites gathered for a ritual meal, the Passover. For this meal they ate the lambs whose blood had already been smeared on their doorposts. This was a common ritual for shepherds in the springtime, to thank God for the birth of new lambs and beg protection during the year that was beginning. The Israelites were probably accustomed to this spring feast, but it took on an entirely new meaning that awful night when they huddled together in their houses, preparing to leave the land where they had lived for four hundred years.

The biblical author gives particular attention to this ritual meal because it was by reenacting that meal each spring that Israelites throughout the ages would experience their connection with the people who fled from Egypt on that fateful night. Still today, the Passover meal is a Jewish family's greatest celebration of freedom.

History that is merely preserved in books is lifeless, but history that is preserved in celebration continues to hold a people together and to have power in their lives. It is hard to imagine Christianity without Christmas and Easter, or Judaism without Passover.

After sharing this last meal in Egypt, the whole people—women, men and children—began their great journey out of the land of slavery.

Read the story of the origin of the Passover feast.

The LORD said to Moses and Aaron in the land of Egypt: This month shall mark for you the beginning of months; it shall be the first month of the year for you. Tell the whole congregation of Israel that on the tenth of this month they are to take a lamb for each family, a lamb for each household.... You shall keep it until the fourteenth day of this month; then the whole assembled congregation of Israel shall slaughter it at twilight. They shall take some of the blood and put it on the two doorposts and the lintel of the houses in which they eat it. They shall eat the lamb that same night; they shall eat it roasted over the fire with unleavened bread and bitter herbs.... This is how you shall eat it: your loins girded, your sandals on your feet, and your staff in your hand; and you shall eat it hurriedly. It is the passover of the LORD. For I will pass through the land of Egypt that night, and I will strike down every firstborn in the land of Egypt, both human beings and animals; on all the gods of Egypt I will execute judgments: I am the LORD. The blood shall be a sign for you on the houses where you live: when I see the blood, I will pass over you, and no plague shall destroy you when I strike the land of Egypt....

Then Moses called all the elders of Israel and said to them, "Go, select lambs for your families, and slaughter the passover lamb. Take a bunch of hyssop, dip it in the blood that is in the basin, and touch the lintel and the two doorposts with the blood in the basin. None of you shall go outside the door of your house until morning. For the Lord will pass through to strike down the Egyptians; when he sees the blood on the lintel and on the two doorposts, the Lord will pass over that door and will not allow the destroyer to enter your houses to strike you down. You shall observe this rite as a perpetual ordinance for you and your children. When you come to the land that the Lord will give you, as he has promised, you shall keep this observance. And when your children ask you, 'What do you mean by this observance?' you shall say, 'It is the passover sacrifice to the Lord, for he passed over the houses of the Israelites in Egypt, when he struck down the Egyptians but spared our houses.'" And the people bowed down and worshiped.

The Israelites went and did just as the LORD had commanded Moses and Aaron.

Exodus 12:1-13; 21-28

—◊◊◊—

The Crossing of the Red Sea

LIBERATION IS NOT A SINGLE, ONCE-FOR-ALL EVENT for the Israelites, any more than it is for us. The people escaped on the night of the Passover and began their journey. But before long they came to an obstacle they could not get across, the Red Sea. With the building of various dams and of the Suez Canal the geography of Egypt has changed so that we can no longer locate the spot where this happened. It is very unlikely that it is the body of water we today call the Red Sea. For that reason some scholars prefer to call it the Sea of Reeds. Perhaps the uncertainty about the location is providential, because it encourages us to think about the "Red Seas" in our own lives: the apparently insuperable obstacles we meet on our spiritual path.

When the great obstacle halts us, evil forces may be very active. In this story, it is Pharaoh, the enemy of life and of God, who gathers all his horses and chariots and comes in pursuit of the escaping slaves. On the night of Passover, it seemed he had finally made up his mind to let them go, but now we see that that was an illusion.

Notice how often the horses and chariots are mentioned in the story. Horses in ancient times were not farm animals or animals to ride for pleasure; they were used mainly for war. In Egyptian art we see many fierce horses pulling small chariots in which warriors ride, weapons at the ready. This was state-of-the-art weaponry, and it terrified the unarmed ex-slaves who travelled by foot. Their horror of and fascination with war equipment is reflected in the frequency with which it is mentioned.

The Israelites, camped by the sea they could not cross, saw the enormous force of Pharaoh's chariots coming down on them. These were slaves, who had spent their lives in dread of their Egyptian masters. Now all that dread returned and overwhelmed them. Their psychology was not so different from ours. When things went badly, they turned on their leader. They lamented to Moses that they had been better off in Egypt. This is the great sin that would recur throughout the forty years of wandering in the desert. They looked back with nostalgia to the comforts of slavery and preferred them to the stress that goes with freedom. The same can happen today to people who have been freed from Communist domination, from some addiction, from an abusive relationship or other slavery.

Moses gave them the message we sometimes need to hear in times of crisis. Do not be afraid; stand firm; be still. There had been a time for flight. There would come a time to fight. This was the time to stand still and wait for God to act. Perhaps it is the hardest time of all.

They did not have as long to wait as we sometimes do. Soon God spoke to Moses and told him what they were to do. Moses was to tell the people to go forward right *through* the sea. We can come to moments as terrifying as this in our lives.

In Ephesus, in present-day Turkey, archaeologists have found an ancient baptismal font shaped in a very strange way. It is a long, thin rectangle, with steps at one end to walk down into it and steps at the other to climb out of it. In between, those being baptized had to walk for some feet through water over their heads. They were to feel a little of the natural dread of drowning that the Israelites must have felt as they began to walk through the sea.

God can ask us at times to walk into situations as frightening as the sea was to the Israelites. If this happens, we can only pray to be as brave as they were.

But God did not plan for the people to drown. God told Moses to stretch out his staff over the sea. He did so, and a path dried up so the people could walk through. Because the biblical account is put together from more than one version of the story, we cannot be clear about exactly what happened. Some seem to have remembered the parting of the sea as happening instantly, forming a wall on each side of the Israelites. (This version is understandably preferred by artists.) Others remembered God sending a strong east wind all night, which eventually dried up the water. It can happen today, too, that different people who witness the same event describe it in quite different ways.

What is important is that by the power of God the people crossed the obstacle that had seemed insuperable. The evil forces of Pharaoh tried to follow them. Now we see why there was so much emphasis on the military equipment of the Egyptians. The chariot wheels of which they were so proud became clogged in the mud of the seabed. The unarmed Israelites could go through easily, but heavy armaments made it impossible. It makes us think of all the ways in which the armaments we obtain for our benefit can turn against us, from nuclear accidents to handguns that kill the children of their owners.

When all the Israelites had passed through the sea, God told Moses to stretch out his staff over the sea again, and the waters returned to their normal course, drowning Pharaoh and all his chariots and charioteers. We are reminded of the time Pharaoh had tried to drown all the Israelite baby boys.

We proclaim this wonderful story every year at the Easter Vigil before the baptisms. We do not proclaim it because of the event that happened over three thousand years ago, the details of which we can never know for certain. We proclaim this story because it expresses our deep faith that, despite all appearances to the contrary, God is in control of our world and will overcome the forces of evil.

Read the famous story of the crossing of the sea.

When the king of Egypt was told that the people had fled, the minds of Pharaoh and his officials were changed toward the people, and they said, "What have we done, letting Israel leave our service?" So he had his chariot made ready, and took his army with him; he took six hundred picked chariots and all the other chariots of Egypt with officers over all of them.... and he pursued the Israelites, who were going out boldly. The Egyptians pursued them, all Pharaoh's horses and chariots, his chariot drivers and his army; they overtook them camped by the sea, by Pi-hahiroth, in front of Baal-zephon.

As Pharaoh drew near, the Israelites looked back, and there were the Egyptians advancing on them. In great fear the Israelites cried out to the LORD. They said to Moses, "Was it because there were no graves in Egypt that you have taken us away to die in the wilderness? What have you done to us, bringing us out of Egypt? Is this not the very thing we told you in Egypt, 'Let us alone and let us serve the Egyptians'? For it would have been better for us to serve the Egyptians than to die in the wilderness." But Moses said to the people, "Do not be afraid, stand firm, and see the deliverance that the LORD will accomplish for you today; for the Egyptians whom you see today you shall never see again. The LORD will fight for you, and you have only to keep still."

Then the LORD said to Moses, "Why do you cry out to me? Tell the Israelites to go forward. But you lift up your staff, and stretch out your hand over the sea and divide it, that the Israelites may go into the sea on dry ground. Then I will harden the hearts of the Egyptians so that they will go in after them; and so I will gain glory for myself over Pharaoh and all his army, his chariots, and his chariot drivers. And the Egyptians shall know that I am the LORD, when I have gained glory for myself over Pharaoh, his chariots, and his chariot drivers."...

Then Moses stretched out his hand over the sea. The LORD drove the sea back by a strong east wind all night, and turned the sea into dry land; and the waters were divided. The Israelites went into the sea on dry ground, the waters forming a wall for them on their right and on their left. The Egyptians pursued, and went into the sea after them, all of Pharaoh's horses, chariots, and chariot drivers. At the morning watch the LORD in the pillar of fire and cloud looked down upon the Egyptian army, and threw the Egyptian army into panic. He clogged their chariot wheels so that they turned with difficulty. The Egyptians said, "Let us flee from the Israelites, for the LORD is fighting for them against Egypt."

Then the LORD said to Moses, "Stretch out your hand over the sea, so that the water may come back upon the Egyptians, upon their chariots and chariot drivers." So Moses stretched out his hand over the sea, and at dawn the sea returned to its normal depth. As the Egyptians fled before it, the LORD tossed the Egyptians into the sea. The waters returned and covered the chariots and the chariot drivers, the entire army of Pharaoh that had followed them into the sea; not one of them remained. But the Israelites walked on dry ground through the sea, the waters forming a wall for them on their right and on their left.

Thus the LORD saved Israel that day from the Egyptians; and Israel saw the Egyptians dead on the seashore. Israel saw the great work that the LORD did against the Egyptians. So the people feared the LORD and believed in the LORD and in his servant Moses.

Exodus 14:5-18; 21-3

Celebration

WHEN THE ISRAELITES HAD EXPERIENCED the wonder of walking through the sea, and had seen the mighty army of Pharaoh drowned in that same sea, they praised God. Moses started a song of praise, and Miriam, Moses' sister, led all the women, playing musical instruments and dancing. This is probably the sister who had so cleverly helped in saving the infant Moses from being drowned by Pharaoh. Now she is well over eighty, but clearly still a leader among the women. She probably played a large part in organizing support for Moses among the Israelites, and now she organizes a celebration. The Scriptures here have something to say to us about the importance of celebration. These people would have a great many more problems to face in the desert, but they were wise enough to pause to thank God and rejoice for the good things that had happened on their journey so far.

Read about the song Moses and Miriam sang after the crossing of the sea.

Then Moses and the Israelites sang this song to the Lord:

"I will sing to the LORD, for he has triumphed
    gloriously;
    horse and rider he has thrown into the sea.

> The LORD is my strength and my might,
>   and he has become my salvation;
> this is my God, and I will praise him,
>   my father's God, and I will exalt him....

Then the prophet Miriam, Aaron's sister, took a tambourine in her hand; and all the women went out after her with tambourines and with dancing. And Miriam sang to them:

> "Sing to the LORD, for he has triumphed
>   gloriously;
> horse and rider he has thrown into the sea."

Exodus 15:1, 2, 20, 21

Questions for Reflection

1. How do you feel about the Israelites taking the gold and silver of the Egyptians? About modern situations where underprivileged people try to get compensation for what they have been deprived of in the past?

2. What meals have special symbolic importance for you, as the Passover supper does for Jews?

3. The most important event for Jews to remember was the Exodus from Egypt. What are the most important events for Christians to remember? How should we pass on these memories to the next generation?

—∾—

4. Do you think that having state-of-the-art military equipment is as important to us, or as frightening to poor nations, as Pharaoh's horses and chariots were?

5. The Red Sea seemed like an obstacle impossible to get through. Has God ever brought you through an obstacle like that?

6. Is there some action of God in your life for which you would like to praise God as Moses and Miriam and the Israelites did for the crossing of the Red Sea?

Suggestions for Further Reading
Exodus 11—15
Acts 6, 7
Psalm 136

Prayer

Yahweh, our Lord and God, we thank you for freeing the Israelites from their bondage in Egypt. By the story of the first Passover and the crossing of the Red Sea, we see clearly that you are in control of our world. The forces of evil were overcome for the Israelites. We believe you will continue to overcome evil in our world as well if we have faith and trust in you.

Just as the Israelites were liberated from slavery with the leadership of Moses, lead us, Lord, from our own slavery to the material attractions of our secular society and keep us focused on you. Help us to appreciate the many freedoms we enjoy each day.

When faced with the obstacle of the Red Sea, the Israelites had to place their faith in your intermediary Moses in order to cross through the sea. Don't let troubling waters overwhelm us but protect and shield us. Help us to overcome obstacles we face that keep us from following you on our spiritual journey. Grant us courage to walk into frightening situations and persevere, knowing you are there to guide us each step of the way.

We pray for victims of oppression and bondage, those facing discrimination, violence, destitution and injustices of all kinds. Give them hope, and shelter them with your boundless love.

We ask this through Christ our Lord. Amen.

Dorothy Liston, 59, Denver, Colorado

CHAPTER TEN

Education
in the Desert

Food and Rest in the Desert

GOD, THROUGH MOSES, PERFORMED AN AMAZING FEAT by bringing
the Israelite slaves out of Egypt. But this was only the beginning. After the Civil War in the United States, we discovered
that it did not do much good to free slaves unless you
provided them with a means of living and education for
taking on the responsibilities of free people. Educating
these Israelite ex-slaves was a challenge for Moses—and
for God.

We used to think of education as something primarily for
children. Today, because of our longer life span and the rapid
rate of change in our whole society, there is much talk of "lifelong learning." Some say that education is such a valuable
thing, it is too bad we waste so much of it on children! God
believed in lifelong learning from the beginning.

The first thing the people experienced when they had
eaten up the food they carried with them was hunger. Of
course this made them homesick for the meat they had eaten
as slaves in Egypt, so they complained against Moses and
Aaron. God heard them grumbling about the lack of food and
decided this was the point at which to begin their education.

Hunger itself was a part of the education. If God provides
our every need before we know we need it, we can develop
an illusion of self-sufficiency. The times when hunger of one
kind or another makes us aware of our need for God are
important times for our spiritual growth. Whether the hunger
is for material things, for companionship, for excitement or
for security, it can draw us toward God if we let it.

Once the people had learned of their need, God provided
a food that would also be an educational tool. God told the
people about a kind of food they could never have imagined

in Egypt. It was desert food. It appeared early each morning, and melted away when the sun became hot. It may have been the secretion of a tamarisk tree which is still eaten by nomads in the desert and called "manna."

God gave careful instructions about gathering the manna. Each morning they were to gather just enough for their families for the day. They were to save none for the next day. Human nature cries out for security. We all want something extra on the shelf or in the freezer in case of emergency. We all want something extra in the bank for the same reason. The Israelites were like us. In spite of God's command, some gathered a little extra. The next morning they found it had turned rotten. God was teaching them to trust divine providence to provide.

God may not be asking us to make a trip to the grocery store every day. But those who hoard the goods of the earth while others have to go hungry could learn something from the punishment of the Israelites who collected more than they needed.

God uses manna as a visual aid to teach the people trust. But it can teach something else also: the importance of the Sabbath rest. Contrary to the general rule that only enough should be gathered for the day, God instructed the people to gather enough on Friday for two days, so that they would not have to gather on Saturday, the Sabbath. In this case the extra did not rot overnight!

It is interesting that at the beginning of the journey God vigorously teaches the law of Sabbath rest. Laws against murder and adultery and idolatry can wait a while, till they arrive at Mount Sinai. But the law of Sabbath rest must be observed from the beginning.

The Israelites had been almost killed with overwork by their slave drivers. Now that they are free they have to learn a healthy balance of work and leisure. Perhaps they felt like people today who retire from high-pressure jobs, yearning for rest, yet not quite knowing how to rest.

Americans value work. The Bible shows surprisingly little interest in it. God probably knows humans can figure out for themselves the need for work. God emphasizes the law of holy rest. Later, Jews, like Christians, will make the day of rest a day of worship. That is surely appropriate, but we should not forget that the original command of God was to rest.

What does it mean to rest? Eventually, Jews and Christians would think up all sorts of rules about what was forbidden on the Sabbath. But God's command is very broad, and leaves it to our creativity to find out how to carry out this solemn rest. It is a real challenge.

God also used the manna to teach a third lesson, the importance of remembering. Though the manna ordinarily rotted if kept over even one night, God ordered that a jar of it be kept permanently in the holy place, so that after the people arrived in their own land and no longer received the manna, they would remember how God had provided for them in the desert and would pass that memory on to their children.

The sacredness of memory is emphasized many times in the Bible. In a human relationship, it is important to remember birthdays, favorite foods and important experiences that have been shared. Memory is also important in our relationship with God. Since this has lasted thousands of years, we need to remember the highlights of a whole history. That is why we read the Scriptures in church and at home.

From the way the Church values our common memories, we learn to value our personal memories. God's care in our lives, even the ordinary daily care that gets us through the desert times, deserves to be remembered with reverence. We rush around so much that we often lose touch with memories instead of cherishing them.

Read about God's great educational tool, the manna.

The whole congregation of the Israelites set out from Elim; and Israel came to the wilderness of Sin, which is between Elim and Sinai, on the fifteenth day of the second month after they had departed from the land of Egypt. The whole congregation of the Israelites complained against Moses and Aaron in the wilderness. The Israelites said to them, "If only we had died by the hand of the LORD in the land of Egypt, when we sat by the fleshpots and ate our fill of bread; for you have brought us out into this wilderness to kill this whole assembly with hunger."

Then the LORD said to Moses, "I am going to rain bread from heaven for you, and each day the people shall go out and gather enough for that day. In that way I will test them, whether they will follow my instruction or not. On the sixth day, when they prepare what they bring in, it will be twice as much as they gather on other days."...

[I]n the morning there was a layer of dew around the camp. When the layer of dew lifted, there on the surface of the wilderness was a fine flaky substance, as fine as frost on the ground. When the Israelites saw it, they said to one another, "What is it?" For they did not know what it was. Moses said to them, "It is the bread that the LORD has given you to eat. This is what the LORD has commanded: 'Gather as much of it as each of you needs, an omer to a person according to the number of persons, all providing for those in their own tents.'" The Israelites did so, some gathering more, some less. But when they measured it with an omer, those who gathered much had nothing over, and those who gathered little had no shortage; they gathered as much as each of them needed. And Moses said to them, "Let no one leave any of it over until morning." But they did not listen to Moses; some left part of it until morning, and it bred worms and became foul. And Moses was angry with them....

On the sixth day they gathered twice as much food, two omers apiece. When all the leaders of the congregation came and told Moses, he said to them, "This is what the LORD has commanded: 'Tomorrow is a day of solemn rest, a holy sabbath to the LORD; bake what you want to bake and boil what you want to boil, and all that is left over put aside to be kept until morning.'" So they put it aside until morning, as Moses commanded them; and it did not become foul, and there were no worms in it. Moses said, "Eat it today, for today is a sabbath to the LORD; today you will not find it in the field. Six days you shall gather it; but on the seventh day, which is a sabbath, there will be none."

On the seventh day some of the people went out to gather, and they found none. The LORD said to Moses, "How long will you refuse to keep my commandments and instructions? See! The LORD has given you the sabbath, therefore on the sixth day he gives you food for two days; each of you stay where you are; do not leave your place on the seventh day." So the people rested on the seventh day.

The house of Israel called it manna; it was like coriander seed, white, and the taste of it was like wafers made with honey. Moses said, "This is what the LORD has commanded: 'Let an omer of it be kept throughout your generations, in order that they may see the food with which I fed you in the wilderness, when I brought you out of the land of Egypt.'" And Moses said to Aaron, "Take a jar, and put an omer of manna in it, and place it before the LORD, to be kept throughout your generations."

Exodus 16:1-34

—⁓—

Advice From a Father-in-law

GOD SAW THAT MOSES HIMSELF needed some education in the art of government. For this purpose God sent Jethro (also called Reuel). Jethro, who had taken Moses in when he was escaping punishment for murder, given him his daughter Zipporah in marriage and employed him for forty years, continued to be his friend and mentor. During the difficult struggle with Pharaoh, Moses had sent his wife and sons back to Jethro, who again provided his daughter and grandsons with a home, as so many grandparents do in difficult situations today.

When Jethro heard that Moses had been successful in freeing the people and had travelled with them back to the mountain where Moses used to pasture his flocks, he brought Zipporah and her sons to the Israelite camp.

Moses welcomed his father-in-law. Together they went into the tent. (The storyteller fails to tell us what happened to Zipporah and the children.) Excitedly, Moses told the old man all his adventures and the wonderful things God had done for the Israelites. Jethro was a good listener. He rejoiced in the good his son-in-law had accomplished.

Jethro listened and learned from his son-in-law. But he also had something to teach his son-in-law. The next day he observed Moses at his work of governing the people. Long lines of Israelites waited all day to have Moses settle their problems. By sunset Moses was exhausted, and so were the people. There are people in authority positions today who have to decide everything themselves, and they are not easy people to deal with.

After observing for a day, Jethro gives clear and sensible advice. Moses needs to decentralize, to learn to delegate his authority to capable people, keeping only policy setting and especially difficult cases for himself. In that way, the talents of more people could be used, the people would be happier and Moses might avoid a heart attack.

Moses was wise enough to accept Jethro's criticism and change his style of leadership. The people would probably never have arrived at the promised land if he had not. It is interesting that the people of Israel remembered and passed on this story that showed that an old pagan priest might be wiser than their wisest leader on some points. The story is a challenge to us to be open to criticism that could be helpful, whatever its source.

The example of Jethro also contains some wisdom for anyone who feels called to be a mentor. He listened for a long time, and enthusiastically affirmed the work of his son-in-law, before putting in his word of advice. He knew that a little advice goes a long way.

Read about Jethro, Moses' father-in-law.

Jethro, the priest of Midian, Moses' father-in-law, heard of all that God had done for Moses and for his people Israel, how the LORD had brought Israel out of Egypt. After Moses had sent away his wife Zipporah, his father-in-law Jethro took her back, along with her two sons.... Jethro, Moses' father-in-law, came into the wilderness where Moses was encamped at the mountain of God, bringing Moses' sons and wife to him. He sent word to Moses, "I, your father-in-law Jethro, am coming to you, with your wife and her two sons." Moses went out to meet his father-in-law; he bowed down and kissed him; each asked after the other's welfare, and they went into the tent. Then Moses told his father-in-law all that the LORD had done to Pharaoh and to the Egyptians for Israel's sake, all the hardship that had beset them on the way, and how the LORD had delivered them. Jethro rejoiced for all the good that the LORD had done to Israel, in delivering them from the Egyptians.

Jethro said, "Blessed be the LORD, who has delivered you from the Egyptians and from Pharaoh. Now I know that the LORD is greater than all gods, because he delivered the people from the Egyptians, when they dealt arrogantly with them."...

The next day Moses sat as judge for the people, while the people stood around him from morning until evening. When Moses' father-in-law saw all that he was doing for the people, he said, "What is this that you are doing for the people? Why do you sit alone, while all the people stand around you from morning until evening?" Moses said to his father-in-law, "Because the people come to me to inquire of God. When they have a dispute, they come to me and I decide between one person and another, and I make known to them the statutes and instructions of God." Moses' father-in-law said to him, "What you are doing is not good. You will surely wear yourself out, both you and these people with you. For the task is too heavy for you; you cannot do it alone. Now listen to me. I will give you counsel, and God be with you! You should represent the people before God, and you should bring their cases before God; teach them the statutes and instructions and make known to them the way they are to go and the things they are to do. You should also look for able men among all the people, men who fear God, are trustworthy, and hate dishonest gain; set such men over them as officers over thousands, hundreds, fifties and tens. Let them sit as judges for the people at all times; let them bring every important case to you, but decide every minor case themselves. So it will be easier for you, and they will bear the burden with you. If you do this, and God so commands you, then you will be able to endure, and all these people will go to their home in peace."

So Moses listened to his father-in-law and did all that he had said. Moses chose able men from all Israel and appointed them as heads over the people, as officers over thousands, hundreds, fifties, and tens. And they judged the people at all times; hard cases they brought to Moses, but any minor case they decided themselves. Then Moses let his father-in-law depart, and he went off to his own country.

Exodus 18:1-27

Sinai

A GOOD TEACHER KNOWS THAT EFFECTIVE EDUCATION does not happen through words alone, but through experience, explained by words. The education of the people reaches a climax of experience and words at Mount Sinai.

After three months their journey through the desert brought them back to the mountain of the burning bush (sometimes called Sinai, sometimes Horeb) just as God had promised. There God spoke to the people through Moses. First God reviewed for the people what they had already experienced: the exodus, the plagues, the divine providence that carried them through the desert as if on eagles' wings. It was important for them to remember all this. The time had come for a formal covenant, an entering into a permanent and binding relationship between God and Israel. It was fundamental to the covenant that it was not made with an unknown God, but with one who had already proved to be powerful and caring.

Now is the point where the people have a choice. If they choose to enter into a covenant relationship with God they will have to obey God's commands. If they agree to the covenant they will be a holy nation, special among all the nations of the earth. This is an amazing promise to make to a motley band of ex-slaves. They know from their years in Egypt what a mighty nation is, and they know they cannot claim to be a nation at all. They say yes. It is like the "I do" of the marriage ceremony: quickly said, but transforming the entire remainder of the lives of those who say it.

This commitment, this special covenant relationship with God, will give Israel its identity for the rest of its history. We all get something of our identity from our relationships. Without God, without our parents, family and friends, we would be different people. This is true in a particularly clear way of the people of Israel.

Three days later the forces of nature joined in a celebration of the covenant. At this same mountain where God had appeared to Moses in a burning bush, God appeared to the people in a fire that transformed the entire mountain. God seems to like the symbol of fire, which is so life-giving yet so awe-inspiring; so beautiful and so uncontrollable. It will appear again at Pentecost. The whole mountain shook. Thunder and lightning and smoke filled the people with awe.

Scholars used to argue about exactly what happened: a volcanic eruption, an earthquake or an extraordinarily violent storm. But this is beside the point. It is quite clear what happened. The entire people met God. The words of God that came out of that experience would be the Ten Commandments.

Read about the encounter of Israel with her God on Mount Sinai.

> On the third new moon after the Israelites had gone out of the land of Egypt, on that very day, they came into the wilderness of Sinai.... Israel camped there in front of the mountain. Then Moses went up to God; the LORD called to him from the mountain, saying, "Thus you shall say to the house of Jacob, and tell the Israelites: You have seen what I did to the Egyptians, and how I bore you on eagles' wings and brought you to myself. Now therefore, if you obey my voice and keep my covenant, you shall be my treasured

possession out of all the peoples. Indeed, the whole earth is mine, but you shall be for me a priestly kingdom and a holy nation....

So Moses came, summoned the elders of the people, and set before them all these words that the LORD had commanded him. The people all answered as one: "Everything that the LORD has spoken we will do." Moses reported the words of the people to the LORD....

On the morning of the third day there was thunder and lightning, as well as a thick cloud on the mountain, and a blast of a trumpet so loud that all the people who were in the camp trembled. Moses brought the people out of the camp to meet God. They took their stand at the foot of the mountain. Now Mount Sinai was wrapped in smoke, because the LORD had descended upon it in fire; the smoke went up like the smoke of a kiln, while the whole mountain shook violently. As the blast of the trumpet grew louder and louder, Moses would speak and God would answer him in thunder.

Exodus 19:1-8; 16-19

As children we memorized the Ten Commandments from the catechism, but we may not have been aware of the living context in which they have to be understood. God first showed immense love for the people, drawing them out of Egypt. God freed the people. Then they were invited to enter freely into covenant with God and granted an extraordinary experience of God at Sinai. Only then were they gifted with instructions so that they would know how to live in a way suitable to this wonderful relationship into which they had entered. The Ten Commandments are like the words of a parent teaching a dearly loved child how to live well.

Questions for Reflection

1. How would you feel if you were allowed to obtain each day just enough food for the day, with nothing on the shelf for an emergency, and no money to enable you to buy

more tomorrow? Are you ever asked to have that much confidence in God?

2. What is the best way for you to observe the Sabbath rest? Is this an easy commandment for you to keep?

3. The Israelites kept a jar of manna so they would always remember the way God cared for them through their years in the desert. Is there something you keep because it reminds you of a time when God was with you in a special way?

—∾∾—

4. Jethro was a friend and mentor to his son-in-law Moses. Do you fill this role for anyone? Has anyone been a mentor for you?

5. The Israelites experienced the presence of God at Sinai. Where do you experience God's presence? How does it make you feel?

6. What are the most important instructions you have given your children or others of the younger generation about how to live life well?

Suggestions for Further Reading

Exodus 19
Exodus 20
Exodus 24
Exodus 25
Exodus 31
Exodus 32
Exodus 33
Exodus 34
Exodus 40
Deuteronomy 5

Prayer

Loving God, you brought freedom from slavery to the Israelite people. We ask you to free each of us from the slavery that we have generated and allowed to exist in our own lives.

Loving God, you provided relief for the Israelite people from their hunger in the desert. We ask that you nourish us in our hunger for a deeper and fuller relationship with you.

Loving God, you taught the Israelite people the importance of observing the Sabbath rest. Help us as we strive to develop a healthy balance of work and leisure in our lives, and especially to rest in your goodness and love on the Sabbath.

We ask all of this in your name. Amen.

Nancy M. Van Anne, 69, Greeley, Colorado

CHAPTER ELEVEN

The End of Moses' Journey

Guidance in the Desert

THE ISRAELITES WANDERED FORTY YEARS IN THE DESERT. They had no map. Just as they depended on God's gift of manna for food each day, they depended on God's guidance by a cloud for directions each day.

It seems that the two symbols through which God most likes to be present are fire and cloud. Both are very real, quite visible, yet neither has a firm shape as pagan idols do. Humans cannot grasp or own or control fire or cloud. Both are life-giving. Without fire we could not survive the cold or cook our food. In the parched Middle East, clouds bring hope of rain without which nothing can live. Clouds are also a gracious presence, shielding humans from the intense sunlight.

My mother suffered from severe memory loss in her last years. The thing to which she remained attuned to the very end was the wonder of clouds. I never took her out in the car that she didn't comment, "Aren't the clouds beautiful!" It seemed that, like the Israelites in the desert, she felt something of the wonder and beauty of the living God in clouds.

Christian mystics have gone deeper into this symbol. They tell us that we sometimes are called to go right into the sacred cloud of God's presence, as was Moses at Mount Sinai. But once inside, we no longer see the beauty of the cloud; it is like walking in fog. We are surrounded by God's presence, but what we feel is our helplessness and inability to see.

The Israelites were not called to go into the cloud, but to watch it, and to follow wherever it led them. This is a story about obedience. It is almost a poem, telling of the people's obedience again and again in different ways, always coming

119

back to the refrain, "At the command of the Lord they...." The repetition is not accidental; it is an indication of the profound importance of this image of the people obediently following the guidance of the cloud through the desert.

Notice that the cloud does not always move. It is just as important, and perhaps more difficult, to remain where you are at God's direction as it is to move when it is time to move. Clearly, the message is that we have to be flexible, willing either to remain still or to move on. We have to leave our schedule in God's hands.

Read about the cloud that guided the Israelites through the desert.

On the day the tabernacle was set up, the cloud covered the tabernacle, the tent of the covenant; and from evening until morning it was over the tabernacle, having the appearance of fire. It was always so: the cloud covered it by day and the appearance of fire by night. Whenever the cloud lifted from over the tent, then the Israelites would set out; and in the place where the cloud settled down, there the Israelites would camp. At the command of the LORD the Israelites would set out, and at the command of the LORD they would camp. As long as the cloud rested over the tabernacle, they would remain in camp. Even when the cloud continued over the tabernacle many days, the Israelites would keep the charge of the LORD, and would not set out. Sometimes the cloud would remain a few days over the tabernacle, and according to the command of the LORD they would remain in camp; then according to the command of the LORD they would set out. Sometimes the cloud would remain from evening until morning; and when the cloud lifted in the morning, they would set out, or if it continued for a day and a night, when the cloud lifted they would set out. Whether it was two days, or a month, or a longer time, that the cloud continued over the tabernacle, resting upon it, the Israelites would remain in camp and would not set out; but when it lifted they would set out. At the command of the LORD they would camp, and at the command of the LORD they would set out. They kept the charge of the LORD, at the command of the LORD by Moses.

Numbers 9:15-23

Problems in the Desert

AS THE PEOPLE JOURNEYED THROUGH THE DESERT, God continued to send them manna each day. It was a nourishing substance, which could be prepared in a variety of ways. The biblical writer remembers it as tasting like something made with olive oil, a great compliment. In the Middle East today olive oil is still preferred for the preparation of every kind of food. But, alas, the Israelites lost their taste for manna. Because it was always there, they grew tired of it, and indulged themselves in nostalgia about the spicy foods of Egypt. They couldn't sit down to their manna breakfast, manna lunch and manna supper without talking about the wonderful fish of Egypt, the cucumbers, melons, onions and garlic. They were disgusted with God's gift of manna.

God was disgusted with their grumbling, too. Poor Moses was in the unenviable position of being the person in the middle, trying to make peace between God and Israel who were angry with each other.

The stress was too much for Moses, and he poured out his frustration to God with great vehemence. Indignantly, he asked God, "Did I conceive all this people? Did I give birth to them...?" (Numbers 11:12). Clearly, this is Moses' indirect way of reminding God of what we read elsewhere in Scripture: that God is like a mother to Israel (Deuteronomy 32:18; Psalm 131:1-2; Isaiah 49:15). Israel is the responsibility of God, not of any human leader. It is a point those in authority in family or church always have to remember.

God listens to Moses and responds graciously. We might wonder why God was angry at the people's complaints, but not at Moses' complaints. Notice that the people complain among themselves; Moses complains to God. God wants to relate to us, and that includes listening to the honest out-pouring of our hearts. God does not want to be forgotten while we continually stir the pot of our grumbles without ever bringing them to prayer.

God offers help which goes a step further than Jethro's earlier advice. Moses is to select a council of seventy elders from among the officials who were already helping him with administration. Ancient societies took it for granted that a council of elders, that is, people who had learned from long experience, provide the wisest guidance for government. Our very word "senate" comes from the Latin for "old person."

These elders were to be more than mere officials. Moses gathered them together, and God took some of the spirit given to Moses, and spread it out among these elders. They would share Moses' special gifts from God, as well as his burden of governing an unruly people.

This idea of a council of seventy elders became a tradition in Israel. In Jesus' time, the chief religious authority was the Sanhedrin, a council of seventy. Jesus himself sent out seventy disciples (Luke 10:1-20).

Read a story about grumbling in the desert.

The rabble among them had a strong craving; and the Israelites also wept again, and said, "If only we had meat to eat! We remember the fish we used to eat in Egypt for nothing, the cucumbers, the melons, the leeks, the onions, and the garlic; but now our strength is dried up, and there is nothing at all but this manna to look at."

Now the manna was like coriander seed, and its color was like the color of gum resin. The people went around and gathered it, ground it in mills or beat it in mortars, then boiled it in pots and made cakes of it; and the taste of it was like the taste of cakes baked with oil. When the dew fell on the camp in the night, the manna would fall with it.

Moses heard the people weeping throughout their families, all at the entrances of their tents. Then the LORD became very angry, and Moses was displeased. So Moses said to the LORD, "Why have you treated your servant so badly? Why have I not found favor in your sight, that you lay the burden of all this people on me? Did I conceive all this people? Did I give birth to them, that you should say to me, 'Carry them in your bosom, as a nurse carries a sucking child,' to the land that you promised on oath to their ancestors? Where am I to get meat to give to all this people? For they come weeping to me and say, 'Give us meat to eat!' I am not able to carry all this people alone, for they are too heavy for me. If this is the way you are going to treat me, put me to death at once—if I have found favor in your sight—and do not let me see my misery."

So the LORD said to Moses, "Gather for me seventy of the elders of Israel, whom you know to be the elders of the people and officers over them; bring them to the tent of meeting, and have them take their place there with you. I will come down and talk with you there; and I will take some of the spirit that is on you and put it on them; and they shall bear the burden of the people along with you so that you will not bear it all by yourself...."

So Moses went out and told the people the words of the LORD; and he gathered seventy elders of the people, and placed them all around the tent. Then the LORD came down in the cloud and spoke to him, and took some of the spirit that was on him and put it on the seventy elders; and when the spirit rested upon them, they prophesied.

Numbers 11:4-17; 24-25

—///—

Moses' Prayer

FOR FORTY YEARS MOSES LED THE PEOPLE through the desert. Miriam, Aaron and almost all who had left Egypt with them died. A tough new generation grew up in the desert. They fought kings who stood in their way and conquered some land on the eastern side of the Jordan River. Soon they would cross the Jordan into the true promised land.

Moses, who must surely have been in the category of the

frail elderly by then, had not lost his zeal for leading the people into the land God had promised them. He prayed.

Read Moses' prayer as he described it later to the people.

> At that time, too, I entreated the LORD, saying: "O Lord GOD, you have only begun to show your servant your greatness and your might; what god in heaven or on earth can perform deeds and mighty acts like yours! Let me cross over to see the good land beyond the Jordan, that good hill country and the Lebanon." But the LORD was angry with me on your account and would not heed me. The LORD said to me, "Enough from you! Never speak to me of this matter again! Go up to the top of Pisgah and look around you to the west, to the north, to the south, and to the east. Look well, for you shall not cross over this Jordan. But charge Joshua, and encourage and strengthen him, because it is he who shall cross over at the head of this people and who shall secure their possession of the land that you will see."
>
> *Deuteronomy 3:23-28*

The Handing Over of Moses' Authority

MOSES WAS NOT ALLOWED TO SEE the completion of his life's work. The Bible is unclear about the reason for this. In the passage above we are told that the Lord was angry with Moses on account of the sins of the people. Elsewhere, Scripture seems to say that it was on account of some sin of his own. Common sense suggests that if Moses was 120 years old, he was entitled to a rest.

The next stage of the journey would be one of fighting for the promised land, and the venerable Moses had never been a warrior. A younger, more warlike leader was needed for the times. There are times when the new thing that needs to happen cannot happen while the old leader is still on the scene. There was not a convenient retirement village for Moses to go to, so his death may have been necessary to give Joshua the opportunity to exercise his different leadership skills. As in so many situations in our lives, we cannot be sure of God's motives in allowing Moses to die without entering the promised land.

Moses' final, important responsibility was to see that the people had good leadership for the next stage of their journey. Joshua, who had been his assistant from the beginning, was God's choice. Moses stressed the continuity. God has been the true leader all along, and will continue to be. Joshua will only replace Moses as human leader.

Moses knows that what a people needs to pull it together is hope. So he assures them that they will be able to conquer the promised land, reminding them that they have already overcome kings on the eastern side of the Jordan.

Then Moses solemnly commissions Joshua to his task of conquering the land, and exhorts him to be strong and bold. Joshua will never be the spiritual leader that Moses was, but he will be the military leader the people need at this point of transition. Finally the aged Moses brings Joshua before God, and God commissions Joshua with the same words Moses had used, "Be strong and bold." And God solemnly promises to be with him. He does not have to face the frightening prospect of battling the inhabitants of Canaan alone.

Joshua will lead the people through the transition into a new era, when they will no longer be ex-slaves wandering in the desert, but farmers settled on their own land. Like most of the transitions in our lives, it will not be easy. But the biblical author, living in the promised land, looks back at these stories of his ancestors and knows that it was worth all it cost.

Read about the commissioning of the new leader.

When Moses had finished speaking all these words to all Israel, he said to them: "I am now one hundred twenty years old. I am no longer able to get about, and the LORD has told me, 'You shall not cross over this Jordan.' The LORD your God himself will cross over before you. He will destroy these nations before you, and you shall dispossess them. Joshua also will cross over before you, as the LORD promised. The LORD will do to them as he did to Sihon and Og, the kings of the Amorites, and to their land, when he destroyed them. The LORD will give them over to you and you shall deal with them in full accord with the command that I have given to you. Be strong and bold; have no fear or dread of them, because it is the LORD your God who goes with you; he will not fail you or forsake you."

Then Moses summoned Joshua and said to him in the sight of all Israel: "Be strong and bold, for you are the one who will go with this people into the land that the LORD has sworn to their ancestors to give them; and you will put them in possession of it. It is the LORD who goes before you. He will be with you; he will not fail you or forsake you. Do not fear or be dismayed."...

The LORD said to Moses, "Your time to die is near; call Joshua and present yourselves in the tent of meeting, so that I may commission him." So Moses and Joshua went and presented themselves in the tent of meeting, and the LORD appeared at the tent in a pillar of cloud; the pillar of cloud stood at the entrance to the tent....

Then the LORD commissioned Joshua son of Nun and said, "Be strong and bold, for you shall bring the Israelites into the land that I promised them; I will be with you."

Deuteronomy 31:1-8; 14, 15, 23

The Death of Moses

MOSES CLIMBED ONE LAST MOUNTAIN before he died. It was Mount Nebo, part of the range called Pisgah. Nebo is just east of the Jordan. It is a low, gentle hill. God knew that Moses was no longer able to climb a great rocky mountain like Sinai. From Mount Nebo God gave him a view of all the land which the Israelites were to conquer on the other side of the Jordan.

The Franciscans have built a lovely little church there, on the site of a much older one. From there I have looked across the Jordan into the promised land, but it is clear that Moses had some special help from God, because I surely could not see the whole land from there.

126

Martin Luther King, Jr., spoke shortly before his death of having climbed up the mountain to see the promised land as Moses did. These great men did not live to see their work completed, but God gave them a glimpse of what was to come.

Moses left the people at the foot of the mountain and climbed alone, as he had climbed Sinai. After his vision of the promised land, he died. If the Bible was the story of Moses, we might think it a tragedy because he died without entering into the promised land. But the Bible is the story of God's people. Each of us plays a part, but no one of us is indispensable. After the customary thirty days of mourning the people crossed the Jordan and entered their own land under the leadership of Joshua.

Read the story of Moses' death and burial.

Then Moses went up from the plains of Moab to Mount Nebo, to the top of Pisgah, which is opposite Jericho, and the LORD showed him the whole land: Gilead as far as Dan, all Naphtali, the land of Ephraim and Manasseh, all the land of Judah as far as the Western Sea, the Negeb, and the Plain—that is, the valley of Jericho, the city of palm trees— as far as Zoar. The LORD said to him, "This is the land of which I swore to Abraham, to Isaac, and to Jacob, saying, 'I will give it to your descendants'; I have let you see it with your eyes, but you shall not cross over there." Then Moses, the servant of the LORD, died there in the land of Moab, at the Lord's command. He was buried in a valley in the land of Moab, opposite Beth-peor, but no one knows his burial place to this day. Moses was one hundred twenty years old when he died; his sight was unimpaired and his vigor had not abated. The Israelites wept for Moses in the plains of Moab thirty days; then the period of mourning for Moses was ended.

Joshua son of Nun was full of the spirit of wisdom, because Moses had laid his hands on him; and the Israelites obeyed him, doing as the LORD had commanded Moses.

Deuteronomy 34:1-9

Questions for Reflection

1. God guided the Israelites by a pillar of cloud and a pillar of fire. How do you think God guides people today?

2. If you had been an Israelite would it have been harder to stay in one spot when the cloud did not move, or to pack up and move when it did? In your life now, is the cloud stopped or moving?

3. When have you experienced losing your taste for something you once liked, as the Israelites lost their taste for manna? Do you think boredom is often a problem in the spiritual life?

4. Can you imagine complaining to God as vehemently as Moses did in Numbers 11:11-15? Would you consider this disrespectful?

5. Do you know people who, like Moses, were not given the opportunity to complete their life's work, but had to leave it for someone else to complete? How do you think they felt about leaving their responsibilities to others?

6. Deuteronomy 34 describes Moses' death. In what ways would you like your death to be like Moses'? In what ways would you like it to be different?

Suggestions for Further Reading

Numbers 11—14
Numbers 20—24
Numbers 27
Psalm 105

Prayer

Father, we are ordinary people,
in ordinary time,
seeking a home.
You led us from bondage
and we grumbled.
You know of our worries;
you know of our needs;
you know of our trials
when our heart bleeds.
So we ask for patience
and enlightenment
and courage
to see our days through
while coming to our home!
Amen.

Lillian Shirk, 69, Aurora, Colorado

Chapter Twelve

The Book of Naomi

A Family in Difficulty

THIS CHAPTER IS ABOUT WHAT IS USUALLY CALLED the Book of Ruth.
That name encourages us to focus on the young woman
Ruth. In the book itself, the chief character is Ruth's mother-
in-law, Naomi. The story begins and ends with her; it is she
who plans and initiates the action.

Whether we call this the Book of Ruth or the Book of
Naomi, it is clearly a book about women. Most of the Bible is
told from the point of view of men. Women are mentioned
only because of their relationship with men, and they are
usually peripheral to the main story. In this book, exactly
the opposite is true. The principal theme is the loving relationship between Naomi and her daughter-in-law Ruth.
Women, generally marginal in the Bible, become central in
this book. Men are mentioned only because of their relationships to women.

Scholars have suggested that this was originally a story
told by women for other women. While we have no information about the author, this certainly seems probable. In the
Bible we find journey stories about Abraham, Jacob, Joseph
and other men. Only the Book of Ruth is clearly a woman's
journey story.

The story of Naomi and Ruth, like the stories of so many
refugees today, is set in a time of political chaos and famine.
The text starts, "In the days when the judges ruled...." This
was the time before monarchy brought some orderly structures into political life. "Judges" were not elected or appointed in any predictable way; they were charismatic figures who
rose up in time of emergency and gathered as many Israelites
as they could to fight whatever enemy was currently threatening Israel. After the battle they retired to private life, and, as

the Book of Judges says so pointedly, "...all the people did what was right in their own eyes" (Judges 21:25). The resulting chaos was probably a bit like America's "Wild West."

When the dreaded famine came to the land, there were no government structures to help the people, no Red Cross or crop failure insurance. Elimelech, Naomi's husband, decided to do what Abraham and Jacob had done before: Take his family away from the promised land to a place where economic conditions were better.

Elimelech and Naomi must have crossed the Jordan River into the pagan land of Moab with heavy hearts. The land of Israel was God's great gift, as precious to Israelites in Old Testament times as to Israelis today. After the forty years of wandering in the desert, Joshua had led the people triumphantly through the Jordan, which parted for them as the Red Sea had, into the land God had promised them. It was painful for the little immigrant family to reverse that great journey.

In Moab they faced the problems poor immigrants face everywhere. We are given no details about these, but we do learn that Naomi's husband and both of her sons died in this foreign land.

After the death of Elimelech, Naomi has to raise her sons alone. When they grow up, they both select Moabite women as wives. It must have been difficult for Naomi to have these pagan women come into her home. Israel and Moab were close neighbors, but not friendly ones. Israelites remembered with horror that when they travelled through Moab on their way to their own land, their men sinned with Moabite women and were led by them into worship of the Moabite god. God's anger was kindled against Israel because of this and many died by the plague (Numbers 25:1-3).

If Naomi was sad at having to accept Moabite daughters-in-law, her sorrow was extreme when both of her sons died without having had children. For an Israelite, the dying out of the family line was the greatest of tragedies.

It was believed that the role of a woman was to continue the family line of her husband. This was such an important value that biblical law tried to make provision for the continuation of the family line even if a man died childless. The levirate law required that when a man died without having had children, his widow should marry his brother, and their son should receive the name and inheritance of the deceased brother (Deuteronomy 25:5-10).

Since Naomi had no other sons and was too old to bear more, the levirate law appeared to offer no help to this stricken family. It seemed there was no way to continue the family line.

In a male-dominated world, the family of Elimelech now consisted only of three widows: Naomi and her two Moabite daughters-in-law, Orpah and Ruth. In Scripture, widows are always seen as examples of poverty. The majority of the world's poor today are women, with widows in the forefront. The situation was even worse in Naomi's time.

Naomi was poor, but not weak. Now that the responsibility for the family was hers, she decided to return to her homeland. She had had no part in her husband's decision to leave Bethlehem for pagan Moab, but now she could follow her own heart, which yearned for the promised land. She was not daunted by the journey of four or five days, across the Jordan River and the Judaean desert. She was like many Jews scattered throughout the world who make great sacrifices to return to the promised land, even if only to die there.

Naomi also reminds me of the many widows I have known who, after a lifetime of subservience to their husbands, take control of their lives for the first time after their husband's death, and show strength and skills no one imagined they had.

Naomi is now the head of a household which includes her two Moabite daughters-in-law. In biblical times men and women lived separate social lives. A woman was subject to her husband, but her main emotional support came from the relationships that developed within the women's quarters of the home. Naomi and her daughters-in-law are models of those relationships at their best. As young widows Orpah and Ruth would normally return to the home of their parents and hope that another marriage could be arranged for them. Instead, they set out with Naomi for Bethlehem, where they would be foreigners as she had been in Moab and where their chances for remarriage would be slight, in view of the Israelites' dislike for Moabite women.

Naomi clearly loves the young women. She loves them enough to offer them the gift of freedom. Much as she needs their support in her poverty and old age, she tries tenderly to persuade them to leave her in order to take care of their own future. This is perhaps Naomi's most heroic moment.

It is clear that she is really giving Orpah and Ruth a choice. We know that there is no subtle manipulation behind her kind words because Orpah takes her advice. With tears at having to depart from the women with whom she had shared her life, she returns to her Moabite family. Orpah's is a sensible decision. There are no villains in this gentle book. Orpah's ordinary goodness serves as a foil for the extraordinary devotion of Naomi and Ruth.

It is interesting to see that, though Naomi had taken on the responsibilities of being head of the family, she did not dominate, but selflessly supported the younger members in making their own decisions. It is not surprising that Ruth loved Naomi so deeply.

Ruth cannot be persuaded to leave Naomi. Hers is a heroic commitment to a poor and elderly relation, to whom she is not even tied by blood. For Naomi's sake she leaves her own country to live in a strange land where she can expect little welcome or respect. The storyteller keeps reminding us of Ruth's status as an outsider by identifying her again and again as "Ruth the Moabite."

Read Naomi's story.

In the days when the judges ruled, there was a famine in the land, and a certain man of Bethlehem in Judah went to live in the country of Moab, he and his wife and two sons. The name of the man was Elimelech and the name of his wife Naomi, and the names of his two sons were

Mahlon and Chilion... They went into the country of Moab and remained there. But Elimelech, the husband of Naomi, died, and she was left with her two sons. These took Moabite wives; the name of the one was Orpah and the name of the other Ruth. When they had lived there about ten years, both Mahlon and Chilion also died, so that the woman was left without her two sons and her husband.

Then she started to return with her daughters-in-law from the country of Moab, for she had heard in the country of Moab that the LORD had considered his people and given them food. So she set out from the place where she had been living, she and her two daughters-in-law, and they went on their way to go back to the land of Judah. But Naomi said to her two daughters-in-law, "Go back each of you to your mother's house. May the LORD deal kindly with you, as you have dealt with the dead and with me. The LORD grant that you may find security, each of you in the house of your husband." Then she kissed them, and they wept aloud. They said to her, "No, we will return with you to your people." But Naomi said, "Turn back, my daughters, why will you go with me? Do I still have sons in my womb that they may become your husbands? Turn back, my daughters, go your way, for I am too old to have a husband. Even if I thought there was hope for me, even if I should have a husband tonight and bear sons, would you then wait until they were grown? Would you then refrain from marrying? No, my daughters, it has been far more bitter for me than for you, because the hand of the LORD has turned against me." Then they wept aloud again. Orpah kissed her mother-in-law, but Ruth clung to her.

So she said, "See, your sister-in-law has gone back to her people and to her gods; return after your sister-in-law." But Ruth said,

> "Do not press me to leave you
>   or to turn back from following you!
> Where you go, I will go;
>   Where you lodge, I will lodge;
> your people shall be my people,
>   and your God my God.

> Where you die, I will die—
> there will I be buried.
> May the LORD do thus and so to me,
> and more as well,
> if even death parts me from you!"

When Naomi saw that she was determined to go with her, she said no more to her....

So Naomi returned together with Ruth the Moabite, her daughter-in-law, who came back with her from the country of Moab. They came to Bethlehem at the beginning of the barley harvest.

Ruth 1:1-22

—~~—

Return to Bethlehem

THE ELDERLY ISRAELITE WOMAN HUNGRY FOR HOME and the young Moabite woman ready for the adventure of a strange land have travelled together across the Jordan River, through the Judean desert, to Bethlehem. There they are faced with the challenge of supporting themselves in a society that offers few career options for women.

It is the strong young Ruth who will be able to support their household. But it is Naomi, who remembers the difficulties of adjusting to a foreign land and knows the customs of Israel, whose wisdom guides Ruth at every step.

Naomi knows that Israelite law makes a kind of provision for people like herself and Ruth. It commands that during the harvest the owner of a field not go over the field a second time to pick up the bits of grain that inevitably drop from the sheaves of the harvesters. The poor are allowed to glean these bits (Deuteronomy 24:19-22). Ruth takes advantage of this minimal welfare system: She knows that she may be insulted or refused when she tries to claim what the law says is hers. As a Moabite, a member of an unpopular minority, she is even more vulnerable than other poor women. So she is surprised and delighted when Boaz, the owner of the field in which she begins to work, greets her kindly and instructs his male workers not to harass her as she works.

Ruth returns to Naomi and reports her good fortune. Naomi's heart leaps. She sees in the courtesy of Boaz a hope for much more.

Read about how Naomi and Ruth begin their new life.

Ruth the Moabite said to Naomi, "Let me go to the field and glean among the ears of grain, behind someone in whose sight I may find favor." She said to her, "Go, my daughter." So she went. She came and gleaned in the field behind the reapers. As it happened, she came to the part of the field belonging to Boaz, who was of the family of Elimelech. Just then Boaz came from Bethlehem. He said to the reapers, "The LORD be with you." They answered, "The LORD bless you." Then Boaz said to his servant who was in charge of the reapers, "To whom does this young woman belong?" The servant who was in charge of the reapers answered, "She is the Moabite who came back with Naomi from the country of Moab. She said, 'Please, let me glean and gather among the sheaves behind the reapers.' So she came, and she has been on her feet from early this morning until now, without resting even for a moment."

Then Boaz said to Ruth, "Now listen, my daughter, do not go to glean in another field or leave this one, but keep close to my young women. Keep your eyes on the field that is being reaped, and follow behind them. I have ordered the young men not to bother you. If you get thirsty, go to the vessels and drink from what the young men have drawn." Then she fell prostrate, with her face to the ground, and said to him, "Why have I found favor in your sight, that you should take notice of me, when I am a foreigner?" But Boaz answered her, "All that you have done for your mother-in-law since the death of your husband has been fully told me, and how you left your father and mother and your native land and came to a people that you did not know before. May the LORD reward you for your deeds, and may you have a full reward from the LORD, the God of

Israel, under whose wings you have come for refuge!" Then she said, "May I continue to find favor in your sight, my lord, for you have comforted me and spoken kindly to your servant, even though I am not one of your servants."...

So she gleaned in the field until evening. Then she beat out what she had gleaned, and it was about an ephah of barley. She picked it up and came into the town, and her mother-in-law saw how much she had gleaned.... Her mother-in-law said to her, "Where did you glean today? And where have you worked? Blessed be the man who took notice of you." So she told her mother-in-law with whom she had worked, and said, "The name of the man with whom I worked today is Boaz." Then Naomi said to her daughter-in-law, "Blessed be he by the LORD, whose kindness has not forsaken the living or the dead!" Naomi also said to her, "The man is a relative of ours, one of our nearest kin." Then Ruth the Moabite said, "He even said to me, 'Stay close by my servants, until they have finished all my harvest.'" Naomi said to Ruth, her daughter-in-law, "It is better, my daughter, that you go out with his young women, otherwise you might be bothered in another field." So she stayed close to the young women of Boaz, gleaning until the end of the barley and wheat harvests; and she lived with her mother-in-law.

Ruth 2:2-23

A Bold Initiative

NAOMI UNDERSTANDS THE PROVISIONS Israelite custom makes to provide for those in need. The right of gleaning is only one. A more important custom is that of the redeemer/kinsman. If an Israelite fell into slavery or debt or other tragedy, there was no government Social Security Administration to help. However, there was always a male relative who was closest of kin. His was the responsibility of redeeming the slave or buying back the property that had been sold because of debt, or meeting whatever other need arose. A particular case of the redeemer's responsibility was that of the levirate marriage, which saved a deceased relative from the shame of having no posterity. Though the levirate marriage law only applied strictly to brothers of the dead man, it might be taken up by another relative if there were no brothers.

Naomi realizes that Boaz is a relative who might assume the responsibilities of the redeemer/kinsman. She could not demand this of him, but his favorable response to Ruth gave her hope that he might do so willingly.

Naomi waits until Boaz has had time to observe Ruth's hard work and proper behavior throughout the barley harvest and the wheat harvest. She waits until the time of threshing. She knows that this is a time of celebration. Those who have gathered the harvest congregate at the large flat rock on which the grain is threshed. They rejoice in the harvest, eat and drink, and sleep there on the threshing floor to protect the precious grain from theft. It was a relaxed time, when the usual sexual standards might be bent a bit.

At the time of threshing Naomi advises Ruth to make herself as attractive as she can. It is surprising that we are never told that Ruth is beautiful. Women's beauty was highly prized in the Ancient Near East, and the Bible emphasizes the beauty of Sarah, Rebekah and Rachel. The fact that physical beauty is not mentioned in connection with Ruth breaks the cultural stereotype that a woman must be physically beautiful to have value.

Dressed in her best, Ruth goes alone at night to the threshing floor where Boaz is sleeping after eating and drinking heavily. There she lies down at the feet of Boaz, waiting for him to awake. When he awakes, groggy and puzzled to see a woman at his feet, she asks him to stretch his cloak over her, a symbol of marriage. It is a shocking and risky action, but Naomi has judged the man and the time well, and everything happens according to her plan. Boaz accepts Ruth's proposal of marriage.

Read the story of Ruth's proposal.

Naomi her mother-in-law said to her, "My daughter, I need to seek some security for you, so that it may be well with you. Now here is our kinsman Boaz, with whose young women you have been working. See, he is winnowing barley tonight at the threshing floor. Now wash and anoint yourself, and put on your best clothes and go down to the threshing floor; but do not make yourself known to the man until he has finished eating and drinking. When he lies down, observe the place where he lies; then, go and uncover his feet and lie down; and he will tell you what to do." She said to her, "All that you tell me I will do."

So she went down to the threshing floor and did just as her mother-in-law had instructed her. When Boaz had eaten and drunk, and he was in a contented mood, he went to lie down at the end of the heap of grain. Then she came stealthily and uncovered his feet, and lay down. At midnight the man was startled, and turned over, and there, lying at his feet, was a woman! He said, "Who are you?" And she answered, "I am Ruth, your servant; spread your cloak over your servant, for you are next-of-kin." He said, "May you be blessed by the LORD, my daughter; this last instance of your loyalty is better than the first; you have not gone after young men, whether poor or rich. And now, my daughter, do not be afraid, I will do for you all that you ask, for all the assembly of my people know that you are a worthy woman."

Ruth 3:1-11

A Family Restored

AT THE THRESHING FLOOR, Ruth took center stage, though only following the advice of Naomi. As the story ends, Naomi again becomes central. Obed, the son born to Ruth and Boaz, is even called Naomi's son. The grandmother has as much joy as the parents in this baby.

Again the main theme of the story is stressed: the loving bond between Ruth and Naomi. Israelite culture said that the most precious gift a woman could receive was a son. But the women of Bethlehem tell Naomi that the daughter-in-law who loves her is worth more to her than seven sons!

This is a domestic story about the providence of God working quietly in the lives of two poor widows. But its conclusion connects it with the great King David who is to come. Ruth's baby Obed will be the grandfather of David! Read the conclusion of the story of Naomi.

> So Boaz took Ruth and she became his wife. When they came together, the LORD made her conceive and she bore a son. Then the women said to Naomi, "Blessed be the LORD, who has not left you this day without next-of-kin; and may his name be renowned in Israel! He shall be to you a restorer of life and a nourisher of your old age; for your daughter-in-law who loves you, who is more to you than seven sons, has borne him." Then Naomi took the child and laid him in her bosom, and became his nurse. The women of the neighborhood gave him a name, saying, "A son has been born to Naomi." They named him Obed; he became the father of Jesse, the father of David.
>
> *Ruth 4:13-17*

Questions for Reflection

1. Do you know of any families like Naomi's that are forced by poverty to move to a foreign land, and then marry natives of that land? What difficulties would you expect in such marriages?

2. Naomi made a special effort to see that Orpah and Ruth felt free to follow their own star rather than be tied down by obligation to care for her in her old age. Do you know an old person who has done the same? One who has done the opposite?

3. Do you know people who sacrificed their own best interests for the sake of an elderly relative, as Ruth did for Naomi? Do you think this was wise?

4. What do you imagine Naomi did to win such love from Ruth?

5. Israelite society provided for the poor by allowing them to glean grain after the harvesters. How does our society provide for the poor? Do you think we provide adequately?

6. In Israelite society, women and children were most likely to suffer from poverty. Do you think this is true today? Why?

7. Do you know anyone who enjoys a grandchild as much as Naomi enjoyed Obed? What do you think it takes to be a good grandparent?

Suggestions for Further Reading

The Book of Esther
The Book of Ruth

Prayer

My Lord, you are Love. When we love, we are sharing you with somebody else. Through this mystery you reveal your presence among us. The love among people of different ages and cultures makes the world glow. Love has no barriers, even if it makes no sense. The happiness of others is ours, too. When we lack that part of you, the world suffers. Most of the sufferings of this world are caused by people because there is not enough love.

As Ruth told Naomi: "Do not press me to leave you or to turn back from following you," so teach us, Lord, to care for others, no matter who they are, whether friends or enemies, of different race or different culture, rich or poor, but to always love. May we be a window of your great love. This we ask in Jesus' name. Amen.

Elena C. Arroyo, 76, Littleton, Colorado

CHAPTER THIRTEEN

Hannah
and Her Son

Hannah Prays

HANNAH, THE MOTHER OF SAMUEL, was like Sarah and Rebekah
and Ruth, a woman who seemed unable to bear children. Her
situation was made even more painful because her husband
had another wife, Peninnah, who did bear him children. In a
society that valued women mainly for their fertility, competition could make life in the women's quarters a misery for a
childless woman like Hannah.

We are not told that Hannah was particularly beautiful or
virtuous, or that she came from an important family. She is a
quite ordinary woman in great distress, which makes it easier
for us to identify with her.

From Hannah we can learn a great deal about prayer. She
did not try to repress her grief, to pretend that everything
was all right. She went into the house of the Lord at Shiloh
and poured out her heart to God. Her emotion was so visible
that the priest Eli, who stood guard at the door of the sanctuary, thought she was drunk, and scolded her angrily for
disrespect for the holy place. He was like people today who
quickly pass judgment on individuals whose behavior in
religious matters does not conform to the proprieties.

Eli was not a perceptive priest, but he meant well. When
Hannah explained to him that she was not drunk but was
pouring out her distress before the Lord he blessed her. After
venting her pain and receiving a word of hope from God's
priest, Hannah returned to her stressful family situation in a
different frame of mind. She still had no child, but she had
hope and peace, and that made all the difference.

Hannah's husband, Elkanah, also tries to comfort her,
though his words do not seem to be as effective as the
priest's. His tenderness toward a wife who had failed to bear

him children is quite unusual in the Old Testament. Strong emotional bonds in the cultures of the Ancient Near East existed between mothers and sons, not between husbands and wives. Marriages were arranged, and women lived with their children in the women's quarters. The daily taunts of her rival Peninnah probably caused Hannah grief that outweighed her husband's extraordinary love.

God heard the prayer of Hannah and she bore a son whom she named Samuel. She had promised God that if she received the precious gift of a male child, she would offer him to God as a Nazirite. Nazirites were Israelites specially dedicated to God. As signs of their dedication, they were not allowed to drink alcohol or to cut their hair. In biblical times, long hair was a sign of special dedication to God.

Women in those days nursed their children for two or three years. We can imagine with what love Hannah nursed this longed-for child. But when he was weaned she brought him to the sanctuary in Shiloh to be raised for God's service by the priest Eli. It must have been a painful parting, but Hannah was still grateful for having borne the child, and she sang a hymn praising God who had brought her through her ordeal. She was not like those who pray fervently in time of need but forget to thank God for gifts received. God had been faithful to Hannah, and Hannah was faithful to God.

Later, when another apparently ordinary woman was made pregnant by a special gift from God, she remembered Hannah's joy at bearing Samuel and sang a song of praise much like Hannah's. Mary's Magnificat, like Hannah's, is a song about God's special care for the poor and those unlikely to succeed.

Read the story of Hannah and her baby son.

There was a certain man of Ramathaim, a Zuphite from the hill country of Ephraim, whose name was Elkanah son of Jeroham son of Elihu son of Tohu son of Zuph, an Ephraimite. He had two wives; the name of the one was Hannah, and the name of the other Peninnah. Peninnah had children, but Hannah had no children.

Now this man used to go up year by year from his town to worship and to sacrifice to the LORD of hosts at Shiloh, where the two sons of Eli, Hophni and Phinehas, were priests of the LORD. On the day when Elkanah sacrificed, he would give portions to his wife Peninnah and to all her sons and daughters; but to Hannah he gave a double portion, because he loved her, though the LORD had closed her womb. Her rival used to provoke her severely, to irritate her, because the LORD had closed her womb. So it went on year by year; as often as she went up to the house of the LORD, she used to provoke her. Therefore Hannah wept and would not eat. Her husband Elkanah said to her, "Hannah, why do you weep? Why do you not eat? Why is your heart sad? Am I not more to you than ten sons?"

After they had eaten and drunk at Shiloh, Hannah rose and presented herself before the LORD. Now Eli the priest was sitting on the seat beside the doorpost of the temple of the LORD. She was deeply distressed and prayed to the LORD, and wept bitterly. She made this vow: "O LORD of hosts, if only you will look on the misery of your servant, and remember me, and not forget your servant, but will give to your servant a male child, then I will set him before you as a nazirite until the day of his death. He shall drink neither wine nor intoxicants, and no razor shall touch his head."

As she continued praying before the LORD, Eli observed her mouth. Hannah was praying silently; only her lips moved, but her voice was not heard; therefore Eli thought she was drunk. So Eli said to her, "How long will you make a drunken spectacle of yourself? Put away your wine." But Hannah answered, "No, my lord, I am a woman deeply troubled; I have drunk neither wine nor strong drink, but I have been pouring out my soul before the LORD. Do not regard your servant as a worthless woman, for I have been speaking out of my great anxiety and vexation all this time." Then Eli answered, "Go in peace; the God of Israel grant the petition you have made to him." And she said, "Let your servant find favor in your sight." Then the woman went to her quarters, ate and drank with her husband, and her countenance was sad no longer.

They rose early in the morning and worshiped before the LORD; then they went back to their house at Ramah. Elkanah knew his wife Hannah, and the LORD remembered her. In due time Hannah conceived and bore a son. She named him Samuel, for she said, "I have asked him of the LORD."...

When she had weaned him, she took him up with her, along with a three-year-old bull, an ephah of flour, and a skin of wine. She brought him to the house of the LORD at Shiloh; and the child was young. Then they slaughtered the bull, and they brought the child to Eli. And she said, "Oh, my lord! As you live, my lord, I am the woman who was standing here in your presence, praying to the LORD. For this child I prayed; and the LORD has granted me the petition that I made to him. Therefore I have lent him to the LORD; as long as he lives, he is given to the LORD." She left him there for the LORD.

Hannah prayed and said,

"My heart exults in the LORD;
    my strength is exalted in my God.
My mouth derides my enemies,
    because I rejoice in my victory.
"There is no Holy One like the LORD,
    no one besides you;
    there is no Rock like our God.

1 Samuel 1:1-20, 24-28; 2:1-2

Eli and Samuel

THE ELDERLY PRIEST, ELI, WAS IN CHARGE of the sanctuary at Shiloh. Age and failing eyesight prevented him from presiding at the sacrifices, so his sons did most of the priestly work. While the people respected the old man, they resented his sons, who treated worshippers rudely and used their priestly privileges for personal benefit. Yet it was expected that the sons would take over their father's place when he died.

Eli took on the responsibility of training young Samuel in

the ways of God, and he was more successful with him than he had been with his own sons. Samuel was a child who truly loved God; he also loved the old priest who taught him about God. As sometimes happens, God gave the child a message for the old man.

For Israel this was a time when God was silent. We have all had times like this in our own lives. Good people tried to live by the words God had spoken in the past, but they did not expect any new revelation. So Eli had not prepared the boy Samuel for what happened to him one night.

It was the child's responsibility to sleep in the sanctuary itself to guard it, and perhaps to tend to the lamp that burned there through the night. Eli slept in an adjoining room. One night the boy was awakened by a voice calling him. Thinking it was Eli, he went to see what the old man wanted. Eli had not called him, and simply told him to go back to sleep. This happened three times before the priest realized that God was calling the boy. Eli was a bit slow in catching on, as he had been when Hannah prayed so fervently in the temple, but once he realized what was going on, he gave proper priestly advice. He told Samuel to go back to sleep, and if the voice came again, to respond, "Speak, Lord, for your servant is listening."

This is the great fundamental prayer we should learn from Samuel. God is willing to listen to us, but also wants us to listen sometimes. God likes us to be really attentive as Eli taught Samuel to be, saying, "Speak, Lord, for your servant is listening." God does not expect us to be always working; Samuel was to go back to bed. But God wants us to be always ready for a divine message, even an unexpected one.

Samuel would be a much greater man than Eli, but he could never have become the spiritual giant he was if he had not followed Eli's wise advice to listen attentively to God.

God did speak to Samuel that night, and the message was not something the boy was prepared to hear or willing to repeat to Eli. It was a strong statement that the family of Eli would be punished forever because Eli had not prevented his sons from misusing the priestly office. This would soon happen when Eli's sons both died in battle; Eli himself died of shock when he heard the news, and the priestly leadership passed from the family of Eli to Samuel.

When Samuel delivers his painful message to Eli, the old priest has his moment of spiritual greatness. He accepts God's judgment humbly. He acknowledges that he has failed as a father and relinquishes his dearest hope: that his sons would carry on his responsibilities after his death. In his old age he is able to give up control and let God be God. It is a grace for which we can all pray.

What God is pointing to, and Eli is embracing without completely understanding it, is a new order in which the boy Samuel, who has been spiritually nurtured by the old priestly family, will replace that family. It is an interesting mixture of discontinuity and continuity. God brought the old priestly line to an unexpected end, but the new priest Samuel had received a spiritual heritage from them that he would carry into new times.

Eli had probably tried from the beginning to teach Samuel obedience to God, but his greatest moment as a teacher came when he accepted God's judgment on him from the mouth of his young pupil.

Read the story of Eli and Samuel.

Now the boy Samuel was ministering to the LORD under Eli. The word of the LORD was rare in those days; visions were not widespread.

At that time Eli, whose eyesight had begun to grow dim so that he could not see, was lying down in his room; the lamp of God had not yet gone out, and Samuel was lying down in the temple of the LORD, where the ark of God was. Then the LORD called, "Samuel! Samuel!" and he said, "Here I am!" and ran to Eli, and said, "Here I am, for you called me." But he said, "I did not call; lie down again." So he went and lay down. The LORD called again, "Samuel!" Samuel got up and went to Eli, and said, "Here I am, for you called me." But he said, "I did not call, my son; lie down again." Now

Samuel did not yet know the LORD, and the word of the LORD had not yet been revealed to him. The LORD called Samuel again, a third time. And he got up and went to Eli, and said, "Here I am, for you called me." Then Eli perceived that the LORD was calling the boy. Therefore Eli said to Samuel, "Go, lie down; and if he calls you, you shall say, 'Speak, LORD, for your servant is listening.'" So Samuel went and lay down in his place.

Now the LORD came and stood there, calling as before, "Samuel! Samuel!" And Samuel said, "Speak, for your servant is listening." Then the LORD said to Samuel, "See, I am about to do something in Israel that will make both ears of anyone who hears of it tingle. On that day I will fulfill against Eli all that I have spoken concerning his house, from beginning to end. For I have told him that I am about to punish his house forever, for the iniquity that he knew, because his sons were blaspheming God, and he did not restrain them. Therefore I swear to the house of Eli that the iniquity of Eli's house shall not be expiated by sacrifice or offering forever."

Samuel lay there until morning; then he opened the doors of the house of the LORD. Samuel was afraid to tell the vision to Eli. But Eli called Samuel and said, "Samuel, my son." He said, "Here I am." Eli said, "What was it that he told you? Do not hide it from me. May God do so to you and more also, if you hide anything from me of all that he told you." So Samuel told him everything and hid nothing from him. Then he said, "It is the LORD; let him do what seems good to him."

As Samuel grew up, the LORD was with him and let none of his words fall to the ground. And all Israel from Dan to Beer-sheba knew that Samuel was a trustworthy prophet of the LORD. The LORD continued to appear at Shiloh, for the LORD revealed himself to Samuel at Shiloh by the word of the LORD. And the word of Samuel came to all Israel.

1 Samuel 3:1-21; 4:1

Samuel's Retirement

SAMUEL WAS AN EXTRAORDINARY FIGURE. He was priest, prophet and judge for the people throughout his life. These are different roles, ordinarily filled by different individuals. The priest carries on the prescribed religious services and explains the law of God to the people. The prophet receives and transmits to the people new messages from God for their times. The judge is not involved primarily in judicial affairs as judges are today. He is both a military and a civil leader, in charge of all secular affairs.

Samuel, unlike any other leader of Israel, carried all three of these responsibilities throughout his long life and fulfilled them well. He was a truly holy man. He was also the man called by God to lead the people through a great transition from the chaotic period of the judges to the more organized period when kings ruled over the nation. Israel moved from being a rather primitive tribal society to being a wealthy and powerful monarchy. Samuel was the last of the judges, and he ushered in the first of the kings.

His was not an easy task. He makes me think of Pope John XXIII, a deeply devout man of the pre-Vatican II era, who was called by God to lead the Church into a new time that he himself could hardly imagine. God can call the old to serve a future they themselves will not live to see. I notice the same pattern in the many senior citizens today who are deeply involved in global and ecological issues that will affect their grandchildren.

God uses our failures as well as our successes to move us into new phases of our lives. Samuel, who tried to raise his sons to continue his dedicated leadership of Israel, failed in this. His sons, whom he had appointed to help him with his responsibilities, accepted bribes and did not govern justly.

The elders, who were respected as the natural leaders of the people, came to Samuel to complain about the behavior of his sons and to demand that Samuel resign and appoint a king to rule over the people. The elders had the political astuteness to see that the powerful nations around them had kings. Kings meant stable leadership, because when a king died his son succeeded him. A nation could not make progress in the circumstances of the new times without a strong person always at its head. The spontaneous rising up of judges to deal with particular crises was no longer enough.

The elders were calling for a new form of government for a new era. Samuel was not pleased by their demand. The old order seemed holy to him. He had long served God in that way. It was doubly hard for him to think of turning his leadership responsibilities over to someone not of his family, knowing that as king the new leader would have the right to pass his position on to his sons.

Because Samuel was truly wise, he did not respond immediately to the elders' demand, but brought the matter to prayer. Perhaps he still prayed as Eli had taught him, "Speak, Lord, your servant is listening." The message he heard in prayer was not the one he wanted. God told him to listen to the elders and give the people the king they asked for. Perhaps Samuel guessed that this would mean a long and painful period of retirement for him, when he would no longer be in control of the political life of the nation, but would be called back into involvement when things were at their worst.

When Samuel heard that God wanted him to anoint a king who would replace his sons as leader, he must have remembered the message he had to deliver to Eli many years before when Eli's sons did not follow the good example their father had given them, and the people refused to accept them as his successors. Samuel tried hard to accept God's will as humbly as Eli had. It would not be easy. He would have to anoint two kings for the people and would have to give them his moral support even though they did not always behave as he would have liked.

The story recurs throughout history. In some way, every generation fails in its responsibilities, but God always sends a new generation to do things in a different way. We may be exhausted, but God's resourcefulness never is. Again and again the old are called both to give way to the new and to support it. It is that giving way and supporting that is their greatest example and their greatest gift.

Please read God's command to the aged Samuel.

Samuel judged Israel all the days of his life. He went on a circuit year by year to Bethel, Gilgal, and Mizpah; and he judged Israel in all these places. Then he would come back to Ramah, for his home was there; he administered justice there to Israel, and built there an altar to the LORD.

When Samuel became old, he made his sons judges over Israel. The name of his firstborn son was Joel, and the name of his second, Abijah; they were judges in Beer-sheba. Yet his sons did not follow in his ways, but turned aside after gain; they took bribes and perverted justice.

Then all the elders of Israel gathered together and came to Samuel at Ramah, and said to him, "You are old and your sons do not follow in your ways; appoint for us, then, a king to govern us, like other nations." But the thing displeased Samuel when they said, "Give us a king to govern us." Samuel prayed to the LORD, and the LORD said to Samuel, "Listen to the voice of the people in all that they say to you; for they have not rejected you, but they have rejected me from being king over them...."

1 Samuel 7:15-17; 8:1-7

Questions for Reflection

1. Have you known anyone who yearned and prayed for a child as Hannah did?

2. When you want something very much, how do you go about praying for it? thanking God for it when you have received it?

3. Hannah gave back to God the precious gift God gave her. Have you ever felt called on to return a gift you received from God?

4. In your life, who has helped you to serve God and listen to God as Eli helped young Samuel? Whom have you helped?

5. Do you know any case where a young person brought God's word to an elder as Samuel did to Eli?

6. Samuel's sons disappointed him, as Eli's sons had disappointed him. Do you know any parents disappointed by their children? Do you think your parents were disappointed in you?

Suggestions for Further Reading
1 Samuel 1—8

Prayer

God, please teach us how to pray with complete abandon as Hannah did. In her distress Hannah poured out her heart to you. You heard and answered her prayer. We know that you always hear our prayers, but sometimes you seem to be silent. Those are very difficult times for us, especially when the prayer is for our children or close family members. Perhaps those are the times we must "listen" more attentively.

We want everything that is good for them. We try to set an example, but sometimes they fail to follow our path and we look on that as failure. Please, God, swiftly help us to give up control. Just because they do things differently than we would have does not make them wrong. Help us to know that your resourcefulness is never exhausted. You will be ready to say to them "Here I am" whenever they are ready to call on you. We pray in Jesus' name. Amen.

Glee Cloos, 70, Denver, Colorado

CHAPTER FOURTEEN

Samuel the Kingmaker

The Anointing of Saul

IN THE FIRST FIVE BOOKS OF THE BIBLE, the Pentateuch, we read mostly stories of family life and the adventures of a small tribe that escaped from Egypt to live in the desert and finally to claim its own land. In the books of Samuel and Kings we move into the world of politics. Israel had become a nation. It was attacked by other nations, especially the Philistines. At the same time, it was torn apart by internal struggles over leadership.

Samuel, the son of Hannah, was an extraordinary man whose religious and political leadership was accepted by all the people. Like any conscientious person with heavy responsibilities, he planned for the time when he would not be able to continue in his position. His plan was that his two sons should succeed him. But God and the people made it clear to Samuel that he would not be allowed to pass the leadership on to his sons.

It became Samuel's responsibility to appoint a king to lead the people into a new era. But we do not hear that he began a training program or sent out a request for resumes. God had turned down his plan, and he did not have a "plan B." He simply continued with his duties as priest, prophet and judge, and continued to follow old Eli's advice to listen for God's voice.

While he waited, the need for a king became increasingly clear. The Philistines, a warlike and well-organized group coming in from the seacoast, encroached more and more on Israelite territory. Though Samuel had led the people in war when he was young, he was no longer able to do so, especially against an enemy so much better armed and organized than any they had faced in the past. The people cried out for deliverance from the Philistine onslaught as their ancestors had cried out for deliverance from Egyptian slavery.

Finally God's voice pointed out to Samuel a total stranger who was God's choice to be Israel's first king. In his old age as in his youth, Samuel's role was simply to wait for God's word and then to obey it. While Samuel was preparing to meet the new king, an insignificant young man named Saul had been sent by his father to search for some donkeys that had strayed from the farmyard. He was accompanied by one servant. They searched for such a long time that they were about to give up, but the servant had an idea. He had heard that a seer named Samuel lived in the nearby town. Perhaps the seer could tell them where the donkeys had wandered. Saul was hesitant, but he agreed to give the seer a try.

Read the story of the meeting of Samuel and Saul.

So [Saul and the servant] went up to the town. As they were entering the town, they saw Samuel coming out toward them on his way up to the shrine.

Now the day before Saul came, the Lord had revealed to Samuel: "Tomorrow about this time I will send to you a man from the land of Benjamin, and you shall anoint him to be ruler over my people Israel. He shall save my people from the hand of the Philistines; for I have seen the suffering of my people, because their outcry has come to me." When Samuel saw Saul, the Lord told him, "Here is the man of whom I spoke to you. He it is who shall rule over my people." Then Saul approached Samuel inside the gate, and said, "Tell me, please, where is the house of the seer?" Samuel answered Saul, "I am the seer; go up before me to the shrine, for today you shall eat with me, and in the morning I will let you go and will tell you all that is on your mind. As for your donkeys that were lost three days ago, give no further thought to them, for they have been found. And on whom is all Israel's desire fixed, if not on you and on all your ancestral house?" Saul answered, "I am only a Benjaminite, from the least of the tribes of Israel, and my family is the humblest of all the families of the tribe of Benjamin. Why then have you spoken to me in this way?"

Then Samuel took Saul and his servant-boy and brought them into the hall, and gave them a place at the head of those who had been invited, of whom there were about thirty. And Samuel said to the cook, "Bring the portion I gave you, the one I asked you to put aside." The cook took up the thigh and what went with it and set them before Saul. Samuel said, "See, what was kept is set before you. Eat; for it is set before you at the appointed time, so that you might eat with the guests."

So Saul ate with Samuel that day. When they came down from the shrine into the town, a bed was spread for Saul on the roof, and he lay down to sleep. Then at the break of dawn Samuel called to Saul upon the roof, "Get up, so that I may send you on your way." Saul got up, and both he and Samuel went out into the street.

As they were going down to the outskirts of the town, Samuel said to Saul, "Tell the boy to go on before us, and when he has passed on, stop here yourself for a while, that I may make known to you the word of God."

Samuel took a vial of oil and poured it on his head, and kissed him; he said, "The LORD has anointed you ruler over his people Israel. You shall reign over the people of the LORD and you will save them from the hand of their enemies all around.

1 Samuel 9:14-27; 10:1

The Anointing of David

THE VIAL OF OIL IS IMPORTANT IN THE STORY. In the dry climate of Israel, olive oil is highly valued for anointing the skin. It is also used in ritual because the way it penetrates and restores the body is like the way the Spirit of God penetrates a person God chooses for a particular task. So anointing, not crowning, became the ritual by which a man was made king. Samuel knew that he was to turn an ordinary man into a king by anointing him. The transformation would not be evident at first, but over time the anointing would work on the man with a power similar to that of a seed in the ground.

After the anointing, Saul returned home. Only he and Samuel knew that he was king of Israel. Later Samuel presented Saul to the people as the new king, and they accepted him. Samuel never had the opportunity to mentor Saul as Eli had mentored him. He did try to guide him on occasion. Samuel had retired from his political and military leadership of the people, but not from his spiritual leadership. However, Saul was not as obedient as Samuel had been. As a result, God regretted having selected him as king.

Samuel, who had been such a success in his day, felt like a failure in his old age. His hope for the future government of the people by his sons had failed. Heroically, he had given up his plan and obeyed the strange command of God to anoint Saul. He had then used his enormous prestige with the people to get Saul accepted as king and had tried to guide Saul in his new role. Now this second plan, God's plan, in which he had invested his reputation, had failed. Retirement was not turning out well for Samuel.

God always has a "plan C." It made no sense whatever to Samuel. He was to travel to a small village far from his home and anoint as king one of the sons of a farmer named Jesse. Samuel probably did not know or care that Jesse was a descendant of Ruth. Not only did he know nothing about Jesse, he saw no way he could even get to Bethlehem. Saul knew that God had told Samuel that Saul had failed and his royal line could not continue. Saul's police would be on the lookout for any move of Samuel's that might mean the anointing of a rival king. God answers the old prophet kindly, suggesting a trick by which he could go to Bethlehem to offer a sacrifice in his role as priest without letting anyone know that anything more than a religious service was planned.

Bethlehem was a tiny place, not accustomed to visits from important people like Samuel. Visits from government officials are frightening to simple people in small towns, but Samuel tried to put them at ease by assuring them that he intended them no harm. He was only fulfilling his priestly duties by offering a sacrifice, which he invited them all to attend.

When the people gathered, Samuel asked to be introduced to the sons of Jesse. Jesse proudly brought forward his handsome eldest son, Eliab. Samuel was impressed, and felt sure this was the man he was to make king. But the voice of God contradicted him. Even a prophet does not see what God sees in a person. So Jesse presented his seven sons, one by one. Of each one God said, "No, not this one." Poor Samuel was thoroughly bewildered by this God of his, who sent him on this bizarre errand, then forbade him to carry it out. As a last resort he asked Jesse if these seven were all the sons he had. Jesse told him the youngest had not come. He was occupied in the lowly task of watching his father's sheep.

Samuel refused to continue with the sacrifice until the youngster was brought. We feel the tension of the scene as the father, the seven older brothers and all the villagers wait till someone can find the youngest brother and bring him back. We, the readers, are waiting, too. For a long time the story has been building up to this climax.

David's insignificance is emphasized even more than Saul's had been. He comes from an unimportant village, and he is the eighth son in a society where the eldest has much higher status than the youngest. He was not important enough even to bring along to the sacrifice Samuel was offering. His task as shepherd was the least valued on a farm. Yet the biblical author emphasizes David as shepherd boy because he will grow to be shepherd of God's people.

Contrary to what human beings would expect, God tells Samuel to anoint the boy David as king of Israel. We can imagine the shock of his big brothers and the villagers when they see the prophet pour the oil over the little brother. In this ritual Samuel accomplishes the great work of his old age. He will die soon, but David will look to him for guidance while he lives, and afterwards will be obedient to other prophets God will send. David, in contrast to Saul, will succeed in establishing a royal line because he obeys the word of God.

As with Saul, the anointing made a profound spiritual change in David. It is the turning point of the story, the moment of God's intervention. Yet there is no immediate visible change. The case here is different from that of Saul; Samuel cannot present David to the people as their new king because Saul is king and has no intention of letting go the reins of power, no matter what Samuel says.

Only by a long and complicated process will David be prepared for the kingship. God's action will be hidden behind a human political process. The anointing is the clue by which all the rest of the story has to be interpreted.

Meet David, the shepherd boy.

The word of the LORD came to Samuel: "I regret that I made Saul king, for he has turned back from following me, and has not carried out my commands." Samuel was angry; and he cried out to the LORD all night....

The LORD said to Samuel, "How long will you grieve over Saul? I have rejected him from being king over Israel. Fill your horn with oil and set out; I will send you to Jesse the Bethlehemite, for I have provided for myself a king among his sons." Samuel said, "How can I go? If Saul hears of it, he will kill me." And the LORD said, "Take a heifer with you, and say, 'I have come to sacrifice to the LORD.' Invite Jesse to the sacrifice, and I will show you what you shall do; and you shall anoint for me the one whom I name to you." Samuel did what the LORD commanded, and came to Bethlehem. The elders of the city came to meet him trembling, and said, "Do you come peaceably?" He said, "Peaceably; I have come to sacrifice to the LORD; sanctify yourselves and come with me to the sacrifice." And he sanctified Jesse and his sons and invited them to the sacrifice.

When they came, he looked on Eliab and thought, "Surely the Lord's anointed is now before the LORD." But the LORD said to Samuel, "Do not look on his appearance or on the height of his stature, because I have rejected him; for the LORD does not see as mortals see; they look on the outward appearance, but the LORD looks on the heart." Then Jesse called Abinadab, and made him pass before Samuel. He said, "Neither has the LORD chosen this one." Then Jesse made Shammah pass by. And he said, "Neither has the LORD chosen this one." Jesse made seven of his sons pass before Samuel, and Samuel said to Jesse, "The LORD has not chosen any of these." Samuel said to Jesse, "Are all your sons here?" And he said, "There remains yet the youngest, but he is keeping the sheep." And Samuel said to Jesse, "Send and bring him; for we will not sit down until he comes here." He sent and brought him in. Now he was ruddy, and had beautiful eyes, and was handsome. The LORD said, "Rise and anoint him; for this is the one." Then Samuel took the horn of oil, and anointed him in the presence of his brothers; and the spirit of the LORD came mightily upon David from that day forward.

Samuel 15:10-11; 16:1-13

A King in Decline

THE SPIRIT OF GOD RUSHED UPON DAVID when he was anointed by Samuel. The spirit had come upon Saul at his anointing, but now it left him. In its place came an evil spirit, what we would probably call mental illness. In his later years the great warrior king Saul became the victim of depression and paranoia. The more the illness progressed, the less he was able to rule effectively and the more he clung to his royal power.

The courtiers who surrounded him were concerned by their erratic king, and they suggested the best treatment they knew for depression: good music. Since they had no compact discs, the only way to provide music was to find a musician to join the court. Whenever Saul had a bad spell, music therapy would be available.

It so happened that Jesse's son David was an excellent musician. Long days watching the sheep gave plenty of time for practice, and David had used it well. So David was called to Saul's court to provide music to soothe the disturbed king. He was a handsome and likeable young man, and Saul soon came to love him. He even honored him by making him his armor bearer. Had Saul known about Samuel's anointing of David, he would have felt different. That remained secret, as God's plan does in many of our lives.

This story illustrates Saul's gradual decline, which will eventually lead to military defeat and suicide. When Saul heard from Samuel that God had taken the kingship from him, he did not retire gracefully as Samuel had done, but held on desperately to his royal power, a power that was no longer based on God's will for him. From that point on things became worse and worse for Saul.

Because we know that David has already been anointed for kingship, we notice another story in the background of this one about Saul: David's rise to popularity. Considering that David has already been anointed king, it is surprising how long and complicated his process of acquiring the kingship will be and how humbly he begins it as Saul's musician. God is giving the shepherd boy time to mature and to learn all that he will need to know when he finally becomes king. We can imagine him in Saul's court, silently keeping his secret, but listening and learning.

Saul wanted to keep his position until he died, then hand it over to his son Jonathan. Jonathan was a good man, but not the one God chose. Saul certainly did not intend to mentor David as his successor, but he probably did so unawares. God used Saul for David's education.

Read about how David is brought to the court of Saul.

Now the spirit of the LORD departed from Saul, and an evil spirit from the LORD tormented him. And Saul's servants said to him, "See now, an evil spirit from God is tormenting you. Let our lord now command the servants who attend you to look for someone who is skillful in playing the lyre; and when the evil spirit from God is upon you, he will play it, and you will feel better." So Saul said to his servants, "Provide for me someone who can play well, and bring him to me." One of the young men answered, "I have seen a son of Jesse the Bethlehemite who is skillful in playing, a man of valor, a warrior, prudent in speech, and a man of good presence; and the LORD is with him." So Saul sent messengers to Jesse, and said, "Send me your son David who is with the sheep." Jesse took a donkey loaded with bread, a skin of wine, and a kid, and sent them by his son David to Saul. And David came to Saul, and entered his service. Saul loved him greatly, and he became his armor-bearer. Saul sent to Jesse, saying, "Let David remain in my service, for he has found favor in my sight." And whenever the evil spirit from God came upon Saul, David took the lyre and played it with his hand, and Saul would be relieved and feel better, and the evil spirit would depart from him.

1 Samuel 16:14-23

A King's Jealousy

SAUL HAD STARTED OUT AS A PERSON OF NO IMPORTANCE at all and had succeeded in becoming Israel's first king, pulling the tribes together and resisting the Philistines in a way none of the judges had been able to do. An outsider would think he had reason to be well satisfied with the accomplishments of his life. But healthy aging requires one to let go of positions one has held and welcome the young who will take one's place. Saul lacked the inner security to rise to the challenge. Saul was a great politician and military leader in his day, but as he aged he was out of tune with God's plan.

God sent Saul a gifted and honorable young man, David, to serve him. Saul, like everyone else, was attracted by David. But because of his own interior deterioration, he was also jealous of him.

David went out to battle with Saul's army, and he contributed mightily to Saul's victory. David is a model of collaboration. But Saul's spirit, in his declining years, was a spirit of competition. He resented the younger man's success and popularity. Tactlessly, the women's chorus which traditionally sang the praises of returning warriors, put more emphasis on the young hero than on the old king. Jealousy led the older man into paranoia, and he imagined that David was a threat to his power.

Actually, David remained heroically loyal to the old king. As Saul was deteriorating, David was maturing, and part of that maturity was the ability to prepare himself for the role for which Samuel had anointed him, but at the same time to wait until the time of Saul's death to actually claim it.

Read about the jealousy of Saul.

David went out and was successful wherever Saul sent him; as a result, Saul set him over the army. And all the people, even the servants of Saul, approved.

As they were coming home, when David returned from killing the Philistine, the women came out of all the towns of Israel, singing and dancing, to meet King Saul, with tambourines, with songs of joy, and with musical instruments. And the women sang to one another as they made merry,

"Saul has killed his thousands,
   and David his ten thousands."

Saul was very angry, for this saying displeased him. He said, "They have ascribed to David ten thousands, and to me they have ascribed thousands; what more can he have but the kingdom?" So Saul eyed David from that day on.

The next day an evil spirit from God rushed upon Saul, and he raved within his house, while David was playing the lyre, as he did day by day. Saul had his spear in his hand; and Saul threw the spear, for he thought, "I will pin David to the wall." But David eluded him twice.

Saul was afraid of David, because the LORD was with him but had departed from Saul. So Saul removed him from his presence, and made him a commander of a thousand; and David marched out and came in, leading the army. David had success in all his undertakings; for the LORD was with him. When Saul saw that he had great success, he stood in awe of him. But all Israel and Judah loved David; for it was he who marched out and came in leading them.

1 Samuel 18:5-16

Questions for Reflection

1. How do you think Samuel felt when his protegé Saul failed to obey God? Do you know of people who suffer because a younger person they tried to guide did not turn out well?

2. Do you know of people like Samuel who, though retired from their jobs, continue to exert great influence? Why are they able to do this?

3. Samuel turned his responsibilities as judge over to Saul, but kept his responsibilities as priest and prophet. As you age, what responsibilities would you like to turn over to others, and what would you like to keep?

—∿∿—

4. Do you know of any people like Saul and David who, in their youth, did not seem likely to succeed, yet accomplished great things?

5. In your experience, how do people who, like Saul, realize that their time of leadership is drawing to an end, feel about popular young subordinates who may take their places?

6. Do you know of any cases of depression and/or paranoia that are at all like Saul's?

Suggestions for Further Reading
1 Samuel 10—18

Prayer

In today's readings we hear the Lord tell Samuel "...the Lord does not see as mortals see, they look on the outward appearance, but the Lord looks on the heart."

Lord God, as we look at the heart of Saul we see jealousy, resentment and willfulness. In contrast, the heart of David shows acceptance, patience and desire to do God's will.

As we reflect on the anointing of King Saul and King David, which brought transformation in them, we recall our anointing at baptism and confirmation which began a transformation in us.

God, our King, anoint us now that in our ongoing transformation we will be less like Saul and more like David; less interested in worldly power and glory, and more focused on what is in our hearts. Anoint us that we will fill our hearts full of surrender, acceptance, patience and your way of loving others unconditionally. Anoint us that we will set aside our own agendas and submit our wills to yours, especially when doubt, hardship, and pain come our way. Anoint us that we may grow in our faith and trust in you, knowing that you will lead us through our lifelong transformations and to eventual greater glory with you. For this we pray. Amen.

Dorothy Liston, 59, Denver, Colorado

CHAPTER FIFTEEN

David the Outlaw

Michal Saves David

THE STORY OF DAVID MIGHT HAVE BEEN DESIGNED to upset the stereotype that human beings fall into two categories: the law-abiding citizens and those who disrupt the social order. David fit into both categories. From the moment of his anointing by Samuel, David's goal was to be king, which meant bringing law and order to his people. Yet he spent years as an outlaw, supporting himself by shrewdness and violence.

David tried to begin his political career in the proper way, by joining the court of King Saul and doing the work Saul assigned to him. He learned much at court, and he won the respect of many people. But Saul was not like Samuel, a man big enough to mentor the one who would succeed him in power, and then to step back to give the newcomer opportunities.

Saul had failed at his life's great project, bringing Israel from the era of the judges into that of the kings. He could still have had an important place in history if he had been able to support David in doing what he could not do himself. But Saul was the victim of his own insane jealousy. Since he failed at establishing the kingship, he tried to kill the young man God had sent to replace him at the task.

Saul's attitude toward David shows his increasing mental instability. At times he loves David. He gives David his daughter Michal as wife. At other times he tries to kill David his son-in-law. On one such occasion, Michal learns of her father's intentions and cleverly plans an escape for David. Like her brother Jonathan, David's friend, she chooses loyalty to David and the future he represents over loyalty to her father, who holds present power. She suffers for her choice. She loses the husband she loves and has to face the rage of her father, who marries her off to a man she does not love.

The escape engineered by Michal is the beginning of David's adventures as an outlaw. By the time the story was written down, David was the famous king and founder of a great dynasty of kings, all of them at least theoretically committed to law and order. The author cannot avoid mention of the irregularities of David's youth, but tries to smooth them over by emphasizing David's basic innocence. He only escaped to save his life and only at the insistence of his wife, the king's daughter.

After escaping from Saul, David went to the aged prophet Samuel, trusting Samuel's wisdom to guide him in his predicament. How many independent young adults turn to a parent or mentor in times of crisis! They are fortunate if they find someone as centered in God as Samuel was.

Read how Michal saved her husband from her father.

Saul sent messengers to David's house to keep watch over him, planning to kill him in the morning. David's wife Michal told him, "If you do not save your life tonight, tomorrow you will be killed." So Michal let David down through the window; he fled away and escaped. Michal took an idol and laid it on the bed; she put a net of goats' hair on its head, and covered it with the clothes. When Saul sent messengers to take David, she said, "He is sick." Then Saul sent the messengers to see David for themselves. He said, "Bring him up to me in the bed, that I may kill him." When the messengers came in, the idol was in the bed, with the covering of goats' hair on its head. Saul said to Michal, "Why have you deceived me like this, and let my enemy go, so that he has escaped?" Michal answered Saul, "He said to me, 'Let me go; why should I kill you?'"

Now David fled and escaped; he came to Samuel at Ramah, and told him all that Saul had done to him. He and Samuel went and settled at Naioth.

1 Samuel 19:11-18

David and Jonathan

DAVID IS NOW A MAN ON THE RUN, trying to escape the pursuit
of Saul and find ways of surviving in the wilderness. Saul's
son Jonathan, who has been David's friend since they met at
Saul's court, sneaks away from his father's army to visit David.

David and Jonathan are a great model of friendship.
Jonathan, as eldest son of King Saul and a famous warrior in
his own right, would in the normal course of things have succeeded Saul as king. He realized that David, not he, would succeed to the kingship, yet he was not jealous. Unlike his father,
he felt no need for royal power, and he became David's friend
and supporter. Saul's insane hatred of David has alienated
both his daughter and his son from him. Saul's family has
become a tangled web of conflicting loyalties.

Jonathan and David met secretly, and Jonathan encouraged David by telling him that both Jonathan and Saul knew
that David would be king. Saul was trying to kill his competi-
tor, but Jonathan wanted only to be his second in command.
In David's wilderness hideout, while Saul searched for David
to kill him, Jonathan and David renewed their covenant of
friendship. It is the last time they will see each other alive.

We are left to imagine the anguish of crazed Saul, whose
son and daughter both side with the young man he fears will
seize his throne. As Eli and Samuel suffered because their
sons did not follow their good example, Saul suffers because
his children do not follow his bad example.

Read about the famous friendship of David and Jonathan.

David remained in the strongholds in the wilderness, in
the hill country of the Wilderness of Ziph. Saul sought him
every day, but the LORD did not give him into his hand.

David was in the Wilderness of Ziph at Horesh when he
learned that Saul had come out to seek his life. Saul's son
Jonathan set out and came to David at Horesh; there he
strengthened his hand through the LORD. He said to him,
"Do not be afraid; for the hand of my father Saul shall not
find you; you shall be king over Israel, and I shall be second

to you; my father Saul also knows that this is so." Then the two of them made a covenant before the LORD; David remained at Horesh, and Jonathan went home.

1 Samuel 23:14-18

David and Saul at En-Gedi

SAUL CONTINUED TO PURSUE DAVID. Having heard that David was hiding in the desert area around En-gedi, near where the Dead Sea Scrolls would later be found, Saul led his army there. He went alone into one of the many caves in the area to relieve himself. He did not know that David and his men were hiding in the deep recesses of the same cave.

Saul is a humorous and pathetic figure, squatting in the cave, unaware of his danger. This is a moment of opportunity for David. He can easily kill Saul and end his own life of constant flight. He can seize the throne for which Samuel has anointed him. However, David knows that the throne is not to be grasped but to be received as a gift at the proper time. He will wait; he will not force the process which is slowly leading him to kingship. His ability to wait is a sign of his strength.

This is also an opportunity for revenge on a man who has made many attempts to kill a loyal follower. But David understands what few people will understand until the coming of Jesus: God is the only one who punishes evildoers, and we seize that prerogative of God at our own risk.

David cuts the edge off of Saul's cloak and allows him to leave the cave unhurt. Later, he shows Saul the bit of his cloak to let him know in what danger he was, and how loyal David is. Saul, in one of his erratic shifts of mood, weeps and admits David's loyalty and his own sinfulness.

In this maudlin mood, Saul even asks David an extraordinary favor. He asks that when David becomes king he not follow the usual procedure of eliminating the family of the previous king, who are always a threat to a new and shaky dynasty. Amazingly, David agrees.

Read the story of the encounter of Saul and David in the cave.

When Saul returned from following the Philistines, he was told, "David is in the wilderness of En-gedi." Then Saul took three thousand chosen men out of all Israel, and went to look for David and his men in the direction of the Rocks of the Wild Goats. He came to the sheepfolds beside the road, where there was a cave; and Saul went in to relieve himself. Now David and his men were sitting in the innermost parts of the cave. The men of David said to him, "Here is the day of which the LORD said to you, 'I will give your enemy into your hand, and you shall do to him as it seems good to you.'" Then David went and stealthily cut off a corner of Saul's cloak. Afterward David was stricken to the heart because he had cut off a corner of Saul's cloak. He said to his men, "The LORD forbid that I should do this thing to my lord, the Lord's anointed, to raise my hand against him; for he is the Lord's anointed." So David scolded his men severely and did not permit them to attack Saul. Then Saul got up and left the cave, and went on his way.

Afterwards David also rose up and went out of the cave and called after Saul, "My lord the king!" When Saul looked behind him, David bowed with his face to the ground, and did obeisance. David said to Saul, "Why do you listen to the words of those who say, 'David seeks to do you harm'? This very day your eyes have seen how the LORD gave you into my hand in the cave; and some urged me to kill you, but I spared you. I said, 'I will not raise my hand against my lord; for he is the Lord's anointed.' See, my father, see the corner of your cloak in my hand; for by the fact that I cut off the corner of your cloak, and did not kill you, you may know for certain that there is no wrong or treason in my hands. I have not sinned against you, though you are hunting me to take my life. May the LORD judge between me and you! May the LORD avenge me on you; but my hand shall not be against you.... Against whom has the king of Israel come out? Whom do you pursue? A dead dog? A single flea? May the LORD therefore be judge, and give sentence between me and you. May he see to it, and plead my cause, and vindicate me against you."

When David had finished speaking these words to Saul, Saul said, "Is this your voice, my son David?" Saul lifted up his voice and wept. He said to David, "You are more righteous than I; for you have repaid me good, whereas I have repaid you evil. Today you have explained how you have dealt well with me, in that you did not kill me when the LORD put me into your hands. For who has ever found an enemy, and sent the enemy safely away? So may the LORD reward you with good for what you have done to me this day. Now I know that you shall surely be king, and that the kingdom of Israel shall be established in your hand. Swear to me therefore by the LORD that you will not cut off my descendants after me, and that you will not wipe out my name from my father's house." So David swore this to Saul. Then Saul went home; but David and his men went up to the stronghold.

1 Samuel 24:1-22

Abigail

SAMUEL, THE WISE ELDER WHO SUPPORTED DAVID, died while David was still in exile in the wilderness, hiding from Saul. All the people mourned the old man who had given them a sense of connection with God even during times of political chaos. David must have felt the loss deeply, but God planned another gift to replace Samuel's wisdom, a wise woman to become David's wife.

David and his band were camped in the wilderness. Near them grazed the large flocks of a very rich man named Nabal. David's men resisted the natural temptation to appropriate a lamb or two to supplement their scanty rations. David treated the shepherds courteously. Here, as everywhere, he made friends, not enemies.

When the time came to shear the sheep, they were brought to Nabal at Carmel. Sheep shearing was a period of festivity, and the culture made it appropriate for David to send some men to ask for a gift, a kind of tip for their protection of the sheep in the wilderness. Nabal was stingy to the point of folly, and rudely refused to give David anything.

A servant realized the folly of Nabal's meanness but did not dare say anything to his master. Nabal did not listen to servants. However, Nabal had a wise and beautiful wife who did. The servant told her what had happened, and she immediately took matters into her own capable hands. Abigail was the competent mistress of her house, who reminds me of the "valiant woman" described in the Book of Proverbs (Proverbs 31:10-31).

Without a word to her husband, Abigail collected a huge amount of the food supplies men hiding in the wilderness would need, and started out to bring them to David. She moved quickly, yet not before David, in hot anger, had set out with an armed band to take bloody revenge on Nabal.

They met on the way, and Abigail showed herself a mistress of diplomacy. By her gifts and her wise words she was able to persuade David to give up his violent errand. It is clear from his behavior toward Saul that in his better moments he realized that vengeance and bloodshed were no base for the kind of kingdom he hoped to build, but in the case of Nabal only Abigail's wisdom saved him from vindictiveness.

David did not forget the wise and beautiful Abigail. When her husband died, David asked her to marry him, and she agreed gladly. As Michal had supported David against her insane father, Abigail supported him against her foolish husband. Michal had stayed behind at Saul's court, but Abigail lived with David in the wilderness. It is easy to imagine this strong woman transforming the rough life of the outlaws into something much more comfortable and civilized.

Read the story of Abigail.

Now Samuel died; and all Israel assembled and mourned for him. They buried him at his home in Ramah. Then David got up and went down to the wilderness of Paran.

There was a man in Maon, whose property was in

Carmel. The man was very rich; he had three thousand sheep and a thousand goats. He was shearing his sheep in Carmel. Now the name of the man was Nabal, and the name of his wife Abigail. The woman was clever and beautiful, but the man was surly and mean.... David heard in the wilderness that Nabal was shearing his sheep. So David sent ten young men; and David said to the young men, "Go up to Carmel, and go to Nabal, and greet him in my name. Thus you shall salute him: 'Peace be to you, and peace be to your house, and peace be to all that you have. I hear that you have shearers; now your shepherds have been with us, and we did them no harm, and they missed nothing, all the time they were in Carmel. Ask your young men, and they will tell you. Therefore let my young men find favor in your sight; for we have come on a feast day. Please give whatever you have at hand to your servants and to your son David.'"

When David's young men came, they said all this to Nabal in the name of David; and then they waited. But Nabal answered David's servants, "Who is David? Who is the son of Jesse? There are many servants today who are breaking away from their masters. Shall I take my bread and my water and the meat that I have butchered for my shearers, and give it to men who come from I do not know where?" So David's young men turned away, and came back and told him all this. David said to his men, "Every man strap on his sword!" And every one of them strapped on his sword; David also strapped on his sword; and about four hundred men went up after David, while two hundred remained with the baggage.

But one of the young men told Abigail, Nabal's wife, "David sent messengers out of the wilderness to salute our master; and he shouted insults at them. Yet the men were very good to us, and we suffered no harm, and we never missed anything when we were in the fields, as long as we were with them; they were a wall to us both by night and by day, all the while we were with them keeping the sheep. Now therefore know this and consider what you should do; for evil has been decided against our master and against all his house; he is so ill-natured that no one can speak to him."

Then Abigail hurried and took two hundred loaves, two skins of wine, five sheep ready dressed, five measures of parched grain, one hundred clusters of raisins, and two hundred cakes of figs. She loaded them on donkeys and said to her young men, "Go on ahead of me; I am coming after you." But she did not tell her husband Nabal. As she rode on the donkey and came down under cover of the mountain, David and his men came down toward her; and she met them. Now David had said, "Surely it was in vain that I protected all that this fellow has in the wilderness, so that nothing was missed of all that belonged to him; but he has returned me evil for good. God do so to David and more also, if by morning I leave so much as one male of all who belong to him."

When Abigail saw David, she hurried and alighted from the donkey, fell before David on her face, bowing to the ground. She fell at his feet and said, "Upon me alone, my lord, be the guilt; please let your servant speak in your ears, and hear the words of your servant. My lord, do not take seriously this ill-natured fellow, Nabal; for as his name is, so is he; Nabal is his name, and folly is with him; but I, your servant, did not see the young men of my lord, whom you sent.

"Now then, my lord, as the LORD lives, and as you yourself live, since the LORD has restrained you from bloodguilt and from taking vengeance with your own hand, now let your enemies and those who seek to do evil to my lord be like Nabal. And now let this present that your servant has brought to my lord be given to the young men who follow my lord. Please forgive the trespass of your servant; for the LORD will certainly make my lord a sure house, because my lord is fighting the battles of the LORD; and evil shall not be found in you so long as you live. If anyone should rise up to pursue you and to seek your life, the life of my lord shall be bound in the bundle of the living under the care of the LORD your God; but the lives of your enemies he shall sling out as from the hollow of a sling. When the LORD has done to my lord according to all the good that he has spoken concerning you, and has appointed you prince over Israel, my lord shall have no cause of grief, or pangs of conscience, for having shed blood without cause or for having saved himself. And when the LORD has dealt well with my lord, then remember your servant."

David said to Abigail, "Blessed be the LORD, the God of Israel, who sent you to meet me today! Blessed be your good sense, and blessed be you, who have kept me today from bloodguilt and from avenging myself by my own hand! For as surely as the LORD the God of Israel lives, who has restrained me from hurting you, unless you had hurried and come to meet me, truly by morning there would not have been left to Nabal so much as one male." Then David received from her hand what she had brought him; he said to her, "Go up to your house in peace; see, I have heeded your voice, and I have granted your petition."

Abigail came to Nabal; he was holding a feast in his house, like the feast of a king. Nabal's heart was merry within him, for he was very drunk; so she told him nothing at all until the morning light. In the morning, when the wine had gone out of Nabal, his wife told him these things, and his heart died within him; he became like a stone. About ten days later the LORD struck Nabal, and he died.

When David heard that Nabal was dead, he said, "Blessed be the LORD who has judged the case of Nabal's insult to me, and has kept back his servant from evil; the LORD has returned the evildoing of Nabal upon his own head." Then David sent and wooed Abigail, to make her his wife. When David's servants came to Abigail at Carmel, they said to her, "David has sent us to you to take you to him as his wife." She rose and bowed down, with her face to the ground, and said, "Your servant is a slave to wash the feet of the servants of my lord." Abigail got up hurriedly and rode away on a donkey; her five maids attended her. She went after the messengers of David and became his wife.

1 Samuel 25:1-42

Questions for Reflection

1. Do you know anyone who, like Jonathan and Michal, suffers inner conflict between loyalty to a parent and other loyalties? Which loyalty seems most important to you?

2. Do you know anyone who, like Saul, resented the young person who seemed likely to take over his or her responsibilities? What qualities would be necessary in both parties to make such relationships work?

3. What is the importance of friendship in your life? Can it ever outweigh family ties, as it did with Jonathan?

———

4. David had the opportunity to take vengeance on Saul, but he left vengeance to God. Do you know of anyone else who did this?

5. Do you know of an older person who was able to be a support to a young adult in crisis as Samuel was to David? What makes the young person choose a particular elder in time of need?

6. Abigail took courageous initiative to make peace between her husband and David. Do you know of anyone today who has taken a courageous initiative in order to make peace?

7. Do you think Abigail did right in bringing a gift to David without her husband's permission? When is it right for married people to take action without consulting their spouses?

Suggestions for Further Reading
1 Samuel 19—30
Proverbs 31:10-31

Prayer

Lord God, as we listen to the words of those events that happened so long ago to David and Saul, we see and appreciate that their humanness is much like ours.

We remember that as we were maturing, like Saul we may not have done as good a job of mentoring our children and others we met as we would have liked. For this we ask your forgiveness.

We pray to you, O Lord, for friends we've met and cherished over the years, especially those like David's friend, Jonathan, who were close for awhile, then through various kinds of circumstances were no longer with us. We remember them, O Lord, as you always remember us.

Lord, as we recall the support Michal and Abigail gave David, help us to be like them as we support others in need. Help us also to thank those who have supported us over time. And most of all we thank you, O Lord, for everything you have given us. We pray in the name of the Father, and of the Son, and of the Holy Spirit. Amen.

Helen Williams, 61, Arvada, Colorado

CHAPTER SIXTEEN

David the King

The Death of Saul

SAUL'S DETERIORATION AS KING CONTINUED. He divided his energies between seeking out his imagined enemy, David, and protecting his people against their real and powerful enemy, the Philistines. In the end he was defeated in battle by the Philistines and came to his low point by falling into despair and killing himself. In the same battle, his son Jonathan and two other sons were also killed, so that any realistic hope of a dynasty to succeed him as king was destroyed. This is the disastrous end of the downward journey that began when Saul refused to obey God's word spoken to him through the prophet Samuel. Perhaps the Scriptures have preserved the memory of this king who failed as a warning to all who are specially chosen by God.

Read about the tragic death of Saul.

Now the Philistines fought against Israel; and the men of Israel fled before the Philistines, and many fell on Mount Gilboa. The Philistines overtook Saul and his sons; and the Philistines killed Jonathan and Abinadab and Malchishua, the sons of Saul. The battle pressed hard upon Saul; the archers found him, and he was badly wounded by them. Then Saul said to his armor-bearer, "Draw your sword and thrust me through with it, so that these uncircumcised may not come and thrust me through, and make sport of me." But his armor-bearer was unwilling; for he was terrified. So Saul took his own sword and fell upon it. When his armor-bearer saw that Saul was dead, he also fell upon his sword and died with him. So Saul and his three sons and his armor-bearer and all his men died together on the same day.

1 Samuel 31:1-6

David Becomes King

EVEN AFTER THE DEATH OF SAUL, David did not rush to claim the kingship. He ordered public mourning for the dead king and his sons. He himself wrote a lament on the death of Saul and Jonathan.

When the time of mourning was over, David asked God for guidance. God told him to move to Hebron, the city where Sarah and Abraham had been buried. This was in the territory of Judah, David's own tribe. The people of Judah anointed him king and he began to rule over this tiny kingdom, always learning and consolidating his position as he went.

Saul left behind a weak son, Ishbaal, who had not fallen in battle. Ishbaal attempted to rule the powerful northern tribes, but he was not capable of holding the people's loyalty and was killed by his own officials.

By this time David was thirty years old, a mature age at a time when the lifespan was much shorter than ours. He had learned from Saul about government and had been toughened by years as an outlaw. Then he had gained experience of government from ruling the tribe of Judah. Throughout, he had carefully avoided doing anything against Saul or Saul's family, so he had not aroused too much hostility from Saul's followers.

The time had come when David was ready to be king of all twelve tribes. The people of Israel came to him to beg him to become their shepherd. The image of shepherd must have brought David's mind back to the day he was tending his father's sheep when Samuel called him in from the fields to anoint him king.

Throughout the Ancient Near East the shepherd was seen as symbol of the king. It was an image that said much about what people hoped for from their kings. The shepherd must be strong to protect the helpless sheep from wild animals and thieves. He must also be gentle and caring, meeting all the needs of the sheep for food, water, rest and healing. The shepherd must be wise, knowing where to lead the sheep so they will find good pasture. He labors day and night for the welfare of the flock. Grown sheep are kept for wool, not for meat, so the shepherd does not kill them or use them without concern for their welfare.

Jesus, the ultimate good shepherd, would give his life for his sheep. The people of Israel never expected that much, but they did expect a great deal of the man they anointed to be their shepherd-like king. David knew from his own experience as a shepherd-boy what they expected.

Read about the anointing of David as shepherd-king.

> Then all the tribes of Israel came to David at Hebron, and said, "Look, we are your bone and flesh. For some time, while Saul was king over us, it was you who led out Israel and brought it in. The LORD said to you: It is you who shall be shepherd of my people Israel, you who shall be ruler over Israel." So all the elders of Israel came to the king at Hebron; and King David made a covenant with them at Hebron before the LORD, and they anointed David king over Israel. David was thirty years old when he began to reign, and he reigned forty years. At Hebron he reigned over Judah seven years and six months; and at Jerusalem he reigned over all Israel and Judah thirty-three years.
>
> *2 Samuel 5:1-5*

God Speaks Through Nathan

WE COME NOW TO AN EPISODE that is central to the whole story of monarchy in Israel and links it most closely to the New Testament.

David overcame the Philistines and conquered Jerusalem, which he made his capital city. There he built himself a luxurious house of imported cedar wood. He was a great king. He had come to success the hard way, and perhaps he felt a bit uncomfortable with his new life-style. It occurred to him that he might feel better if he built a house for God as fine as the house in which he himself lived.

When David told his court prophet Nathan about his pious plan, Nathan was enthusiastic. Nathan was a professional religious man and had no doubt that what seemed good to him also seemed good to God. It is a mistake to which professional religious people are susceptible. But sometimes it is only in sleep, when we are totally defenseless, that we truly hear God. That night God gave Nathan a message quite opposite the words Nathan had spoken to the king.

The embarrassed prophet had to return to court the next day and tell David that after all God did not want that house David wanted to build. God had always been present among the people where the ark of the covenant was kept in a tent. The tent symbolized God's ability to move with the people. God was not ready to be restricted to a solid building. God did not want any appearance of being domesticated or co-opted and did not hanker for the luxury that David offered.

However, God was not displeased with David, but offered him a gift beyond anything he expected. God wished to be the giver of a house, not the recipient of one. To understand the wordplay in this conversation, it is necessary to know that in Hebrew, as in English, the word *house* sometimes has the meaning "dynasty."

God promises David a dynasty that will last forever. This is not a conditional promise like the covenant made at Sinai. David's kingship will not be taken away from his family as Saul's had been.

This promise is the basis of the expectation of a messiah from the family of David. Gabriel refers to it when speaking to Mary, "And now, you will conceive in your womb and bear a son, and you will name him Jesus. He will be great, and will be called the Son of the Most High, and the Lord God will give to him the throne of his ancestor David. He will reign over the house of Jacob forever, and of his kingdom there will be no end" (Luke 1:31-33).

Read this great promise pronounced by the prophet Nathan.

Now when the king was settled in his house, and the LORD had given him rest from all his enemies around him, the king said to the prophet Nathan, "See now, I am living in a house of cedar, but the ark of God stays in a tent." Nathan said to the king, "Go, do all that you have in mind; for the LORD is with you."

But that same night the word of the LORD came to Nathan: Go and tell my servant David: Thus says the LORD: Are you the one to build me a house to live in? I have not lived in a house since the day I brought up the people of Israel from Egypt to this day, but I have been moving about in a tent and a tabernacle. Wherever I have moved about among all the people of Israel, did I ever speak a word with any of the tribal leaders of Israel, whom I commanded to shepherd my people Israel, saying, "Why have you not built me a house of cedar?" Now therefore thus you shall say to my servant David: Thus says the LORD of hosts: I took you from the pasture, from following the sheep to be prince over my people Israel; and I have been with you wherever you went, and have cut off all your enemies from before you; and I will make for you a great name, like the name of the great ones of the earth.... Moreover the LORD declares to you that the LORD will make you a house. When your days are fulfilled and you lie down with your ancestors, I will raise up your offspring after you, who shall come forth from your body, and I will establish his kingdom. He shall build a house for my name, and I will establish the throne of his kingdom forever. I will be a father to him, and he shall be a son to me. When he commits iniquity, I will punish him with a rod such as mortals use, with blows inflicted by human beings. But I will not take my steadfast love from him, as I took it from Saul, whom I put away from before you. Your house and your kingdom shall be made sure forever before me; your throne shall be established forever. In accordance with all these words and with all this vision, Nathan spoke to David.

Then King David went in and sat before the LORD, and said, "Who am I, O Lord GOD, and what is my house, that you have brought me thus far? And yet this was a small thing in your eyes, O Lord GOD; you have spoken also of your servant's house for a great while to come. May this be instruction for the people, O Lord GOD! And what more can David say to you? For you know your servant, O Lord GOD! Because of your promise, and according to your own heart, you have wrought all this greatness, so that your servant may know it.

2 Samuel 7:1-21

Bathsheba

DAVID'S CAREER HAS REACHED ITS PINNACLE with the prophecy of Nathan. Soon after, it begins its decline with the famous story of his adultery with Bathsheba. It is a classic tale of illicit sexual desire and improper use of power.

The great warrior David has retired from battle. He can now stay at home and issue orders. He sends his general Joab out to conquer the neighboring country of Ammon (in present-day Jordan). David himself stays home in his cedar palace where he can enjoy a siesta on the flat roof. I was never able to visualize the scene until I visited Jerusalem. We were staying at a hospice four stories high and there was a lovely area on the roof where we did our laundry. From here we had a clear view of the roofs of smaller buildings around us, where much household activity was going on. In a crowded city, the rooftop is the only place to catch a breeze as well as a view. It is valuable living space.

Looking down from his large palace, David had a good view of the rooftop of his neighbor Uriah, whose wife Bathsheba was taking a bath there. This was probably the ritual bath a Jewish woman takes after her menstrual period before resuming intercourse with her husband.

David was stricken with lust for the beautiful Bathsheba. Her husband Uriah was with Joab's army in Ammon. David had power to do what he wanted, so he had Bathsheba brought to the palace and he slept with her. There is no conversation, no expression of affection; this is pure lust. We hear no word about Bathsheba's feelings; it is taken for granted that she is at the mercy of the king.

Soon Bathsheba sends David word that she is pregnant. He faces the dilemma so many men have faced. Because he is king, he has power to resolve his dilemma in an extraordinary way. He calls Uriah back from the battlefield, receives him kindly, and urges him to go down to his house and "wash his feet," a euphemism for having intercourse with his wife.

The unprincipled David did not reckon with a highly principled Uriah. It was customary for soldiers in the Israelite army to abstain from sex in time of war. Uriah, even though he had been sent to Jerusalem, thought of himself as part of the army that was fighting, so he refused to sleep with his wife. Even the power of the king could not corrupt a man of Uriah's integrity.

Since there was now no way to pretend that the child was Uriah's, David descended further along the slippery path of sin. He arranged for Uriah's death. David is a man corrupted by his own power.

Bathsheba went through the period of mourning that custom demanded. Then David took her into his harem, and she gave birth to their son.

Read the story of the sin that was the beginning of David's troubles.

In the spring of the year, the time when kings go out to battle, David sent Joab with his officers and all Israel with him; they ravaged the Ammonites, and besieged Rabbah. But David remained at Jerusalem.

It happened, late one afternoon, when David rose from his couch and was walking about on the roof of the king's house, that he saw from the roof a woman bathing; the woman was very beautiful. David sent someone to inquire about the woman. It was reported, "This is Bathsheba daughter of Eliam, the wife of Uriah the Hittite." So David sent messengers to get her, and she came to him, and he lay with her. (Now she was purifying herself after her period.)

Then she returned to her house. The woman conceived; and she sent and told David, "I am pregnant."

So David sent word to Joab, "Send me Uriah the Hittite." And Joab sent Uriah to David. When Uriah came to him, David asked how Joab and the people fared, and how the war was going. Then David said to Uriah, "Go down to your house, and wash your feet." Uriah went out of the king's house, and there followed him a present from the king. But Uriah slept at the entrance of the king's house with all the servants of his lord, and did not go down to his house. When they told David, "Uriah did not go down to his house," David said to Uriah, "You have just come from a journey. Why did you not go down to your house?" Uriah said to David, "The ark and Israel and Judah remain in booths; and my lord Joab and the servants of my lord are camping in the open field; shall I then go to my house, to eat and to drink, and to lie with my wife? As you live, and as your soul lives, I will not do such a thing."...

In the morning David wrote a letter to Joab, and sent it by the hand of Uriah. In the letter he wrote, "Set Uriah in the forefront of the hardest fighting, and then draw back from him, so that he may be struck down and die." As Joab was besieging the city, he assigned Uriah to the place where he knew there were valiant warriors. The men of the city came out and fought with Joab; and some of the servants of David among the people fell. Uriah the Hittite was killed as well.

When the wife of Uriah heard that her husband was dead, she made lamentation for him. When the mourning was over, David sent and brought her to his house, and she became his wife, and bore him a son. But the thing that David had done displeased the LORD....

2 Samuel 11:1-11, 14-17; 26-27

God Speaks Again Through Nathan

WHEN KINGS APPEAR IN ISRAEL, prophets also become important. The danger of kingship is that power corrupts, as in the case of David. The balance God provides to the royal power is the prophetic ministry. Prophets challenge the king by speaking God's word to him. The king's power is never absolute; he is subject to God as represented by the prophet.

The prophet Nathan speaks to David through a parable, as Jesus will do so often. The purpose of a parable is to get the listener involved in the story and led to drawing conclusions about it before realizing that the story is actually about him or herself. It can be much more effective than a more direct statement of the same message.

When Nathan told the king about a man who owned great flocks, yet stole the single lamb treasured by his poor neighbor, we see that David took seriously his royal role as upholder of justice and defender of the poor. He is full of indignation and promises to punish the wealthy man. Only then does Nathan speak the crucial words, "You are the man." David, who had a large harem, was not content with what God had given him but wanted more, even at the cost of taking the only wife of a poor and honest soldier.

Nathan was a brave man to speak this word to the king. Many powerful people would have destroyed the bearer of such a message. But David shows his true greatness here. Unlike Saul, who refused correction from Samuel, David admits that Nathan is right, and repents. He is forgiven, but will suffer severely as a result of his sin. He will have trouble from within his house. The immediate trouble is the death of Bathsheba's child. For the rest of David's life the trouble will escalate, all from his sons.

Yet God did not abandon David. Bathsheba bore him another son named Solomon who would inherit the blessing Nathan had pronounced for the house of David. No matter how badly we sin, God is always able to give us a new start.

Read about the prophet confronting the king.

[A]nd the LORD sent Nathan to David. He came to him, and said to him, "There were two men in a certain city, the one rich and the other poor. The rich man had very many flocks and herds; but the poor man had nothing but one little ewe lamb, which he had bought. He brought it up, and it grew up with him and with his children; it used to eat of his meager fare, and drink from his cup, and lie in his bosom, and it was like a daughter to him. Now there came a traveler to the rich man, and he was loath to take one of his own flock or herd to prepare for the wayfarer who had come to him, but he took the poor man's lamb, and prepared that for the guest who had come to him." Then David's anger was greatly kindled against the man. He said to Nathan, "As the LORD lives, the man who has done this deserves to die; he shall restore the lamb fourfold, because he did this thing, and because he had no pity."

Nathan said to David, "You are the man! Thus says the LORD, the God of Israel: I anointed you king over Israel, and I rescued you from the hand of Saul; I gave you your master's house, and your master's wives into your bosom, and gave you the house of Israel and of Judah; and if that had been too little, I would have added as much more. Why have you despised the word of the LORD, to do what is evil in his sight? You have struck down Uriah the Hittite with the sword, and have taken his wife to be your wife, and have killed him with the sword of the Ammonites...

Thus says the LORD: I will raise up trouble against you from within your own house; and I will take your wives before your eyes, and give them to your neighbor, and he shall lie with your wives in the sight of this very sun. For you did it secretly; but I will do this thing before all Israel, and before the sun." David said to Nathan, "I have sinned against the LORD." Nathan said to David, "Now the LORD has put away your sin; you shall not die. Nevertheless, because by this deed you have utterly scorned the LORD, the child that is born to you shall die." Then Nathan went to his house....

[After the death of the child] David consoled his wife Bathsheba, and went to her, and lay with her; and she bore a son, and he named him Solomon. The LORD loved him....

2 Samuel 12:1-9; 11-15; 24

Questions for Reflection

1. Saul is one of the few biblical figures who committed suicide. How does his story help you to understand people who commit suicide today?

2. The people selected David to be king because they believed God had appointed him to be shepherd over them. What characteristics of a shepherd would you like your political leaders to have?

3. Nathan at first thought God would be pleased with a temple built by David. He later realized he had been mistaken. Have you ever realized you were mistaken about God's will on some point?

4. David was not allowed to build the temple of which he dreamed. What have you dreamed of doing, but not been allowed to do?

5. In what ways will Jesus be like his ancestor David? Unlike him?

—◊—

6. When David retired from personally leading his army it seems he had more time to get into trouble. Does this ever happen to people in the process of retirement today?

7. Do you know of anyone who saw his or her error when corrected, and repented as David did?

Suggestions for Further Reading

1 Samuel 31
2 Samuel 1—12
Psalm 89

Prayer

All-powerful God, you know our every action, our every fear, our hopes and our failures. When we suffer disaster in our world as Saul did, do not let us give in to despair. Thank you for your gift of hope that gives us comfort and guidance.

All-loving God, do not hold our faults and failings against us. Grant us the humility to admit our mistakes and to ask for forgiveness just as David asked for forgiveness for his great sin. Look on us with kindness and compassion and teach us to walk in your ways. We thank you for your gift of love which brings us peace. Amen.

Mary Finch, 71, Lakewood, Colorado

CHAPTER SEVENTEEN

The Decline of David

The Rape of Tamar

DAVID'S ADULTERY WITH BATHSHEBA marked the beginning of his downward path. The prophecy of Nathan that God would raise up trouble for David from within his house (2 Samuel 12:11) is fulfilled in a long series of events beginning with the rape of David's daughter Tamar.

To understand this story, we need to keep in mind the kind of blended family typical of ancient kings. Kings had many wives in their harems. Each wife had her own household in which she raised her children. Children born of the same mother were raised together and usually had great affection and loyalty for each other. Since the various wives competed to gain the king's favor and especially to obtain advancement for their children, relationships among the half brothers and sisters might be much less affectionate, though they were all part of the same court. The king had complete power over the whole family, but was not personally involved in childrearing.

One of David's wives, Ahinoam, bore his first son, Amnon, the crown prince. Another wife, Maacah, the daughter of Talmai the king of Geshur, bore David's third son, Absalom, and a beautiful daughter, Tamar. Amnon was overcome by lust for his half-sister Tamar. In Egypt and other nations of the ancient Near East, it was common for royal brothers to marry their sisters, but in Israel this was considered incest.

Powerful people such as crown princes are always surrounded by courtiers eager to give the kind of advice the powerful one wants to hear. Such a one was Jonadab, Amnon's cousin and friend. When Jonadab discovers the intensity of Amnon's passion for Tamar, he suggests a trick by which Amnon can get what he wants. If Amnon had sought advice from a prophet like Nathan, he would have heard something very different.

Jonadab suggests that Amnon pretend to be sick. When David comes to the sickroom to visit, Amnon is to say that he has no appetite, but he could eat if his half-sister Tamar was to come and prepare food for him with her own hands. David will surely be willing to humor his ailing eldest son.

Amnon takes Jonadab's advice. David acts as expected, unaware that his power is being used for the downfall of his daughter. Tamar obeys David. It would have been unthinkable for her to do otherwise. When she comes to bake for Amnon he rapes her.

When Amnon makes his intention clear, Tamar speaks for the first time. She is a model of a wise woman attempting to deflect the passion of an evil man. She suggests that David's love for Amnon is so great that he will make an exception to the Israelite custom forbidding marriage of brother and half-sister. In that way Amnon could have her without shame. Amnon ignores her words and overcomes her by force.

No sooner has he raped her than his passion for her turns into hatred, and he puts her out of his house. Again Tamar speaks with wisdom and pathos. Virginity was considered essential for a woman to be marriageable. Therefore biblical law required that a man who raped a woman marry her (Deuteronomy 22:28, 29). We see the extremity of Tamar's situation in that she pleads to become the wife of her rapist. Amnon refuses.

Tamar has only two choices. She might try to cover up the incident as David tried to cover up his adultery with Bathsheba. Or she could acknowledge what has happened, knowing full well that in the case of rape it is the victim who is punished. She would never find a husband. She chooses not to hide the truth.

David was angry at what had happened, but did nothing to punish the crown prince. For the first time we see how helpless this great man was to deal with the problems within his own family. Perhaps the memory of his own adultery made him embarrassed to correct his sons.

Tamar lived the rest of her life as a spinster in her brother Absalom's house. In the culture of her time, this was seen as a tragic fate. He tried to comfort her. He felt her disgrace deeply, but bided his time for vengeance.

Read the story of the rape of David's daughter Tamar.

David's son Absalom had a beautiful sister whose name was Tamar; and David's son Amnon fell in love with her. Amnon was so tormented that he made himself ill because of his sister Tamar, for she was a virgin and it seemed impossible to Amnon to do anything to her. But Amnon had a friend whose name was Jonadab, the son of David's brother Shimeah; and Jonadab was a very crafty man. He said to him, "O son of the king, why are you so haggard morning after morning? Will you not tell me?" Amnon said to him, "I love Tamar, my brother Absalom's sister." Jonadab said to him, "Lie down on your bed, and pretend to be ill; and when your father comes to see you, say to him, 'Let my sister Tamar come and give me something to eat, and prepare the food in my sight, so that I may see it and eat it from her hand.'" So Amnon lay down, and pretended to be ill; and when the king came to see him, Amnon said to the king, "Please let my sister Tamar come and make a couple of cakes in my sight, so that I may eat from her hand."

Then David sent home to Tamar, saying, "Go to your brother Amnon's house, and prepare food for him." So Tamar went to her brother Amnon's house, where he was lying down. She took dough, kneaded it, made cakes in his sight, and baked the cakes. Then she took the pan and set them out before him, but he refused to eat. Amnon said, "Send out everyone from me." So everyone went out from him. Then Amnon said to Tamar, "Bring the food into the chamber, so that I may eat from your hand." So Tamar took the cakes she had made, and brought them into the chamber to Amnon her brother. But when she brought them near him to eat, he took hold of her, and said to her, "Come, lie with me, my sister." She answered him, "No, my brother, do not force me; for such a thing is not done in Israel; do not do anything so vile! As for me, where could I carry my shame? And as for you, you would be as one of the scoundrels in Israel. Now therefore, I beg you, speak to the king; for he will not withhold me from you." But he would not listen to her; and being stronger than she, he forced her and lay with her.

Then Amnon was seized with a very great loathing for her; indeed, his loathing was even greater than the lust he had felt for her. Amnon said to her, "Get out!" But she said to him, "No, my brother; for this wrong in sending me away is greater than the other that you did to me." But he would not listen to her. He called the young man who served him and said, "Put this woman out of my presence, and bolt the door after her." (Now she was wearing a long robe with sleeves; for this is how the virgin daughters of the king were clothed in earlier times.) So his servant put her out, and bolted the door after her. But Tamar put ashes on her head, and tore the long robe that she was wearing; she put her hand on her head, and went away, crying aloud as she went.

Her brother Absalom said to her, "Has Amnon your brother been with you? Be quiet for now, my sister; he is your brother; do not take this to heart." So Tamar remained, a desolate woman, in her brother Absalom's house. When King David heard of all these things, he became very angry, but he would not punish his son Amnon, because he loved him, for he was his firstborn. But Absalom spoke to Amnon neither good nor bad; for Absalom hated Amnon, because he had raped his sister Tamar.

2 Samuel 13:1-22

Tamar Avenged

IN ISRAEL EACH PERSON HAS A *GO'EL* or redeemer. This is the nearest male relative. He is responsible for providing care or taking vengeance in situations such as rape. Boaz took on the responsibilities of *go'el* for Naomi and Ruth. Since Tamar's father David refused to accept this responsibility for her, it fell to her brother Absalom.

Absalom was a man with a long fuse. For two years he brooded over the injury done to his sister and waited for an opportunity to avenge her. His righteous anger was no doubt nurtured by the fact that the death of Amnon would put Absalom in line to inherit the throne.

He saw the right opportunity when everyone but he and Tamar had forgotten the incident. It was sheepshearing time, when celebration was in order. (It had been at sheepshearing time that David sent to ask a gift from Nabal.) Absalom invited the royal family to a feast at his farm. When they came and had eaten and drunk deeply he ordered his servants to murder Amnon. We are reminded of Absalom's father David ordering Joab to murder Uriah.

The rest of the family fled in disorder back to Jerusalem. Absalom escaped the country by crossing the Jordan to his mother's parents in Geshur, a foreign land. David mourned for his firstborn Amnon and also for the exiled Absalom.

Read the story of Absalom's revenge for Tamar.

> After two full years Absalom had sheepshearers at Baal-hazor, which is near Ephraim, and Absalom invited all the king's sons. Absalom came to the king, and said, "Your servant has sheepshearers; will the king and his servants please go with your servant?" But the king said to Absalom, "No, my son, let us not all go, or else we will be burdensome to you." He pressed him, but he would not go but gave him his blessing. Then Absalom said, "If not, please let my brother Amnon go with us." The king said to him, "Why should he go with you?" But Absalom pressed him until he let Amnon and all the king's sons go with him. Absalom made a feast like a king's feast. Then Absalom commanded his servants, "Watch when Amnon's heart is merry with wine, and when I say to you, 'Strike Amnon,' then kill him. Do not be afraid; have I not myself commanded you? Be courageous and valiant." So the servants of Absalom did to Amnon as Absalom had commanded. Then all the king's sons rose, and each mounted his mule and fled...

> But Absalom fled, and went to Talmai son of Ammihud, king of Geshur. David mourned for his son day after day.

2 Samuel 13:23-29, 37

Absalom Plots Against David

ABSALOM WAS EXILED FROM DAVID'S COURT for five years. David gradually got over his grief at the murder of Amnon and allowed Absalom to come home. However, he did not delegate any authority to Absalom.

Absalom by now was in the prime of life. He was handsome and had inherited his father's political skills. He took every opportunity to build up a following for himself. This was not difficult, because the old king was no longer able to fulfil all that was expected of him by his people, nor did he assign others to do what he could not. Perhaps that would have been too much like acknowledging his own diminishment.

Absalom cultivated the discontent of the people. Like any candidate who has not yet been in office, he found it easy to claim that if he were in charge things would be much better. People were impressed by the handsome son of the king who rode around in such a fine chariot with fifty servants, and many were persuaded by his preelection promises.

For four years Absalom prepared the ground for a rebellion against his father. Perhaps David was afflicted by the blindness that comes to those who are in power too long. He did not see that he was not meeting the needs of his people, and he did not notice that the son to whom he had forgiven so much was conniving against him.

When Absalom asked his father's permission to go to offer sacrifice at Hebron, David agreed willingly. He did not realize that at this sacred spot where Abraham and Sarah were buried and where David had been anointed king, Absalom would gather the people to proclaim him king.

David has deteriorated since his youth when he was so

bold and politically astute and able to win such popular support. He is now at the stage of life when he should have been mentoring a successor as Eli mentored Samuel and Samuel attempted to mentor both Saul and David. Instead, he clings to the royal prerogatives he should be delegating to others.

Like the attitude of many parents toward their adult children, David's attitude toward Absalom is profoundly ambivalent. He loves him deeply. That love is great enough to make him forgive Absalom for the murder of Amnon. Yet he does not trust him and gives him no outlet for his energies. It is a recipe for disaster.

Read about the rebellion of Absalom.

Absalom got himself a chariot and horses, and fifty men to run ahead of him. Absalom used to rise early and stand beside the road into the gate; and when anyone brought a suit before the king for judgment, Absalom would call out and say, "From what city are you?" When the person said, "Your servant is of such and such a tribe in Israel," Absalom would say, "See, your claims are good and right; but there is no one deputed by the king to hear you." Absalom said moreover, "If only I were judge in the land! Then all who had a suit or cause might come to me, and I would give them justice." Whenever people came near to do obeisance to him, he would put out his hand and take hold of them, and kiss them. Thus Absalom did to every Israelite who came to the king for judgment; so Absalom stole the hearts of the people of Israel.

At the end of four years Absalom said to the king, "Please let me go to Hebron and pay the vow that I have made to the LORD. For your servant made a vow while I lived at Geshur in Aram: If the LORD will indeed bring me back to Jerusalem, then I will worship the LORD in Hebron." The king said to him, "Go in peace." So he got up, and went to Hebron. But Absalom sent secret messengers throughout all the tribes of Israel, saying, "As soon as you hear the sound of the trumpet, then shout: Absalom has become king at Hebron!"

2 Samuel 15:1-10

The Flight of the King

THE AGED DAVID, SURROUNDED BY HIS COURTIERS, had been unaware of his growing unpopularity. When he heard of Absalom's revolt, he seemed to be too astonished even to organize the defenses of his capital Jerusalem. He fled across the Jordan, away from the promised land. He went weeping, making no effort to hide his feelings.

The path he takes east from Jerusalem to the Mount of Olives is one Jesus will take on the night his passion begins. David, as he begins his passion, reminds us in many ways of Jesus.

On this painful journey David is met by a member of the family of Saul. Now that David has lost his grip on royal power, a ghost from his past arises to curse him. David thought he had won over Saul's followers long ago, but some had carried resentment against him through the forty years of his reign. This man accuses David of murdering Saul and his family, a charge the biblical account has carefully denied. There is probably no rumor so discredited that someone does not cling to it.

David's followers would like to kill the man who is throwing old accusations against the king just when he is suffering the supreme humiliation of the disloyalty of his son. But David forbids them. It is as if the huge pain he suffers from Absalom swallows up any pain this lesser enemy might cause.

In this time of David's humiliation, the deep trust in God which he had in his youth returns to him. He realizes that God is in charge of his life. He believes that his present humiliation comes from God and only God can save him. As he did long ago with Saul, he leaves vengeance to God and waits for God's time of salvation. The weak old man is like the weak young man: he knows his need for God.

Absalom was killed in his war against his father. David grieved over his death, but resumed his responsibilities as king. However, political unrest continued and his position was no longer secure.

Read about David's humiliation.

A messenger came to David, saying, "The hearts of the Israelites have gone after Absalom." Then David said to all his officials who were with him at Jerusalem, "Get up! Let us flee, or there will be no escape for us from Absalom. Hurry, or he will soon overtake us, and bring disaster down upon us, and attack the city with the edge of the sword." The king's officials said to the king, "Your servants are ready to do whatever our lord the king decides." So the king left, followed by all his household, except ten concubines whom he left behind to look after the house. The king left, followed by all the people; and they stopped at the last house. All his officials passed by him; and all the Cherethites, and all the Pelethites, and all the six hundred Gittites who had followed him from Gath, passed on before the king....

The whole country wept aloud as all the people passed by; the king crossed the Wadi Kidron, and all the people moved on toward the wilderness....

David went up the ascent of the Mount of Olives, weeping as he went, with his head covered and walking barefoot; and all the people who were with him covered their heads and went up, weeping as they went....

When King David came to Bahurim, a man of the family of the house of Saul came out whose name was Shimei son of Gera; he came out cursing. He threw stones at David and at all the servants of King David; now all the people and all the warriors were on his right and on his left. Shimei shouted while he cursed, "Out! Out! Murderer! Scoundrel! The LORD has avenged on all of you the blood of the house of Saul, in whose place you have reigned; and the LORD has given the kingdom into the hand of your son Absalom. See, disaster has overtaken you; for you are a man of blood."

Then Abishai son of Zeruiah said to the king, "Why should this dead dog curse my lord the king? Let me go over and take off his head." But the king said, "What have I to do with you, you sons of Zeruiah? If he is cursing because the LORD has said to him, 'Curse David,' who then shall say, 'Why have you done so?'" David said to Abishai and to all his servants, "My own son seeks my life; how much more now may this Benjaminite! Let him alone, and let him curse; for the LORD has bidden him. It may be that the LORD will look on my distress, and the LORD will repay me with good for this cursing of me today." So David and his men went on the road, while Shimei went along on the hillside opposite him and cursed as he went, throwing stones and flinging dust at him.

2 Samuel 15:13-18, 23,30; 16:5-13

Questions for Reflection

1. Many rapes today, like Tamar's, occur within the family circle. What effects do you think these have on the family?

2. Compare the way in which Amnon and Tamar are treated to the way in which rapists and their victims are treated today.

3. Do you know cases of young people who, like Absalom, when they are in trouble flee to their grandparents? Do you think this is a good idea?

—⁓—

4. Does Absalom's maneuvering to attain kingship have any similarities to modern politics?

5. Do you know of families where a long-term grudge like Absalom's festers and surfaces at an unexpected time?

6. Do parents today have mixed feelings toward their problematic adult children, as David had toward Absalom?

Suggestions for Further Reading

2 Samuel 13—24

Prayer

Dearest Lord, we humbly acknowledge the same human frailties that were so evident in the family of King David.

We often are indifferent to the injustice and disgrace that are inflicted on others.

We can become envious, reacting with false self-righteousness, and exercising our powers with no sense of shame.

We are so vulnerable to our own weaknesses, and so blind to what is truth!

Most loving and forgiving God, banish these selfish ways that we possess. Gently nourish within our families and communities a respect for others and an open heart for reconciliation and peace.

For this we pray, through your infinite goodness, in the name of Jesus. Amen.

Barbara Tapp, 58, Parker, Colorado

CHAPTER EIGHTEEN

King Solomon

David Retires

SINCE THE PEOPLE DEMANDED THAT SAMUEL give them a king, the issue has been, "Who will replace Samuel?" The issue arose when Samuel became too old to meet all the people's needs and his sons were not acceptable as a replacement for him. Previously, there had been no established process for selecting leaders; judges simply arose in time of emergency and returned to private life when the emergency was over.

The Philistine threat required clear authority at all times. The only system known in those days for providing such leadership was kingship. A king, unlike a judge, ruled for his whole life and handed his authority over to his son at death. Thus there was no interval during which an enemy could overcome a leaderless people.

Saul became king for his lifetime, but he did not succeed in handing his authority over to his son. David has made a new start at kingship, and everyone is waiting with bated breath to see if he will succeed in establishing a stable dynasty. God, through Nathan, has promised that he will, but prospects do not look good.

The assumption was that the oldest son would inherit his father's position, but there were not yet any precedents to assure people that this would actually happen. David's oldest son, Amnon, had been murdered. The next heir apparent, Absalom, had been killed in his rebellion against his father. Adonijah, the next in line, was eager to take over, but David did not delegate any responsibility to him or give any assurance that he would be king.

If a king died without assuring a peaceful succession, civil war was to be expected, with the brothers ambitious for the throne killing off one another. The whole nation is waiting for David to act.

David is now in advanced old age. We do not see Samuel or Saul or any other biblical character lose their grip on things in the aging process as David does. The symbols of his loss of control are his inability to get warm and his sexual impotence. His staff brings in a beautiful young virgin, Abishag, to revitalize the old David by nursing him and sleeping in his bed. The hope is that David, so lusty in earlier years, will be sexually aroused by her. This does not happen. In the culture of the time, impotence is a sign that David is no longer capable of ruling.

This creates a political crisis, into which Adonijah leaps. Like his brother Absalom, he schemes to gather support for a coup. He has shown signs of arrogance for some time, but David has done nothing about it, as Eli and Samuel had done nothing to control their misbehaving sons. David has lost control of the country and of his family.

The prophet Nathan sees the crisis. He believes that God has chosen one of David's younger sons, Solomon, to be the next king. This is in keeping with God's countercultural choice of other younger sons: Isaac, Jacob and David himself. Nathan knows who may still be able to persuade the confused king: David's great love, Bathsheba.

Bathsheba now has a place of honor as David's favorite wife, but she is ambitious for yet higher status. In that society, the queen was not any one of the king's many wives, but his mother. To be queen mother is the highest honor and the most powerful position a woman can attain. Ancient history is full of harem intrigues in which various wives scheme to attain the throne for their sons and the position of queen mother for themselves.

Nathan and Bathsheba scheme to manipulate David into naming Bathsheba's son, Solomon, king. To arouse the feeble king to his responsibility, they paint a vivid picture of Adonijah's ambition, one that makes him sound like a second Absalom. This finally draws the old man's attention, and he uses his royal power one last time to order the anointing of Solomon.

He gives detailed orders for the ceremony. Solomon is to ride David's own mule, the equivalent of the presidential plane. We are more likely to imagine kings on horseback, but in Israel the horse was a war animal. In times of peace, the king rode a fine mule, as Jesus would do on Palm Sunday. David had been anointed by Samuel, who was both priest and prophet. Solomon is to be anointed by the priest Zadok and the prophet Nathan.

The intrigue by which Solomon became king could be criticized. However, rarely are political processes without ambiguity. Our author emphasizes that Solomon himself had nothing to do with the conniving. There is no suggestion that he was ambitious for the throne; he accepted it as a gift when David gave it to him, just as David himself had accepted it as a gift from God. It even seems that God uses the conspiracy of Nathan and Bathsheba to carry out the divine plan. "God writes straight with crooked lines."

Solomon, like David, knew how to wait for the proper time. Absalom and Adonijah, the logical successors, lost the throne by grasping for it before it was theirs.

This vivid passage brings the dramatic power struggle that began with Absalom to its conclusion. It would make a great play.

Read about how David finally handed his power over to his son Solomon.

King David was old and advanced in years; and although they covered him with clothes, he could not get warm. So his servants said to him, "Let a young virgin be sought for my lord the king, and let her wait on the king, and be his attendant; let her lie in your bosom, so that my lord the king may be warm." So they searched for a beautiful girl throughout all the territory of Israel, and found Abishag the Shunammite, and brought her to the king. The girl was very beautiful. She became the king's attendant and served him, but the king did not know her sexually.

Now Adonijah son of Haggith exalted himself, saying, "I will be king"; he prepared for himself chariots and horsemen, and fifty men to run before him. His father had never at any time displeased him by asking, "Why have you done thus and so?" He was also a very handsome man, and he was born next after Absalom. He conferred with Joab son of Zeruiah and with the priest Abiathar, and they supported Adonijah. But the priest Zadok, and Benaiah son of Jehoiada, and the prophet Nathan, and Shimei, and Rei, and David's own warriors did not side with Adonijah.

Adonijah sacrificed sheep, oxen, and fatted cattle by the stone Zoheleth, which is beside En-rogel, and he invited all his brothers, the king's sons, and all the royal officials of Judah, but he did not invite the prophet Nathan or Benaiah or the warriors or his brother Solomon.

Then Nathan said to Bathsheba, Solomon's mother, "Have you not heard that Adonijah son of Haggith has become king and our lord David does not know it? Now therefore come, let me give you advice, so that you may save your own life and the life of your son Solomon. Go in at once to King David, and say to him, 'Did you not, my lord the king, swear to your servant, saying: Your son Solomon shall succeed me as king, and he shall sit on my throne? Why then is Adonijah king?' Then while you are still there speaking with the king, I will come in after you and confirm your words."

So Bathsheba went to the king in his room. The king was very old; Abishag the Shunammite was attending the king. Bathsheba bowed and did obeisance to the king, and the king said, "What do you wish?" She said to him, "My lord, you swore to your servant by the LORD your God, saying: Your son Solomon shall succeed me as king, and he shall sit on my throne. But now suddenly Adonijah has become king, though you, my lord the king, do not know it. He has sacrificed oxen, fatted cattle, and sheep in abundance, and has invited all the children of the king, the priest Abiathar, and Joab the commander of the army; but your servant Solomon he has not invited. But you, my lord the king—the eyes of all Israel are on you to tell them who shall sit on the throne of my lord the king after him.

Otherwise it will come to pass, when my lord the king sleeps with his ancestors, that my son Solomon and I will be counted offenders."

While she was still speaking with the king, the prophet Nathan came in. The king was told, "Here is the prophet Nathan." When he came in before the king, he did obeisance to the king, with his face to the ground. Nathan said, "My lord the king, have you said, 'Adonijah shall succeed me as king, and he shall sit on my throne'? For today he has gone down and has sacrificed oxen, fatted cattle, and sheep in abundance, and has invited all the king's children, Joab the commander of the army, and the priest Abiathar, who are now eating and drinking before him, and saying, 'Long live King Adonijah!' But he did not invite me, your servant, and the priest Zadok, and Benaiah son of Jehoiada, and your servant Solomon. Has this thing been brought about by my lord the king and you have not let your servants know who should sit on the throne of my lord the king after him?"

King David answered, "Summon Bathsheba to me." So she came into the king's presence, and stood before the king. The king swore, saying, "As the LORD lives, who has saved my life from every adversity, as I swore to you by the LORD, the God of Israel, 'Your son Solomon shall succeed me as king, and he shall sit on my throne in my place,' so will I do this day." Then Bathsheba bowed with her face to the ground, and did obeisance to the king, and said, "May my lord King David live forever!"

King David said, "Summon to me the priest Zadok, the prophet Nathan, and Benaiah son of Jehoiada." When they came before the king, the king said to them, "Take with you the servants of your lord, and have my son Solomon ride on my own mule, and bring him down to Gihon. There let the priest Zadok and the prophet Nathan anoint him king over Israel; then blow the trumpet, and say, 'Long live King Solomon!' You shall go up following him. Let him enter and sit on my throne; he shall be king in my place; for I have appointed him to be ruler over Israel and over Judah." Benaiah son of Jehoiada answered the king, "Amen! May the LORD, the God of my lord the king, so ordain. As the

LORD has been with my lord the king, so may he be with Solomon, and make his throne greater than the throne of my lord King David."

So the priest Zadok, the prophet Nathan, and Benaiah son of Jehoiada, and the Cherethites and the Pelethites, went down and had Solomon ride on King David's mule, and led him to Gihon. There the priest Zadok took the horn of oil from the tent and anointed Solomon. Then they blew the trumpet, and all the people said, "Long live King Solomon!" And all the people went up following him, playing on pipes and rejoicing with great joy, so that the earth quaked at their noise.

1 Kings 1:1-40

Solomon Prays for Wisdom

THE NEW KING FACED MANY CHALLENGES that made him aware of his need for God. He went to a shrine to pray. It may have been one of those ancient shrines where worshippers are invited to take a holy nap in the hope that the god would speak to them in a dream. In any case, Solomon did have a dream there that is key to the rest of his life.

In the dream, God appeared to Solomon and asked him what he wanted. This is perhaps the deepest question God is constantly asking us, "What is the desire of your heart?" If we can answer it honestly, we can learn a great deal about our spiritual state.

Solomon prayed for wisdom with which to carry out his great responsibilities well. In this prayer, we see that he wants to be shepherd of the people as his father David was. He looks to the welfare of the flock before his own. God was pleased with this prayer. He promised Solomon wisdom, but also the wealth and worldly success for which he had not asked.

From this time on, Solomon became famous for his wisdom. In the ancient world, wisdom was thought to come from experience, so only the old could be wise. It was an extraordinary gift of God that made Solomon wise even in his youth.

Read about Solomon's famous dream.

The king went to Gibeon to sacrifice there, for that was the principal high place; Solomon used to offer a thousand burnt offerings on that altar. At Gibeon the LORD appeared to Solomon in a dream by night; and God said, "Ask what I should give you." And Solomon said, "You have shown great and steadfast love to your servant my father David, because he walked before you in faithfulness, in righteousness, and in uprightness of heart toward you; and you have kept for him this great and steadfast love, and have given him a son to sit on his throne today. And now, O LORD my God, you have made your servant king in place of my father David, although I am only a little child; I do not know how to go out or come in. And your servant is in the midst of the people whom you have chosen, a great people, so numerous they cannot be numbered or counted. Give your servant therefore an understanding mind to govern your people, able to discern between good and evil; for who can govern this your great people?"

It pleased the Lord that Solomon had asked this. God said to him, "Because you have asked this, and have not asked for yourself long life or riches, or for the life of your enemies, but have asked for yourself understanding to discern what is right, I now do according to your word. Indeed I give you a wise and discerning mind; no one like you has been before you and no one like you shall arise after you. I give you also what you have not asked, both riches and honor all your life; no other king shall compare with you. If you will walk in my ways, keeping my statutes and my commandments, as your father David walked, then I will lengthen your life."

Then Solomon awoke; it had been a dream. He came to Jerusalem where he stood before the ark of the covenant of the LORD. He offered up burnt offerings and offerings of well-being, and provided a feast for all his servants.

1 Kings 3:4-15

Solomon Builds a Temple

THE GREAT WORK OF SOLOMON'S LIFE was the building of a temple for God. For this he utilized the cedar wood and the skill of his pagan neighbors, suggesting that even those things that we might consider unworthy can be used in God's service.

Solomon and his priests and builders are excited about the temple. It is less clear how God feels about it. In ancient times, most temples were built at the order of some God, but that is not the case here. God had refused David's offer of a temple. God does not refuse Solomon's temple, but subtly suggests that a building cannot buy divine favor; what is important is obedience to the divine law. Religious structures are good, but not if we place too much importance on them.

Read about the beginning of the famous temple of Solomon.

Now King Hiram of Tyre sent his servants to Solomon, when he heard that they had anointed him king in place of his father; for Hiram had always been a friend to David. Solomon sent word to Hiram, saying, "You know that my father David could not build a house for the name of the LORD his God because of the warfare with which his enemies surrounded him, until the LORD put them under the soles of his feet. But now the LORD my God has given me rest on every side; there is neither adversary nor misfortune. So I intend to build a house for the name of the LORD my God, as the LORD said to my father David, 'Your son, whom I will set on your throne in your place, shall build the house for my name.'...

Now the word of the LORD came to Solomon, "Concerning this house that you are building, if you will walk in my statutes, obey my ordinances, and keep all my commandments by walking in them, then I will establish my promise with you, which I made to your father David. I will dwell among the children of Israel, and will not forsake my people Israel."

1 Kings 5:1-5; 6:11-13

The Queen of Sheba

SOLOMON BROUGHT ISRAEL TO THE PINNACLE of its power and prosperity. For the only time in its history, God's people played a part with dignity on the world scene. This is illustrated by the visit of the queen of Sheba to Solomon's court.

She is an exotic figure from a faraway country bringing lavish gifts. She is also a wise woman, able to enter into intellectual conversation with a king world famous for his wisdom. The form of the conversation is one common in the wisdom tradition shared by all the nations of the Ancient Near East: the riddle.

Ethiopian tradition says that she was from Ethiopia, and returned there pregnant with Solomon's son, who would be the ancestor of the family that ruled Ethiopia until modern times. Ethiopians have always felt a special link with Jerusalem. Today a tiny Ethiopian chapel perches on the roof of the ancient Church of the Holy Sepulcher in Jerusalem. Inside, an Ethiopian monk welcomes the pilgrim and points out a wall covered with an extremely colorful painting of the queen of Sheba bearing her exotic gifts to King Solomon.

Solomon, in the magnanimous style of the East, gives the queen gifts even richer than those she brought.

Solomon extended his influence to many nations. Israelites before and after his time were rarely seafaring people, but Solomon had a fleet of ships that kept Jerusalem supplied with imports from the whole world. It was a brief moment of glory that Israel would never forget.

Read about the queen of Sheba.

> When the queen of Sheba heard of the fame of Solomon, she came to test him with hard questions. She came to Jerusalem with a very great retinue, with camels bearing spices, and very much gold, and precious stones; and when she came to Solomon, she told him all that was on her mind. Solomon answered all her questions; there was nothing hidden from the king that he could not explain to her. When the queen of Sheba had observed all

the wisdom of Solomon, the house that he had built, the food of his table, the seating of his officials, and the attendance of his servants, their clothing, his valets, and his burnt offerings that he offered at the house of the LORD, there was no more spirit in her.

So she said to the king, "The report was true that I heard in my own land of your accomplishments and of your wisdom, but I did not believe the reports until I came and my own eyes had seen it. Not even half had been told me; your wisdom and prosperity far surpass the report that I had heard. Happy are your wives! Happy are these your servants, who continually attend you and hear your wisdom! Blessed be the LORD your God, who has delighted in you and set you on the throne of Israel! Because the LORD loved Israel forever, he has made you king to execute justice and righteousness." Then she gave the king one hundred twenty talents of gold, a great quantity of spices, and precious stones; never again did spices come in such quantity as that which the queen of Sheba gave to King Solomon....

For the king had a fleet of ships of Tarshish at sea with the fleet of Hiram. Once every three years the fleet of ships of Tarshish used to come bringing gold, silver, ivory, apes, and peacocks. Thus King Solomon excelled all the kings of the earth in riches and in wisdom. The whole earth sought the presence of Solomon to hear his wisdom, which God had put into his mind.

1 Kings 10:1-10; 22-24

Questions for Reflection

1. Do you know any old people who, like David, are manipulated by others because they are unable to handle their responsibilities? How can such situations be avoided?

2. Do you know people today who, like David, in their old age procrastinate in making decisions which others depend on them to make?

3. What do you think David could have done that might have

prevented Absalom and Adonijah from trying to seize the throne from him?

—∾—

4. Can you think of someone besides Solomon who heard a message from God in a dream? Have you ever had a dream that helped you in your Christian life?

5. If God told you, like Solomon, to ask for whatever you wanted, for what one thing would you ask?

6. How important do you think it was for Solomon to build a temple? Why? Compare this to some church or shrine you have been involved in building.

7. Solomon had commercial and cultural relations with many nations, as the United States does today. What advantages and disadvantages do you see in these relationships?

Suggestions for Further Reading
1 Kings 1—11

Prayer

Dearest Father, just as Solomon prayed for wisdom with which to carry out his responsibilities, hear our prayers for wisdom as well.

Grant us the wisdom to rejoice in each and every part of your creation and find joy in living one day at a time.

Enlighten us to know your will so that your wisdom can lead us, not our own.

Imbue us with the spirit of wisdom that comes from reading and hearing your word given to us in the Bible.

Inspire us in our daily challenges and in always choosing good over evil.

Grant us wisdom in dealing with our family members, in mending broken relationships and in knowing when and how to listen, and how to speak words of encouragement rather than judgment.

Make us wise in unselfishness. Show us the best ways to share our time and talents and treasure in service to you.

Inspire us in coping and accepting our own aging process and in supporting our aging parents, spouses and loved ones.

While we learn from the past and look with hope toward the future, teach us to live in the present moment.

Teach us wisdom. Teach us love. For this we pray. Amen.

Dorothy R. Liston, 59, Denver, Colorado

CHAPTER NINETEEN

Jeremiah:
A Prophet Who Failed

The Call of Jeremiah

THE BOOK OF JEREMIAH BEGINS by setting the prophet Jeremiah in time and place. Prophets do not speak from the clouds, but from some particular historical context. We cannot understand them well if we ignore their setting.

Jeremiah was the son of Hilkiah, a priest from the little village of Anathoth, three miles northeast of Jerusalem. His ancestor, Abiathar, a descendant of Eli, the priest of Shiloh who raised Samuel, had become David's priest. However, when he supported Adonijah instead of Solomon to succeed to David's throne, Solomon exiled him from the capital and the temple to Anathoth. Jeremiah was trained by descendants of this out-of-favor priest. He understood deeply the religious traditions of Israel, but he had no opportunity to perform priestly duties in Solomon's great temple.

Jeremiah worked as a prophet for over forty years. This was during a time of crisis in the history of Judah. The Assyrian power, which had dominated the Ancient Near East for more than two centuries, was on the decline. The Babylonian Empire, which would replace it, had not yet shown its strength. During this interval between oppressors a mood of naive optimism filled the country. King Josiah carried out liturgical reforms, and people rejoiced in a sense of national independence. They did not see, as Jeremiah did, that they were actually poised on the edge of a precipice. Babylonian oppression would be worse than the Assyrian domination had been. Throughout his ministry Jeremiah predicted disaster to a people unwilling to hear such a message.

At the time when God calls Jeremiah to his work as a prophet, he is a young man, perhaps about twelve. He is clearly horrified by the call and complains that he certainly cannot fulfill it because he is too young. In his society, a young man was expected to listen to his elders and learn. Only an old man would be listened to with respect. The values of our society are so reversed that we can best understand Jeremiah's feelings by imagining a person of eighty being called by God to a strenuous ministry of preaching to the nation.

Like Moses and Samuel before him, Jeremiah resists the divine call. This seems to be the ordinary pattern of vocation. If we feel we have never resisted God's call, it is possible that we have merely evaded it so successfully we did not even realize we were being called.

As with Moses and Samuel, God is not easily discouraged, but insists, and promises to be with Jeremiah. It is not a promise of peace or of success, only of the divine presence through hard times.

Jeremiah's call was to be a prophet, that is, a messenger for God. God will place the divine word on the human lips of this young man. God's word has power to build and to destroy, so Jeremiah will become in some way an instrument of God's power working in the world. It is not surprising that the boy felt overwhelmed.

Read the beginning of the Book of Jeremiah.

The words of Jeremiah son of Hilkiah, of the priests who were in Anathoth in the land of Benjamin, to whom the word of the LORD came in the days of King Josiah son of Amon of Judah, in the thirteenth year of his reign. It came also in the days of King Jehoiakim son of Josiah of Judah, and until the end of the eleventh year of King Zedekiah son of Josiah of Judah, until the captivity of Jerusalem in the fifth month.

Now the word of the LORD came to me saying,

"Before I formed you in the womb I knew you,
and before you were born I consecrated you;
I appointed you a prophet to the nations."

Then I said, "Ah, Lord GOD! Truly I do not know how to speak, for I am only a boy." But the LORD said to me,

> "Do not say, 'I am only a boy';
> for you shall go to all to whom I send you,
> and you shall speak whatever I command you,
> Do not be afraid of them,
> for I am with you to deliver you,
>   says the LORD."

Then the LORD put out his hand and touched my mouth; and the LORD said to me,

> "Now I have put my words in your mouth...."

Jeremiah 1:1-9

A Sermon for Templegoers

JEREMIAH FOUND, AS HE HAD SUSPECTED from the beginning, that being God's prophet was no easy task. God commanded him to stand at the gate of the Jerusalem temple, where pious crowds were always passing through, and proclaim what must have sounded like a sacrilegious message.

When Solomon built the temple, God came down in the form of a cloud as a sign of a special divine presence in this building. A century before Jeremiah, when the Assyrian army surrounded Jerusalem and seemed sure to destroy it, the prophet Isaiah promised the people that, contrary to all human expectation, God would protect the temple and its city. In Jeremiah's own time, King Josiah had instituted a liturgical renewal by closing all the rival shrines and calling everyone to worship only in the Jerusalem temple.

No matter what was going on in the world of politics, the people who came in and out of the gate of the temple had a great sense of spiritual security. They knew that long ago the temple at Shiloh, where Hannah had brought her little son Samuel, had been destroyed. But they were comfortable in the assurance that such a thing could never happen to their temple.

The problem was that they were too comfortable. They were applying God's words of assurance, given in a different situation, to themselves. The wealthy were living in luxury while the poor starved and foreign residents suffered from discrimination. People imagined that God would pay no attention to their failures at social justice as long as they were enthusiastic in coming to the temple to worship.

Jeremiah shocks these devout worshippers by proclaiming that their temple will be destroyed, just as the old temple at Shiloh was. Imagine a preacher shouting to the thousands of pilgrims coming to St. Peter's in Rome that unless they change their ways and feed the poor of the world, God will destroy this church.

Jeremiah is not opposed to the great temple, but to the way people are using it as a substitute for obeying God's law. The temple is a value, but not an absolute value. Every symbol of God should be treated with reverence, but God is greater than any symbol. When we forget that, we turn the symbol into an idol.

Much later, when Jesus drove the buyers and sellers out of the temple in Jerusalem, he quoted this "temple sermon" of Jeremiah (Mark 11:17; Jeremiah 7:11). Immediately after this quotation, Mark tells us, "...when the chief priests and the scribes heard it, they kept looking for a way to kill him" (Mark 11:18).

The response of the leaders and people of Jeremiah's time was similar. They were willing to kill God's messenger to avoid having to listen to God's message that temple worship was not enough and that if they failed to change their lives the temple itself would be demolished.

The story challenges us to look carefully at the religious institutions we value, whether buildings or groups or religious practices, to be sure that they do not become substitutes for doing what God is really asking of us.

Read Jeremiah's famous "temple sermon."

> The word that came to Jeremiah from the LORD: Stand in the gate of the LORD's house, and proclaim there this word, and say, Hear the word of the LORD, all you people of Judah, you that enter these gates to worship the LORD. Thus says

the LORD of hosts, the God of Israel: Amend your ways and your doings, and let me dwell with you in this place. Do not trust in these deceptive words: "This is the temple of the LORD, the temple of the LORD, the temple of the LORD."

For if you truly amend your ways and your doings, if you truly act justly one with another, if you do not oppress the alien, the orphan, and the widow, or shed innocent blood in this place, and if you do not go after other gods to your own hurt, then I will dwell with you in this place, in the land that I gave of old to your ancestors forever and ever.

Here you are, trusting in deceptive words to no avail. Will you steal, murder, commit adultery, swear falsely, make offerings to Baal, and go after other gods that you have not known, and then come and stand before me in this house, which is called by my name, and say, "We are safe!"—only to go on doing all these abominations? Has this house, which is called by my name, become a den of robbers in your sight? You know, I too am watching, says the LORD. Go now to my place that was in Shiloh, where I made my name dwell at first, and see what I did to it for the wickedness of my people Israel. And now, because you have done all these things, says the LORD, and when I spoke to you persistently, you did not listen, and when I called you, you did not answer, therefore I will do to the house that is called by my name, in which you trust, and to the place that I gave to you and to your ancestors, just what I did to Shiloh....

The priests and the prophets and all the people heard Jeremiah speaking these words in the house of the LORD. And when Jeremiah had finished speaking all that the LORD had commanded him to speak to all the people, then the priests and the prophets and all the people laid hold of him, saying, "You shall die! Why have you prophesied in the name of the LORD, saying, 'This house shall be like Shiloh, and this city shall be desolate, without inhabitant'?"

Jeremiah 7:1-14; 26:7-9

Jeremiah's Call to Celibacy

JEREMIAH DID NOT JUST SPEAK HIS MESSAGE. He was required to express his message in his life. God is a good teacher who knows that humans are more impressed by what they see than by what they hear.

One way in which Jeremiah was told to act out his message was particularly difficult. God forbade him to marry or have children. People in Jeremiah's time did not know about life after death, so they believed that the person who died childless was totally extinguished. This seemed to them a most terrible thing, so it was unheard of for anyone to choose not to marry.

Inevitably, people would ask this strange young man why he was not married. He was to tell them that he saw no point in bringing children into the world because in the coming disaster everyone would die and there would be no one to bury the corpses. The coming devastation was Jeremiah's continual message, but this way of communicating it probably caught the attention of more people than all his sermons on the subject.

We are left to imagine the impact this command to celibacy had on Jeremiah himself. Jeremiah's temperament was sensitive and loving. He suffered terribly from the isolation of his life. He had to go contrary to the currents of popular opinion. He offended the people he wanted as friends by the shocking things he said. His neighbors plotted against him. In the midst of this painful alienation, he had no wife or children to support him.

There are parts of the Book of Jeremiah where Jeremiah pours out the anguish of his lonely life. To whom does he pour it out? To God. It may be the very loneliness of his life that led Jeremiah to the most intense and intimate relationship with God in the Old Testament. Perhaps Jeremiah is in the Scriptures as a message to those deprived of the joys of family life, and to all of us in our times of loneliness.

Read God's command to Jeremiah to remain celibate.

The word of the Lord came to me: You shall not take a wife, nor shall you have sons or daughters in this place. For thus says the Lord concerning the sons and daughters who are born in this place, and concerning the mothers who bear them and the fathers who beget them in this land: They shall die of deadly diseases. They shall not be lamented, nor shall they be buried; they shall become like dung on the surface of the ground. They shall perish by the sword and by famine, and their dead bodies shall become food for the birds of the air and for the wild animals of the earth.

Jeremiah 16:1-4

―⁓―

Jeremiah Visits the Potter

IN THE PARABLES OF JESUS WE SEE how powerfully God can use the most commonplace things of everyday life to get a message across. That happened to Jeremiah when God ordered him to go to the potter's house. Potters were not an elite kind of artist in Jeremiah's day. They were like factory workers today: the people who make objects needed for daily life. No one paid much attention to how they worked.

But Jeremiah obediently went and watched the potter at work. The potter shaped the clay with strong hands, but it did not turn out properly, so he squashed it back into a lump of clay and began again.

The people of God are like the lump of clay. God is lovingly shaping the clay, but if the clay does not cooperate, God will abandon the project and reduce what was being shaped back to a lump of clay. This is the same message Jeremiah gave in the "temple sermon," by his celibacy and in many other ways. God is about to destroy Jerusalem. Jeremiah is still trying to undermine the false security the people feel.

However, the image of the potter adds a note of hope. It is not hope of avoiding disaster, but hope for a new creation by God after disaster. What appears to be a catastrophic end is also a new beginning. The future is open-ended. There may be no hope for the particular structure on which the people depend. God is not committed to any particular shape for the clay. God, like the potter, is creative and will eventually find another, perhaps better, shape.

It is a comforting image for the Church, but also for each of us individually. When everything we value seems to be falling apart, God may be moving us toward a future we cannot imagine. Throughout our lives, we are called to be flexible like the clay, and to trust the potter. Death itself is like the destruction of one shape our life has had to allow God to give it a new shape.

Read about Jeremiah's visit to the potter.

> The word that came to Jeremiah from the LORD: "Come, go down to the potter's house, and there I will let you hear my words." So I went down to the potter's house, and there he was working at his wheel. The vessel he was making of clay was spoiled in the potter's hand, and he reworked it into another vessel, as seemed good to him.
>
> Then the word of the LORD came to me: Can I not do with you, O house of Israel, just as this potter has done? says the LORD. Just like the clay in the potter's hand, so are you in my hand, O house of Israel. At one moment I may declare concerning a nation or a kingdom, that I will pluck up and break down and destroy it, but if that nation, concerning which I have spoken, turns from its evil, I will change my mind about the disaster that I intended to bring on it. And at another moment I may declare concerning a nation or a kingdom that I will build and plant it, but if it does evil in my sight, not listening to my voice, then I will change my mind about the good that I had intended to do to it. Now, therefore, say to the people of Judah and the inhabitants of Jerusalem: Thus says the LORD: Look, I am a potter shaping evil against you and devising a plan against you. Turn now, all of you from your evil way, and amend your ways and your doings.
>
> *Jeremiah 18:1-11*

The Suffering of an Old Prophet

FINALLY, WHAT JEREMIAH HAD BEEN PREDICTING for so many years came to pass. The Babylonians marched on Jerusalem and surrounded it. The people rallied to defend their sacred city. Jeremiah gave them no encouragement. He tried to persuade them to escape the besieged city and go over to the Babylonians (who are also called Chaldeans in this passage). In wartime, such a voice sounds anti-patriotic, and it is not surprising that Jeremiah was arrested as a traitor. Those who protested the Vietnam War often remembered this time in Jeremiah's life.

The king had mixed feelings toward Jeremiah. He did not like the prophet's message, but he suspected that it was truly from God. He did not want to harm Jeremiah, but he was a weak ruler, and his officials pressured him into letting them throw Jeremiah into a cistern. In Jerusalem, then and now, water is scarce, so every home has an open cistern to catch precious rainwater when it comes. Since it had not rained recently, the cistern into which Jeremiah was thrown contained no water, but it was muddy on the bottom.

Jeremiah would probably have died of starvation in the cistern if he had not been rescued by a most surprising person, Ebed-Melech. Ebed-Melech was an Ethiopian, probably a black man, who had come as a foreigner to Jerusalem and taken a job working for King Zedekiah. He saw the injustice of what the officials had done to Jeremiah, and had the courage to confront the weak king about it. So Zedekiah allowed the Ethiopian to rescue Jeremiah. This man's courage brings a ray of light into the desperate situation of the city which is about to be conquered and devastated by the Babylonians. There is no situation so bad that a good person cannot do what is right.

Please read how Ebed-Melech saved Jeremiah on the eve of the destruction of Jerusalem.

Now Shephatiah son of Mattan, Gedaliah son of Pashhur, Jucal son of Shelemiah, and Pashhur son of

223

Malchiah heard the words that Jeremiah was saying to all the people, Thus says the LORD, Those who stay in this city shall die by the sword, by famine, and by pestilence; but those who go out to the Chaldeans shall live; they shall have their lives as a prize of war, and live. Thus says the LORD, This city shall surely be handed over to the army of the king of Babylon and be taken. Then the officials said to the king, "This man ought to be put to death, because he is discouraging the soldiers who are left in this city, and all the people, by speaking such words to them. For this man is not seeking the welfare of this people, but their harm." King Zedekiah said, "Here he is; he is in your hands; for the king is powerless against you." So they took Jeremiah and threw him into the cistern of Malchiah, the king's son, which was in the court of the guard, letting Jeremiah down by ropes. Now there was no water in the cistern, but only mud, and Jeremiah sank in the mud.

Ebed-melech the Ethiopian, a eunuch in the king's house, heard that they had put Jeremiah into the cistern. The king happened to be sitting at the Benjamin Gate, so Ebed-melech left the king's house and spoke to the king, "My lord king, these men have acted wickedly in all they did to the prophet Jeremiah by throwing him into the cistern to die there of hunger, for there is no bread left in the city." Then the king commanded Ebed-melech the Ethiopian, "Take three men with you from here, and pull the prophet Jeremiah up from the cistern before he dies." So Ebed-melech took the men with him and went to the house of the king, to a wardrobe of the storehouse, and took from there old rags and worn-out clothes, which he let down to Jeremiah in the cistern by ropes. Then Ebed-melech the Ethiopian said to Jeremiah, "Just put the rags and clothes between your armpits and the ropes." Jeremiah did so. Then they drew Jeremiah up by the ropes and pulled him out of the cistern. And Jeremiah remained in the court of the guard.

King Zedekiah sent for the prophet Jeremiah and received him at the third entrance of the temple of the LORD.... Then Jeremiah said to Zedekiah, "Thus says the LORD, the God of hosts, the God of Israel, If you will only surrender to the officials of the king of Babylon, then your life shall be spared, and this city shall not be burned with fire, and you and your house shall live. But if you do not surrender to the officials of the king of Babylon, then this city shall be handed over to the Chaldeans, and they shall burn it with fire, and you yourself shall not escape from their hand."

Jeremiah 38:1-18

The Babylonians did destroy Jerusalem and level its glorious temple to the ground, just as Jeremiah had predicted. Those who survived were carried off into exile. Jeremiah, the prophet of doom, then became a prophet of hope, assuring them that God would not abandon them, but would eventually bring them home again. Since his prophecies of doom had proved true, the suffering exiles were able to trust his message of hope beyond doom. This man, who had failed to reach the people for over forty years, became a source of comfort to them in his final years and long after his death.

Questions for Reflection

1. In your youth, did you ever feel God calling you in some special way? How important do you think the religious experiences of youth are?

2. Have you ever, like Jeremiah, felt doubtful about your ability to do what God asked of you?

3. Jeremiah's "temple sermon" complains that people were making religious practice a substitute for obeying God's law. Do you think this ever happens today? Give examples.

4. Jeremiah's loneliness led him to a close relationship with God. Do you know of situations where that happens today?

—◊◊◊—

5. Have you had any experience in which God the Potter seemed to be shaping things in one way, then suddenly changed?

6. Do you know of people in the world today who, like Jeremiah, are imprisoned and tortured for doing God's work?

7. During the siege of Jerusalem, Jeremiah tells the people that it is time to admit defeat. When have you come to such a time in your life?

8. Do you know of any ordinary person of modern times who, like Ebed-Melech, had the courage to resist those in power who were doing wrong?

Suggestions for Further Reading

Jeremiah 1
Jeremiah 11—12
Jeremiah 18—20
Jeremiah 26—28
Jeremiah 36—38
Jeremiah 52

Prayer

Gracious Lord, your prophet Jeremiah suffered much because he fulfilled your commands and yet he was misunderstood by the people of his time. So are we, Lord. We are to follow your call at a time when the concept of sin does not seem relevant.

Give us the courage to be your prophets, to face the criticism and mockery of others as we seek to be faithful to you. Help us to witness to the sanctity of all human life. Give us the courage to stand in the convictions of our faith, to hate the sin but to love the sinners and to pray, pray that we all turn our hearts to you. We are all sinners and are called to repent.

Have mercy on us, give us courage and the redeeming love that we need to be one with you. This we ask in Jesus' name. Amen.

Elena Arroyo, 77, Littleton, Colorado

CHAPTER TWENTY

The Widow Judith

Bethulia Under Attack

IN THIS CHAPTER WE LEAVE THE REALM OF HISTORY for that of fiction. As Jesus liked to use fictional stories like the Good Samaritan to get across his message, a few Old Testament authors do the same. The author of the Book of Judith makes his intention of writing fiction clear by using an abundance of historical names and places that do not fit together at all. An author who wanted to do the same thing today might write a novel about George Washington flying to China during the time of the American Civil War to discuss with the Chinese the threat posed by Alexander the Great.

It is not only the names and places that are fantastic. Judith is an independent woman who takes a leading role in public life, which was almost unheard of in biblical times. In some ways she provides a model for women who want to take part in national affairs today. Her story is told with special relish by Latin American women as they seek to grow beyond old stereotypes of women's roles to play an active part in the liberation of their countries.

This book is unique in that the action that saves the people is initiated and carried out by two women, Judith and her companion. The close relationship between the two women throughout the story reminds us of that between Ruth and Naomi, though the issues with which they deal are very different. Judith's companion is described as her maid, but she is far more than an ordinary maid. She is in charge of Judith's large estate, a surprising role for a woman at her time.

The setting for the story is a time of crisis for Bethulia, a town of Israel. The Assyrian emperor Nebuchadnezzar has sent his general Holofernes to conquer Bethulia. Since the city is in the mountains and well defended, Holofernes decides the easiest way to conquer it is simply to take over the water supply, a spring outside the city walls, and wait for the people to die of thirst.

After being cut off from their water supply for thirty-four days, the people are in a state of panic and beg their leaders to surrender. The leaders believe that they should trust God and continue their resistance, but under severe pressure from the people they come to a compromise. They will hold out for five more days. Then, if God has not sent help, they will surrender.

At this point, we meet Judith, the hero of the story. (I hesitate to call her a heroine, as this calls to mind a damsel in distress rescued by a gallant man. Judith's case is quite the opposite.) Judith is a pious and wealthy widow who lives a contemplative life-style in a tent on top of her house. Though she does not leave her retreat, she hears of the decision the leaders have reached.

Judith recognizes the five-day compromise for what it is, an attempt to set conditions for God. She believes that God is not to be negotiated with but obeyed. She will not set any limit to her confidence in God. The emergency situation suddenly transforms this retiring widow into a powerful woman of action. She calls the leaders to her and roundly scolds them for their lack of courage.

Meet the extraordinary widow Judith.

Now in those days Judith heard about these things.... Her husband Manasseh, who belonged to her tribe and family, had died during the barley harvest.... Judith remained as a widow for three years and four months at home where she set up a tent for herself on the roof of her house. She put sackcloth around her waist and dressed in widow's clothing. She fasted all the days of her widowhood, except the day before the sabbath and the sabbath itself, the day before the new moon and the day of the new moon, and the festivals and days of rejoicing of the house of Israel. She was beautiful in appearance, and was very lovely to behold. Her husband Manasseh had left her gold and silver, men and women slaves, livestock, and fields; and she maintained this estate. No one spoke ill of her, for she feared God with great devotion.

When Judith heard the harsh words spoken by the people against the ruler, because they were faint for lack of water, and when she heard all that Uzziah said to them, and how he promised them under oath to surrender the town to the Assyrians after five days, she sent her maid, who was in charge of all she possessed, to summon Uzziah and Chabris and Charmis, the elders of her town. They came to her, and she said to them.

"Listen to me, rulers of the people of Bethulia! What you have said to the people today is not right; you have even sworn and pronounced this oath between God and you, promising to surrender the town to our enemies unless the Lord turns and helps us within so many days. Who are you to put God to the test today, and to set yourselves up in the place of God in human affairs? You are putting the Lord Almighty to the test, but you will never learn anything! You cannot plumb the depths of the human heart or understand the workings of the human mind; how do you expect to search out God, who made all these things, and find out his mind or comprehend his thought? No, my brothers, do not anger the Lord our God. For if he does not choose to help us within these five days, he has power to protect us within any time he pleases, or even to destroy us in the presence of our enemies. Do not try to bind the purposes of the Lord our God; for God is not like a human being, to be threatened, or like a mere mortal, to be won over by pleading. Therefore, while we wait for his deliverance, let us call upon him to help us, and he will hear our voice, if it pleases him.

Judith 8:1-17

Judith's Adventure Begins

THE ELDERS LEFT JUDITH'S HOUSE SHAMEFACEDLY. Judith herself turned to prayer, reminding God "...your strength does not depend on numbers, nor your might on the powerful. But you are the God of the lowly, helper of the oppressed, upholder of the weak, protector of the forsaken, savior of those without hope" (Judith 9:11).

Then the ascetic widow transformed herself into an alluring sexual object, using all the beauticians' skills of her culture. She is a dramatic reminder of the hidden potential so many of us have and can call forth in time of need.

She filled a lunch bag with kosher food and utensils. As a pious Jewess, she could not eat food or use dishes that did not fulfil all the kosher requirements. The lunch bag will play an important role later in the story. Then Judith and her maid left the besieged city to face the Assyrian army that surrounded it.

It is clear that Judith has a plan, though she has consulted no one and explained her intentions to no one. She did not even ask God for guidance, but only for strength to carry out her plan. God remains in the background of this story. The action is initiated by Judith alone.

Judith now appears as sex object, and others react to her as such. The reader knows there is something much deeper in Judith than what appears. In real life we may not see beneath the surface of women who look like Judith.

Judith is profoundly committed to the old religious values, but she is flexible enough to use highly unconventional methods to support those values when the circumstances call for them.

Read how Judith begins to carry out her plan.

When Judith had stopped crying out to the God of Israel...she rose from where she lay prostrate. She called her maid and went down into the house where she lived on sabbaths and on her festal days. She removed the sackcloth she had been wearing, took off her widow's garments, bathed her body with water, and anointed herself with precious ointment. She combed her hair, put on a tiara, and dressed herself in the festive attire that she used to wear while her husband Manasseh was living. She put sandals on her feet, and put on her anklets, bracelets, rings, earrings, and all her other jewelry. Thus she made herself very beautiful, to entice the eyes of all the men who might see her. She gave her maid a skin of wine and a flask of oil, and filled a bag with roasted grain, dried fig cakes, and fine bread; then she wrapped up all her dishes and gave them to her to carry....

As the women were going straight on through the valley, an Assyrian patrol met her and took her into custody. They asked her, "To what people do you belong, and where are you coming from, and where are you going?" She replied, "I am a daughter of the Hebrews, but I am fleeing from them, for they are about to be handed over to you to be devoured. I am on my way to see Holofernes the commander of your army, to give him a true report; I will show him a way by which he can go and capture all the hill country without losing one of his men, captured or slain."

When the men heard her words, and observed her face—she was in their eyes marvelously beautiful—they said to her, "You have saved your life by hurrying down to see our lord. Go at once to his tent; some of us will escort you and hand you over to him...."

Judith 10:1-15

Judith's Great Moment

THE BEAUTIFUL JEWESS CREATED A GREAT STIR in the enemy camp. She was escorted to the tent of Holofernes, who was struck by her beauty and beguiled by her clever flattery. He assigned her a tent and a servant, Bagoas, to look after her. He also offered her food and drink. She insisted that she was a God-fearing woman and could eat only the kosher food she had brought with her. She also needed to go each night into the valley between the Assyrians and Bethulia to the spring where she could perform her ritual purification and pray. Holofernes willingly gave in to her religious oddities.

On the fourth day Holofernes set in motion his plan to seduce Judith. This was the day she had anticipated, and she entered into her work wholeheartedly, though she had to pause at the climax to pray for strength.

Listen to the story of Judith.

> On the fourth day Holofernes held a banquet.... He said to Bagoas, the eunuch who had charge of his personal affairs, "Go and persuade the Hebrew woman who is in your care to join us and to eat and drink with us. For it would be a disgrace if we let such a woman go without having intercourse with her. If we do not seduce her, she will laugh at us."
>
> So Bagoas left the presence of Holofernes, and approached her and said, "Let this pretty girl not hesitate to come to my lord to be honored in his presence, and to enjoy drinking wine with us, and to become today like one of the Assyrian women who serve in the palace of Nebuchadnezzar." Judith replied, "Who am I to refuse my lord? Whatever pleases him I will do at once, and it will be a joy to me until the day of my death." So she proceeded to dress herself in all her woman's finery....
>
> Holofernes' heart was ravished with her and his passion was aroused, for he had been waiting for an opportunity to seduce her from the day he first saw her. So Holofernes said to her, "Have a drink and be merry with us!" Judith said, "I will gladly drink, my lord, because today is the greatest day in my whole life." Then she took what her maid had prepared and ate and drank before him. Holofernes was greatly pleased with her, and drank a great quantity of wine, much more than he had ever drunk in any one day since he was born.
>
> When evening came, his slaves quickly withdrew. Bagoas closed the tent from outside and shut out the attendants from his master's presence. They went to bed, for they all were weary because the banquet had lasted so long. But Judith was left alone in the tent, with Holofernes stretched out on his bed, for he was dead drunk.
>
> Now Judith had told her maid to stand outside the bedchamber and to wait for her to come out, as she did on the other days; for she said she would be going out for her prayers. She had said the same thing to Bagoas. So every-

one went out, and no one, either small or great, was left in the bedchamber. Then Judith, standing beside his bed, said in her heart, "O Lord God of all might, look in this hour on the work of my hands for the exaltation of Jerusalem. Now indeed is the time to help your heritage and to carry out my design to destroy the enemies who have risen up against us."

She went up to the bedpost near Holofernes' head, and said, "Give me strength today, O Lord God of Israel!" Then she struck his neck twice with all her might, and cut off his head. Next she rolled his body off the bed and pulled down the canopy from the posts. Soon afterward she went out and gave Holofernes' head to her maid, who placed it in her food bag.

Then the two of them went out together, as they were accustomed to do for prayer. They passed through the camp, circled around the valley, and went up the mountain to Bethulia, and came to its gates. From a distance Judith called out to the sentries at the gates, "Open, open the gate! God, our God is with us, still showing his power in Israel and his strength against our enemies, as he has done today!"

When the people of her town heard her voice, they hurried down to the town gate and summoned the elders of the town.... Then she pulled the head out of the bag and showed it to them, and said, "See here, the head of Holofernes, the commander of the Assyrian army.... The Lord has struck him down by the hand of a woman. As the Lord lives, who has protected me in the way I went, I swear that it was my face that seduced him to his destruction, and that he committed no sin with me, to defile and shame me."

Judith 12:10-20; 13:1-15

The Assyrians Routed

THE SCENE OF JUDITH CUTTING OFF Holofernes' head has been the subject of many lurid paintings. It has also shocked many people. The fictional hero is not, on the surface, a model any of us would like to follow. Yet she is a woman using the only weapon she had to save her people. Her determination, resourcefulness and courage provide a good model, if her method does not.

The Israelites praised both God and Judith for the deliverance given them. Judith wasted no time accepting compliments, but instructed the men about the military strategy to use in following up on her work. They obeyed her instructions to the letter.

Read about the defeat of the Assyrians.

As soon as it was dawn they hung the head of Holofernes on the wall. Then they all took their weapons, and they went out in companies to the mountain passes. When the Assyrians saw them they sent word to their commanders, who then went to the generals and the captains and to all their other officers. They came to Holofernes' tent and said to the steward in charge of all his personal affairs, "Wake up our lord, for the slaves have been so bold as to come down against us to give battle, to their utter destruction."

So Bagoas went in and knocked at the entry of the tent, for he supposed that he was sleeping with Judith. But when no one answered, he opened it and went into the bedchamber and found him sprawled on the floor dead, with his head missing. He cried out with a loud voice and wept and groaned and shouted, and tore his clothes. ...he rushed out to the people and shouted, "The slaves have tricked us! One Hebrew woman has brought disgrace on the house of King Nebuchadnezzar. Look, Holofernes is lying on the ground, and his head is missing!"...

When the men in the tents heard it, they were amazed at what had happened. Overcome with fear and trembling, they did not wait for one another, but with one impulse all rushed out and fled by every path across the plain and through the hill country.

Judith 14:11-19; 15:1-2

Celebration and Retirement

BIBLICAL PEOPLE KNEW HOW TO CELEBRATE. After the defeat of the Assyrians, Judith leads the women and men of Israel in singing, dancing and rejoicing. They all go in joyous pilgrimage to Jerusalem, where they bring gifts from the spoil of the Assyrians to the temple and continue to celebrate for three months.

Perhaps the most amazing part of the story is what happens when they return home to Bethulia. This fearless young woman, effective leader in war and in worship, retires again to her quiet contemplative life-style. She could surely have taken advantage of her vast popularity, but she preferred a private life. She received many proposals of marriage, but she chose to remain a widow. She stands out in the Old Testament as the only woman who anticipated the many women of New Testament times who recognized the value of a single life dedicated to God, and remained virgins or widows till death. Judith is in sharp contrast to the culture of her own times, which valued women chiefly as bearers of children. In every way this is an extraordinary story.

Having accomplished the active work of her life in a few months, Judith lived in retirement to the age of 105, reminding us of the patriarchs and their wives, and also of the widow Anna, who welcomed the infant Jesus in the temple. Judith must have continued to exercise a strong influence in a quiet way, because the people loved her, and when she died the whole nation mourned for her for seven days.

Read the conclusion of Judith's life.

All the people plundered the camp [of the Assyrians] for thirty days. They gave Judith the tent of Holofernes and all his silver dinnerware, his beds, his bowls, and all his furniture. She took them and loaded her mules and hitched up her carts and piled the things on them.

All the women of Israel gathered to see her, and blessed her, and some of them performed a dance in her honor. She took ivy-wreathed wands in her hands and distributed them to the women who were with her; and she and those who were with her crowned themselves with olive wreaths. She went before all the people in the dance, leading all the women, while all the men of Israel followed, bearing their arms and wearing garlands and singing hymns.

When they arrived at Jerusalem they worshiped God. As soon as the people were purified they offered their burnt offerings, their freewill offerings, and their gifts. Judith also dedicated to God all the possessions of Holofernes, which the people had given her.... For three months the people continued feasting in Jerusalem, before the sanctuary, and Judith remained with them.

After this they all returned home to their own inheritances. Judith went to Bethulia, and remained on her estate. For the rest of her life she was honored throughout the whole country. Many desired to marry her, but she gave herself to no man all the days of her life after her husband Manasseh died and was gathered to his people. She became more and more famous, and grew old in her husband's house, reaching the age of one hundred five. She set her maid free. She died in Bethulia, and they buried her in the cave of her husband Manasseh; and the house of Israel mourned her for seven days.

Judith 15:11-13; 16:18-24

Questions for Reflection

1. Do you know any individuals who, like Judith, retired from active life while grieving the loss of a relationship or a job, but returned to productive action when they realized they were needed?

2. Do you know any cases of a woman who, like Judith, challenged local authorities whom she felt were misusing their position?

3. When have you been faced by a task that seemed too much for you, and prayed for help as Judith did before beheading Holofernes?

4. Do you know any two people who worked together for the Lord as closely as Judith and her maid?

—∕∕∕—

5. Judith and the Israelites spent three months celebrating the victory God had won for them. How do you think we today could better show our appreciation for what God does for us?

6. Why do you think a person like Judith might remain a widow even though she had offers of remarriage?

7. What do you think it was like for a person as famous and capable as Judith to go into early retirement?

Suggestions for Further Reading
Judith 4—16

Prayer

Loving Father, you gather us around you to teach us in many different ways. With childlike trust we listen to the lessons that you make known to us in the story of Judith. She shows us that like her we should begin and end all that we do with prayer. We see that you give us strength when we are faced with insurmountable tasks and we acknowledge with hope that you always bring good from evil. We recognize that in this life, like Judith, we must pull away from the crowd and stand up for those things in which we believe. Chosen by you to save the afflicted people, she models for us the courage and perseverance that we must practice in our lives. Help us to humbly recognize our own unique gifts and to utilize them for the good of others. We ask that you endow us with a strong hope that our faith in you will overcome all things. You are a God who has made a covenant with us at our baptism, and we know that you will never abandon us. You show us

Holofernes as a symbol of evil and we pray that we will see and recognize the evils of our time and that we will have the courage to fight them as Judith did. In the present world so full of dangers to our families give us the strength to protect those we love from a culture that would destroy them. We raise our voices with Judith and the Israelites in their final hymn of praise:

"O Lord, great are you and glorious,
wonderful in power and unsurpassable"
(Judith 16:13). Amen.

Rosemary Angelos, 76, Littleton, Colorado

CHAPTER TWENTY-ONE

Tobit:
Touched by an Angel

Tobit: A Troubled Senior

IT IS UNFORTUNATE THAT SO FEW PEOPLE READ the Book of Tobit. It provides religious instruction in the appealing form of an adventure story. It is among the most charming books of the Bible, and one of the best biblical descriptions of family life, especially of relationships between parents and adult children. We also learn much from Tobit about angels and about prayer: the kind we should use in times of trouble and the kind we should use in times of joy.

The book is named after the old man Tobit, though most of the action is performed by his son Tobias. Tobit, an orphan, had been raised by his grandmother Deborah, who taught him love for God and God's law. He married an Israelite woman named Anna, and they had one son, Tobias, whom they raised in an atmosphere of love and piety.

When the Assyrians conquered Israel, this little family was among those taken captive to the Assyrian capital Nineveh. All those who went into exile with him gave up the demanding kosher food laws, but Tobit did not. He also continued to practice charity toward the needy, with special emphasis on burying the dead. The Assyrians ruled by terror and would often kill those suspected of not supporting them, leaving the bodies out in the open as a warning to others. Again and again, Tobit risked his life to give decent burial to these victims.

He had a high post in the Assyrian government, but when the king discovered his burial activities, he had to flee and all his property was confiscated. Later the king was assassinated by his own sons, and Tobit returned to Nineveh.

Our story begins with a typical scene of his life in Nineveh. Listen as Tobit tells his own story.

At our festival of Pentecost, which is the sacred festival of weeks, a good dinner was prepared for me and I reclined to eat. When the table was set for me and an abundance of food placed before me, I said to my son Tobias, "Go, my child, and bring whatever poor person you may find of our people among the exiles in Nineveh, who is wholeheartedly mindful of God, and he shall eat together with me...." So Tobias went to look for some poor person of our people. When he had returned he said, "Look father, one of our own people has been murdered and thrown into the market place, and now he lies there strangled." Then I sprang up, left the supper before even tasting it, and removed the body from the square and laid it in one of the rooms until sunset when I might bury it....

When the sun had set, I sent and dug a grave and buried him. And my neighbors laughed and said, "Is he still not afraid? He has already been hunted down to be put to death for doing this, and he ran away; yet here he is again burying the dead!" That same night I washed myself and went into my courtyard and slept by the wall of the courtyard; and my face was uncovered because of the heat. I did not know that there were sparrows on the wall; their fresh droppings fell into my eyes and produced white films. I went to physicians to be healed, but the more they treated me with ointments the more my vision was obscured by the white films, until I became completely blind. For four years I remained unable to see.... Then with much grief and anguish of heart I wept, and with groaning began to pray:

> "...command my spirit to be taken from me,
> so that I may be released from the face of the
> earth and become dust.
> For it is better for me to die than to live...."

Tobit 2:1-10; 3:1,6

Sarah: A Young Woman in Distress

THE BOOK OF TOBIT BEGINS WITH TWO PARALLEL SCENES of ordinary people overwhelmed by tragedy in their personal lives: the old man Tobit and the young woman Sarah. Sarah is not only named after the wife of Abraham, but has problems similar to hers: She is childless and as a result she is mocked by her own maids. This Sarah's childlessness is of a special kind, common in folklore. She has been married seven times, but each time the demon Asmodeus, who wants to possess her himself, kills the bridegroom on the wedding night. She needs to be delivered from Asmodeus as the original Sarah needed to be delivered from the harem of Pharaoh.

While the story is farfetched, it reminds us of situations we may know in which a troubled person, perhaps possessed by some inner demon, tries again and again to establish a permanent relationship but seems to bring only disaster.

Sarah, to whom life appears pointless if she cannot marry, is tempted to commit suicide, as are so many adolescents unable to see beyond the pain of the moment. What prevents her is concern for the disgrace such an act would bring on her aging parents. So instead of killing herself, she turns to God. At the moment when Tobit in faraway Nineveh is praying for death, Sarah pours out her pain and begs God to take her life.

Read about Sarah.

> On the same day, at Ecbatana in Media, it also happened that Sarah, the daughter of Raguel, was reproached by one of her father's maids. For she had been married to seven husbands, and the wicked demon Asmodeus had killed each of them before they had been with her as is customary for wives. So the maid said to her, "You are the one who kills your husbands! See, you have already been married to seven husbands and have not borne the name of a single one of them. Why do you beat us? Because your husbands are dead? Go with them! May we never see a son or daughter of yours!"
>
> On that day she was grieved in spirit and wept. When she had gone up to her father's upper room, she intended to hang herself. But she thought it over and said, "Never shall they reproach my father, saying to him, 'You had only

one beloved daughter but she hanged herself because of
her distress.' And I shall bring my father in his old age
down in sorrow to Hades. It is better for me not to hang
myself, but to pray the Lord that I may die and not listen to
these reproaches anymore." At that same time, with hands
outstretched toward the window, she prayed and said,

"...now, Lord, I turn my face to you,
and raise my eyes toward you.
Command that I be released from the earth
and not listen to such reproaches any more....
Why should I still live?"

Tobit 3: 7-13, 15

Raphael

IN THE NEXT SCENE WE MOVE FROM EARTH TO HEAVEN, where the
angels stand before God. Among them is Raphael, whose
name means "God heals." He appears only in the Book of Tobit
in the Bible, but is popular as a patron of travellers.

In this scene we see that God is interested both in healing
and in matchmaking. It is in the Book of Tobit that we learn
that "marriages are made in heaven."

Read about what happens in heaven.

At that very moment, the prayers of both of them were
heard in the glorious presence of God. So Raphael was sent
to heal both of them: Tobit, by removing the white films
from his eyes, so that he might see God's light with his
eyes; and Sarah, daughter of Raguel, by giving her in marriage to Tobias son of Tobit, and by setting her free from
the wicked demon Asmodeus.

Tobit 3:16-17

Tobit Prepares for Death

IN THE NEXT SCENE WE RETURN FROM HEAVEN to the blind old man, Tobit. Tobit takes prayer seriously and expects God to respond to his prayer for death. This leads to concern about leaving a legacy for his wife and son. He remembers that twenty years before, when travelling on the king's business, he left a large amount of money in trust with a friend. He did not know about electronic transfer of funds, and chaotic political conditions made it impossible to travel to retrieve the money. However, the roads are again safe, so he decides to send his son Tobias to reclaim the money.

When Tobias goes to look for a guide for his journey, the angel Raphael is waiting for him in the form of a young man named Azariah. As the two set off on their great adventure, the author focuses on the feelings of the parents, who are being left behind. It seems it was no easier in those days than today to allow a cherished only child to leave the safety of home for a dangerous world.

Read about how Tobit sends Tobias on his quest.

> That same day Tobit remembered the money that he had left in trust with Gabael at Rages in Media, and he said to himself, "Now I have asked for death. Why do I not call my son Tobias and explain to him about the money before I die?" Then he called his son Tobias, and when he came to him he said, "... now, my son, let me explain to you that I left ten talents of silver in trust with Gabael son of Gabrias, at Rages in Media.... So now, my son, find yourself a trust-worthy man to go with you, and we will pay him wages until you return. But get back the money from Gabael."
>
> So Tobias went out to look for a man to go with him to Media.... and found the angel Raphael standing in front of him; but he did not perceive that he was an angel of God....
>
> Before he went out to start his journey, he kissed his father and mother. Tobit then said to him, "Have a safe journey."
>
> But his mother began to weep, and said to Tobit, "Why is it that you have sent my child away? Is he not the staff of our

hand as he goes in and out before us? Do not heap money upon money, but let it be as ransom for our child. For the life that is given to us by the Lord is enough for us." Tobit said to her, "Do not worry; our child will leave in good health and return to us in good health.... For a good angel will accompany him; his journey will be successful, and he will come back in good health." So she stopped weeping.

Tobit 4:1-4, 20; 5:3-4, 17-22; 6:1

The Hero's Journey

JOSEPH CAMPBELL HAS MADE US AWARE that the journey of the hero is a common theme in the world's folklore, a deep universal experience that is expressed in different stories in different cultures. The basic pattern is that a young man leaves the security of home and parents to travel on a quest that will lead eventually to a treasure or a bride or both. On the way he has many adventures, usually including a battle with a monster of some kind. After overcoming the monster and finding the treasure, the hero returns home, bringing the bride and/or treasure back with him. The underlying process is of an adolescent going out to find a personal identity, then returning home.

The young hero usually finds a wise guide at some point in the story. The angel Raphael is Tobias's guide. Notice that Raphael is not a warrior angel like Michael. He gives Tobias instructions about how to overcome the monster; he does not take part in the battle.

Read about the journey of the hero Tobias.

The young man went out and the angel went with him; and the dog came out with him and went along with them. So they both journeyed along, and when the first night overtook them they camped by the Tigris river. Suddenly a large fish leaped up from the water and tried to swallow the young man's foot, and he cried out. But the angel said to the young man, "Catch hold of the fish and hang on to it!" So the young man grasped the fish and drew it up on the land. Then the angel said to him, "Cut open the fish and take out its gall, heart, and liver. Keep them with you.... For its gall, heart, and liver are useful as medicine." So after cutting open the fish the young man gathered together the gall, heart, and liver; then he roasted and ate some of the fish, and kept some to be salted.

Tobit 6:1-6

The Second Challenge

NOW WE SEE THAT THE MAIN ROLE OF RAPHAEL is to unite the families of Tobit and Sarah in a marriage that will answer the prayers of both, though not in the way either expected. It can happen to us, too, that our prayers are answered in ways quite the opposite of what we had in mind, but much better.

Tobit's second adventure will be overcoming the demon that kills Sarah's bridegrooms. Raphael urges the understandably hesitant young man to take on the challenge. He can succeed with a combination of prayer and the medicine he acquired by overcoming the monster that rose up from the water.

Read about how Raphael continues to guide Tobias.

When he entered Media and already was approaching Ecbatana, Raphael said to the young man "...We must stay this night in the home of Raguel. He is your relative, and he has a daughter named Sarah. He has no male heir and no daughter except Sarah only, and you, as next of kin to her, have before all other men a hereditary claim on her. Also, it is right for you to inherit her father's possessions. Moreover the girl is sensible, brave, and very beautiful, and her father is a good man.... You have every right to take her in marriage. So listen to me, brother; tonight I will speak to her father about the girl, so that we may take her to be your bride...."

Then Tobias said in answer to Raphael, "Brother Azariah, I have heard that she already has been married to seven husbands and that they died in the bridal chamber. On the night when they went in to her, they would die.... So now, since I am the only son my father has, I am afraid that I may die and bring my father's and mother's life down to their grave, grieving for me—and they have no other son to bury them."

But Raphael said to him, "...Take her.... When you enter the bridal chamber, take some of the fish's liver and heart, and put them on the embers of the incense. An odor will be given off; the demon will smell it and flee, and will never be seen near her any more. Now when you are about to go to bed with her, both of you must first stand up and pray, imploring the Lord of heaven that mercy and safety may be granted to you. Do not be afraid, for she was set apart for you before the world was made...."

Tobit 6:10-18

The Wedding Night

WHEN TOBIAS AND RAPHAEL ARRIVE at the home of Raguel, he and his wife Edna welcome them with a warm hospitality that reminds us of Abraham's. However, when Tobias makes his request for Sarah's hand, Raguel hesitates. He admits that the seven previous bridegrooms have died on the night of the wedding. Tobias will not be dissuaded, so Raguel finally agrees, and the wedding ceremony is performed.

The painful concern of Raguel and Edna over this marriage makes us think of the anxiety of every parent at the marriage of a beloved child. However, it is magnified by their previous experiences to such a degree that Raguel has a grave dug during the wedding night just in case. This is the first time the recurring burial theme has been treated with humor.

Read about the wedding night.

Raguel called his wife Edna and said to her, "Sister, get the other room ready, and take her there." So she went and made the bed in the room as he had told her, and brought Sarah there. She wept for her daughter. Then, wiping away the tears, she said to her, "Take courage, my daughter; the

Lord of heaven grant you joy in place of your sorrow. Take courage, my daughter." Then she went out.

When they had finished eating and drinking they wanted to retire; so they took the young man and brought him into the bedroom. Then Tobias remembered the words of Raphael, and took the fish's liver and heart out of the bag where he had them and put them on the embers of the incense. The odor of the fish so repelled the demon that he fled....

When the parents had gone out and shut the door of the room, Tobias got out of bed and said to Sarah, "Sister, get up, and let us pray and implore our Lord that he grant us mercy and safety." So she got up, and they began to pray and implore that they might be kept safe. Tobias began by saying,

> Blessed are you, O God of our ancestors,
> and blessed is your name in all generations
> forever.
> Let the heavens and the whole creation bless
> you forever.
> You made Adam, and for him you made his
> wife Eve
> as a helper and support.
> From the two of them the human race has sprung.
> You said, 'It is not good that the man should
> be alone;
> let us make a helper for him like himself.'
> I now am taking this kinswoman of mine....
> Grant that she and I may find mercy
> and that we may grow old together."

And they both said, "Amen, Amen." Then they went to sleep for the night.

But Raguel arose and called his servants to him, and they went and dug a grave, for he said, "It is possible that he will die and we will become an object of ridicule and derision." When they had finished digging the grave, Raguel went into his house and called his wife, saying, "Send one of the maids and have her go in to see if he is alive. But if he is dead, let us bury him without anyone knowing it." So they sent the maid, lit a lamp, and opened the door; and she went in and found them sound asleep together.... So

they blessed the God of heaven.... Then he ordered his servants to fill in the grave before daybreak.

Tobit 7:15-8:15

Other Worried Parents

IN THEIR RELIEF OVER THE SUCCESSFUL WEDDING NIGHT, Raguel and
Edna became more hospitable than ever and insisted on a
fourteen-day celebration of the wedding. Tobias, knowing his
parents would worry, sent Raphael to make the rest of the
journey alone and bring Gabael, with the money, back to the
wedding celebration.

Back home, however, Tobit and Anna were worrying, like
so many parents whose children are testing their wings in the
great world and fail to call home every week. As can happen
so easily, their shared anxiety came out in one parent being
cross with the other.

Read about the parents back in Nineveh.

Now, day by day, Tobit kept counting how many days
Tobias would need for going and for returning. And when
the days had passed and his son did not appear, he said, "Is it
possible that he has been detained? Or that Gabael has died,
and there is no one to give him the money?" And he began
to worry. His wife Anna said, "My child has perished and is no
longer among the living." And she began to weep and mourn
for her son, saying, "Woe to me, my child, the light of my eyes,
that I let you make the journey." But Tobit kept saying to her,
"Be quiet and stop worrying, my dear, he is all right. Probably
something unexpected has happened there. The man who
went with him is trustworthy and is one of our own kin. Do
not grieve for him, my dear; he will soon be here." She
answered him, "Be quiet yourself! Stop trying to deceive me!
My child has perished." She would rush out every day and
watch the road her son had taken, and would heed no one.
When the sun had set she would go in and mourn and weep
all night long, getting no sleep at all.

Tobit 10:1-7

Homecoming

Anna continues to watch for Tobias's return until she sees him coming. This leads to the grand climax of the book: the return of the hero with his bride and his treasure, a treasure that includes healing for Tobit's blindness.

We are not surprised that Tobit and Anna insist on another wedding feast—this one for seven days! The characters in this book do not stint either on lamentations or on celebrations.

Read about Tobias's homecoming.

> Anna sat looking intently down the road by which her son would come. When she caught sight of him coming, she said to his father, "Look, your son is coming, and the man who went with him!"
>
> Raphael said to Tobias, before he had approached his father, "I know that his eyes will be opened. Smear the gall of the fish on his eyes; the medicine will make the white films shrink and peel off from his eyes, and your father will regain his sight and see the light."
>
> Then Anna ran up to her son and threw her arms around him, saying, "Now that I have seen you, my child, I am ready to die." And she wept. Then Tobit got up and came stumbling out through the courtyard door. Tobias went up to him, with the gall of the fish in his hand and holding him firmly, he blew into his eyes, saying, "Take courage, father." With this he applied the medicine on his eyes, and it made them smart. Next, with both his hands he peeled off the white films from the corners of his eyes. Then Tobit saw his son and threw his arms around him, and he wept and said to him, "I see you, my son, the light of my eyes!" Then he said,
>
> "Blessed be God,
> and blessed be his great name,
> and blessed be all his holy angels...."

Tobit 11:5-14

A Peaceful End

A BOOK SO CONCERNED WITH intergenerational relationships and with the burial of the dead cannot end without assuring us that the major characters received the gift of a long life and were buried with honor by their children.

Read the conclusion of the story of Tobit.

> Tobit died in peace when he was one hundred twelve years old...they laid him on his bed, and he died; and he received an honorable funeral. When Tobias's mother died, he buried her beside his father. Then he and his wife and children returned to Media and settled in Ecbatana with Raguel his father-in-law. He treated his parents-in-law with great respect in their old age, and buried them in Ecbatana of Media.... He died highly respected at the age of one hundred and seventeen years.

Tobit 14:2, 12-14

Questions for Reflection

1. Tobit thought it very important to give proper burial to the dead. How do you feel about this?

2. The temptation to suicide can come either to an old person like Tobit or a young person like Sarah. What motives are likely to prevent suicide in the young? in the old?

3. Sarah's maids make her tragic situation harder to bear. How should we respond to people who are suffering?

4. What role do angels have in your life?

5. When your children have left home to make their own journey through life, have you felt more like Tobit, urging them on, or like Anna, wanting to keep them safely at home?

6. Can you remember a particular time when you worried about your grown children as Anna and Tobit worried about Tobias while he was on his journey?

7. Do you know of young people who, like Tobit, left home for faraway adventures, but later returned to be near their parents in their old age?

Suggestions for Further Reading
Book of Tobit

Prayer

We have heard your word, O Lord, in the prayers of your servants Tobit, Tobias and Sarah. Help us to imitate their great trust in you as we, too, offer you praise and thanksgiving.

For the many surprising ways in which you answer our prayers,
Blessed be you, O Lord, our God.
For the gift of patience in waiting for your answer,
Blessed be you, O Lord, our God.
For the guidance of your holy angels,
Blessed be you, O Lord, our God.
For sustaining us in times of sorrow and loss,
Blessed be you, O Lord, our God.
For schooling us in love for our parents and our children,
Blessed be you, O Lord, our God.
For showing us the rewards of fidelity in marriage,
Blessed be you, O Lord, our God.
For courage and support in our times of need,
Blessed be you, O Lord, our God.
For guiding us in our blindness to the needs of others,
Blessed be you, O Lord, our God.
For teaching us reverence for the dead and dying,
Blessed be you, O Lord, our God.
For your loving Providence that is ever with us,
Blessed be you, O Lord, our God.
We humbly thank you, God and Father, through Christ our Lord. Amen.

Rosemary Angelos, 76, Littleton, Colorado

CHAPTER TWENTY-TWO

The Patience of Job?

Job

THE BOOK OF JOB IS ABOUT A MAN who knows his religion well and practices it faithfully, but comes up against a situation with which the religion he knows cannot cope.

As the story begins, Job is at the pinnacle of success. He is of mature years and has an ideal family and many faithful employees. His investments are diversified into the three industries known in his culture. His sheep point to ranching pursuits, his oxen to agricultural and his camels to commercial ventures across the desert. All are thriving. He is known far and wide for his wisdom and his good works.

Job's children have been blessed with all the good things of life, and they celebrate with much feasting. Job, the anxious parent, worries that during their parties they may commit some sin, so to be on the safe side, he offers sacrifices for them.

The surprising thing is that this paragon of wisdom and virtue is not an Israelite but a pagan from the faraway land of Uz. This is the only narrative book in the Bible which is entirely about pagan people. It is a strong reminder to us that God's relationships with humans are not limited to our particular faith community. The wisdom and virtues of Job would put many a good Jew or Christian to shame.

Meet the hero of our story, Job.

There was once a man in the land of Uz whose name was Job. That man was blameless and upright, one who feared God and turned away from evil. There were born to him seven sons and three daughters. He had seven thousand sheep, three thousand camels, five hundred yoke of oxen, five hundred donkeys, and very many servants; so that this man was the greatest of all the people of the east.

His sons used to go and hold feasts in one another's houses in turn; and they would send and invite their three sisters to eat and drink with them. And when the feast days
had run their course, Job would send and sanctify them,
and he would rise early in the morning and offer burnt
offerings according to the number of them all; for Job said,
"It may be that my children have sinned, and cursed God
in their hearts." This is what Job always did.

Job 1:1-5

The Satan

SUDDENLY, THE SCENE SHIFTS TO HEAVEN. There God, like a great
Eastern king, is holding court. His servants come to report
about their work. One of them seems to have the responsibilities of a royal spy, the kind ancient rulers would send
throughout the realm to be their eyes and ears. He is called
"the satan," which means "the adversary." In later books of the
Bible, the name "Satan" would be given to a fallen angel who
tries to lead humans into sin. The "satan" of Job is looking for
something amiss, but not causing it.

This is a highly imaginative tale of God and Satan, like *The
Screwtape Letters* by C. S. Lewis. Satan appears here as a cata-
lyst to get the action of the story started. The main story occurs
on earth, and at its climax God will come down to earth.

God, like a proud parent, boasts to the court about Job, his
pride and joy. Satan is more cynical and suggests that Job is
only virtuous because he is so well rewarded. If his wealth is
taken away, another side of Job will be seen. God trusts Job,
and always refers to him proudly as "my servant," but rises to
Satan's challenge. God allows Satan to experiment to find out
if Job's devotion is really selfless.

Listen to the conversation in God's court.

One day the heavenly beings came to present themselves before the Lord, and Satan also came among them.
The Lord said to Satan, "Where have you come from?" Satan

answered the Lord, "From going to and fro on the earth, and from walking up and down on it." The Lord said to Satan, "Have you considered my servant Job? There is no one like him on the earth, a blameless and upright man who fears God and turns away from evil." Then Satan answered the Lord, "Does Job fear God for nothing? Have you not put a fence around him and his house and all that he has, on every side? You have blessed the work of his hands, and his possessions have increased in the land. But stretch out your hand now, and touch all that he has, and he will curse you to your face." The Lord said to Satan, "Very well, all that he has is in your power; only do not stretch out your hand against him!" So Satan went out from the presence of the Lord.

Job 1:6-12

Disaster Strikes

THE SCENE SHIFTS BACK TO EARTH. Job receives four messengers, each telling a dramatic tale of devastation affecting Job's family. The reports are of robbers, lightning or tornado, from which the messenger alone escaped alive. All of Job's children and possessions are gone. Job is like many a millionaire when the stock market crashed.

Job's response must have been disappointing to Satan. In a culture which does not believe in repressing feelings, he does what is appropriate: he tears his robe, shaves his head and falls prostrate on the ground, all expressions of grief. After all this, he responds out of a deep traditional piety that puts the present disaster in a wider perspective. He remembers that all that he has received came as a gift from God and would be lost at death. The present crisis is simply anticipating by a few years what everyone knew would happen eventually.

The story appears to be over. Actually, it is only beginning. Read about the first trials of Job.

One day when his sons and daughters were eating and drinking wine in the eldest brother's house, a messenger came to Job and said, "The oxen were plowing and the donkeys were feeding beside them, and the Sabeans fell on them and carried them off, and killed the servants with the edge of the sword; I alone have escaped to tell you." While he was still speaking, another came and said, "The fire of God fell from heaven and burned up the sheep and the servants, and consumed them; I alone have escaped to tell you." While he was still speaking, another came and said, "The Chaldeans formed three columns, made a raid on the camels and carried them off, and killed the servants with the edge of the sword; I alone have escaped to tell you." While he was still speaking, another came and said, "Your sons and daughters were eating and drinking wine in their eldest brother's house, and suddenly a great wind came across the desert, struck the four corners of the house, and it fell on the young people, and they are dead; I alone have escaped to tell you."

Then Job arose, tore his robe, shaved his head, and fell on the ground and worshiped. He said, "Naked I came from my mother's womb, and naked shall I return there; the Lord gave, and the Lord has taken away; blessed be the name of the Lord."

In all this Job did not sin or charge God with wrongdoing.

Job 1:13-22

Satan Persists

THE SCENE SHIFTS BACK to the heavenly court. God is aglow with pride over Job's virtuous behavior, but Satan will not give up. He claims that possessions are not that important to human beings. To find out what they are really like, one needs to touch their bodies. Anyone who has ever been sick or disabled can see the force of the argument. God, determined to show Job's goodness, allows Satan to afflict Job with a horrible illness.

Back on earth, Job's illness, perhaps leprosy, makes him so miserable he sits on an ash heap and uses a piece of broken pottery, the trash of the ancient world, to scratch his itching skin. He makes no attempt to hide his misery, but bares it for the whole world to see.

Job's wife is still with him. We would like to know more about her, but this is Job's story, and she appears only here, and only to raise a question. At this point Job silences her with a pious saying, but later he will spend many chapters struggling with the same question.

Read about the continuing trials of Job.

One day the heavenly beings came to present themselves before the Lord, and Satan also came among them to present himself before the Lord. The Lord said to Satan, "Where have you come from?" Satan answered the Lord, "From going to and fro on the earth, and from walking up and down on it." The Lord said to Satan, "Have you considered my servant Job? There is no one like him on the earth, a blameless and upright man who fears God and turns away from evil. He still persists in his integrity, although you incited me against him, to destroy him for no reason." Then Satan answered the Lord, "Skin for skin! All that people have they will give to save their lives. But stretch out your hand now and touch his bone and his flesh, and he will curse you to your face." The Lord said to Satan, "Very well, he is in your power; only spare his life."

So Satan went out from the presence of the Lord, and inflicted loathsome sores on Job from the sole of his foot to the crown of his head. Job took a potsherd with which to scrape himself, and sat among the ashes.

Then his wife said to him, "Do you still persist in your integrity? Curse God, and die." But he said to her, "You speak as any foolish woman would speak. Shall we receive the good at the hand of God, and not receive the bad?" In all this Job did not sin with his lips.

Job 2:1-10

Job's Friends

NOW THREE CHARACTERS APPEAR who will be crucial for the next 40 chapters. These are three old friends of Job, wise pagans like himself, who have come from distant lands to comfort him in his misery.

The main part of the book is now beginning. This part, in total contrast to the introductory chapters, is about the long, untidy process by which Job struggles with his pain and is transformed by it. The three friends will represent Job as he was before his ordeal. His long debate with them will be a struggle with his old self, a struggle he needs to carry on until the experience of God transforms him into a new person.

The friends are wise enough not to begin by speaking. They are shocked to see Job, who is so disfigured by his illness that they do not even recognize him. I remember going to visit a friend with cancer, and not recognizing her when I came into her room. The friends show their sympathy in the rituals that their culture provided: weeping, tearing their clothes and throwing dust on their heads. They then sit in silence for seven days with Job. It is the best thing they do in the whole book.

Meet Job's friends.

> Now when Job's three friends heard of all these troubles that had come upon him, each of them set out from his home—Eliphaz the Temanite, Bildad the Shuhite, and Zophar the Naamathite. They met together to go and console and comfort him. When they saw him from a distance, they did not recognize him, and they raised their voices and wept aloud; they tore their robes and threw dust in the air upon their heads. They sat with him on the ground seven days and seven nights, and no one spoke a word to him, for they saw that his suffering was very great.
>
> *Job 2:11-13*

Job's Lament

THE FIRST PART OF THE BOOK OF JOB, written in prose, is probably an old folktale, a simple story of a man too good to be true, his sufferings and his eventual reward. These two chapters are the source of the expression "the patience of Job." The biblical author has inserted into this old tale a long and complex poetic dialogue in which Job and his friends process the perennial question, "Why do bad things happen to good people?" Simple answers may seem satisfactory at first, but as suffering continues, one has to go deeper. Job's patience becomes less noticeable.

The beginning of the process is to express the pain in words. It is a great mistake to try to repress the expression of pain with pious sayings. Now Job tells us how he really feels, and it is not theologically tidy. In fact, his feelings are much like those for which he scolded his wife. The old answers are not enough, and he has to confront them with his new experience. Only through this process can growth come. The old answers may prove in the end to be true, but the process by which they move from the head to the heart is an agonizing one.

After seven days of silence, the smoldering volcano of Job's feelings erupts. His grief takes the form of cursing the hour when he was conceived, the day when he was born, and his survival as an infant. It is a poetic way of proclaiming that life is not a gift but a burden. It is a profound denial of the goodness of God, the giver of life. We are reminded of the lamentations of Tobit and Sarah in which they, too, expressed the feeling that death would be better than the kind of life they had to live. These are legitimate feelings and need to be expressed in prayer. We are mistaken if we imagine that God cannot cope with our real feelings.

We may not have been in a situation like Job's, but we know there are dying people in Calcutta and starving children in Africa whose situation is really as drastic as his. We can think of them as well as of ourselves as we read Job's words.

Read a few verses of Job's lament.

After this Job opened his mouth and cursed the day of his birth. Job said:

259

"Let the day perish in which I was born,
    and the night that said,
    'A man-child is conceived.'...
"Why did I not die at birth,
    come forth from the womb and expire?...
"O that my vexation were weighed,
    and all my calamity laid in the balances!
For then it would be heavier than the sand of
    the sea;
    therefore my words have been rash.
For the arrows of the Almighty are in me;
    my spirit drinks their poison;
    the terrors of God are arrayed against me....
"O that I might have my request,
    and that God would grant my desire;
    that it would please God to crush me,
        that he would let loose his hand and cut
        me off!..."

Job 3:1-3, 11; 6:2-4, 8-9

Life After Death?

GOD DID NOT REVEAL THE EXISTENCE OF LIFE AFTER DEATH until long
after the Book of Job was written. So Job, like many people
today, had to struggle with his problem without the help of
believing in an afterlife where he would receive justice.

As he searches in every direction for a way to make sense
of his predicament, he almost glimpses the possibility of life
after death, but quickly dismisses it as a foolish dream.
Looking at a tree that has been cut down, he notices that
there is life in the roots that enables it to put out new shoots.
He wishes the same might be true for humans, but everything
he has been taught tells him it is impossible. The Christian,
looking at the same tree at which Job looked, comes up with
a conclusion quite opposite to Job's.

Read Job's sad denial of life after death.

"For there is hope for a tree,
    if it is cut down, that it will sprout again,

and that its shoots will not cease.
Though its root grows old in the earth,
    and its stump dies in the ground,
yet at the scent of water it will bud
    and put forth branches like a young plant.
But mortals die, and are laid low;
    humans expire, and where are they?
As waters fail from a lake,
    and a river wastes away and dries up,
so mortals lie down and do not rise again...."

Job 14:7-12

The Friends' Responses

AFTER JOB'S OPENING LAMENT there are three cycles of speeches by the friends, with responses from Job to each. Some of the most beautiful poetry in the Bible is found in these long poetic discourses, but it is not easy to follow the thread of thought. It is much like the inner process we often go through when struggling with some problem. The human mind seems to go round and round a difficult issue, repeating familiar ideas with new variations, coming gradually toward a new idea, then backing nervously away, only to return later on.

In the few verses given here, Zophar is quoting the common wisdom that claimed that the prosperity of the wicked is short lived, thus implying that Job's current troubles prove that he is wicked. Zophar seems almost to exult in the downfall of the great Job. Eliphaz is even more direct in his accusations against Job. He lists the sins Job must have committed to deserve such punishment. They are the sins of which the poor in every age accuse the rich. We know that in Job's case they are false accusations.

It is important to remember that the friends are only expressing the general belief of the ancient world, which is also found in many other places in the Bible. This wisdom says that the good prosper and the wicked suffer punishment. If this is the teaching of your theology, it is logical to believe that anyone who suffers must have sinned. This theology was held by some even in New Testament times. When Jesus and the disciples pass a blind man, the disciples ask Jesus whether the man is being punished for his own sins or those of his parents (John 9:2). Jesus firmly denies either, yet there are Christians who assume that those who suffer are somehow responsible for their suffering. If people are poor, they must be lazy. If your prayers for healing are not answered, you must lack faith. So the friends are not unique; they represent a universal human type, and the ideas they express are ideas Job himself might have expressed before his experience of multiple loss.

Listen to Job's friends.

Then Zophar the Naamathite answered:

"...Do you not know this from of old,
    ever since mortals were placed on earth,
that the exulting of the wicked is short,
    and the joy of the godless is but for a moment?
Even though they mount up high as the heavens,
    and their head reaches to the clouds,
they will perish forever like their own dung;
    those who have seen them will say, 'Where
    are they?'..."

Then Eliphaz the Temanite answered:
"...Is not your wickedness great?
    There is no end to your iniquities.
For you have exacted pledges from your family for no reason,
    and stripped the naked of their clothing.
You have given no water to the weary to drink,
    and you have withheld bread from the hungry.
The powerful possess the land,
    and the favored live in it.
You have sent widows away empty-handed,
    and the arms of the orphans you have crushed.

Therefore snares are around you,
and sudden terror overwhelms you...."

Job 20:1, 4-7; 22:1, 5-10

Questions for Reflection

1. Is there a saintly person not of your faith from whom you can learn as the Israelites learned from Job?

2. Give an example of someone in modern times who was as highly respected as Job and lost everything.

3. What should Job's wife have said to him when he hit bottom?

4. What do you think of the three friends sitting on the ground with Job in silence for seven days? What would you want from your friends if disaster struck you?

—•—

5. Do you know anyone who has felt as Job did when he cursed the day of his birth?

6. Give a modern example of someone who, like Zophar and Eliphaz, presumes that a person who suffers a terrible tragedy is somehow to blame for it.

7. In hard times, what difference does belief in life after death make to you?

Suggestions for Further Reading
Job 1—15

Prayer

Lord our God! The incomprehensible One!

Job cried out to you in pain. We, also, cry out to you in the mystery of pain and distress that come into our lives.

Will the Lord reject us forever and nevermore be favorable toward us? Is he withholding compassion and pity from us?

We know that we cannot make it on our own, and, like Job, we cry out to the Lord. Hear us, O Lord!

Lord, grant that we may be disciples of Christ and follow in his footsteps, sharing in the pain, suffering and joy that are part of the mystery of life. Amen.

Joan Lennon, 62, Littleton, Colorado

CHAPTER TWENTY-THREE

The Agony of Job

Job Responds to His Friends

THE BOOK OF JOB IS UNIQUE among the books of the Bible. Though it is told in the form of a story, the author is not interested primarily in the story as such. It is a vehicle for a discussion of an issue that has always distressed humankind: Why do bad things happen to good people?

In the first chapters, Job is so perfect he is almost an abstraction. The things that happen to him are so terrible they are hard to imagine. All this sets the scene for a discussion of suffering. The author sees that suffering is a universal fact of life, but does not understand the reason for it. He is not satisfied with the simplistic theories that claim that suffering is punishment for sin. He puts the many conflicting ideas that come to him on the lips of Job and three friends who arrive to comfort Job after he has lost his children, possessions and health.

Job is sitting on an ash heap scratching with pieces of broken pottery at the sores that cover his whole body. The friends have repeated to Job the common explanations of suffering they have all been taught. They are not helpful because Job knows these things, too. In fact, the friends' words are making matters worse because those who are not suffering are in a singularly poor position to advise those who are. This is probably why support groups are so popular today. It is more possible to listen to someone who is going through the same ordeal as your own.

There may be a deeper reason why Job reacts so negatively to his friends. They are what he used to be; they are saying what he used to say. But the experience of multiple losses is changing Job. It is not yet clear what it is changing him into, but he senses that he must not go back.

Read a little of Job's response to his friends' advice.

Then Job answered:

> "I have heard many such things;
> miserable comforters are you all.
> Have windy words no limit?
>> Or what provokes you that you keep on talking?
> I also could talk as you do,
>> if you were in my place;
> I could join words together against you,
>> and shake my head at you...."

Job 16:1-4

God as Enemy

CARDINAL CARLO MARIA MARTINI SAYS, "It is likely that if the Book of Job were presented today to a doctrinal or theological commission for a decision whether or not to accept it as part of the canon, the decision would be not to admit it lest it cause uneasiness and prove disturbing" *(Perseverance in Trials: Reflections on Job*, page 52).

One can see the cardinal's point as Job claims belligerently that God has treated him unjustly. God has turned against Job with violence, like a great army besieging a pathetic little tent. When Job calls for justice, there is no one to help him. God, who is expected to protect the innocent, is the criminal attacking him. There is no hope.

These are wild statements no theologian could support. Yet they are true expressions of the way Job feels. The patient Job of the first chapters has given way to a tormented and angry Job. Perhaps that pious acceptance of his ills in the first chapters was too quick. The challenge of suffering is long and drawn out, and calls for perseverance through months and years, as all of us know who have seen loved ones dying by inches. After two chapters of proper pious response, Job spends thirty-five chapters in bitter complaints. Only after all that will we see where his anguish is leading him.

Job's friends tried to give him the wisdom from the past, but he had to struggle through his pain to come to a new wisdom.

It may be helpful to imagine these desperate words on the lips of really desperate people in parts of today's world where hunger, AIDS or oppressive governments make life a hell.

Read Job's feelings about God.

"...If indeed you magnify yourselves against me,
    and make my humiliation an argument against me,
know then that God has put me in the wrong,
    and closed his net around me.
Even when I cry out, 'Violence!' I am not answered;
    I call aloud, but there is no justice.
He has walled up my way so that I cannot pass,
    and he has set darkness upon my paths.
He has stripped my glory from me,
    and taken the crown from my head.
He breaks me down on every side, and I am gone,
    he has uprooted my hope like a tree.
He has kindled his wrath against me,
    and counts me as his adversary.
His troops come on together;
    they have thrown up siegeworks against me,
    and encamp around my tent...."

Job 19:5-12

God as Redeemer

FEELING ABANDONED BY GOD, Job turns again to his friends, pleading for pity. Then, realizing that they too are against him, he cries out in longing to have his story written down so that at least future generations will recognize how unjustly he has suffered. We, the readers, smile to see how abundantly this wish has been fulfilled through the ages, but for Job it is only another fantasy, as it would be on the lips of one of the suffering millions in today's poor nations.

In his agony, Job's mind searches everywhere for a glimmer of hope, as people with terminal illnesses today will sometimes jump frantically from one unlikely cure to another.

The next idea that comes to him seizes him with special force. He remembers the *go'el*, the kinsman/redeemer, who is supposed to be there for any person in time of disaster. In the culture of his time, this would be the closest male relative, but Job's relatives are conspicuously absent during his trials. It seems that under the image of redeemer, he has come back to trust in God. Through all his confusion and darkness, his faith bursts forth in the immortal words, "I know that my Redeemer lives...and in my flesh I shall see God" (Job 19:25, 26).

This passage, which has been made so famous by Handel's *Messiah*, is actually a difficult one in the original Hebrew, and can be translated in various ways. We already know from the passage about the tree that is cut down that Job does not believe in life after death. Yet his yearning here is pointing in that direction, and we Christians, who do believe in the resurrection of the dead, easily pray it as a proclamation of our faith. Job probably spoke more truly than he realized. It can happen to us, too, that we have glimpses of truths that we never firmly grasp.

Listen again to Job's struggles.

> "...Have pity on me, have pity on me, O you
>   my friends,
>   for the hand of God has touched me!
> Why do you, like God, pursue me,
>   never satisfied with my flesh?
> O that my words were written down!
>   O that they were inscribed in a book!
> O that with an iron pen and with lead
>   they were engraved on a rock forever!
> For I know that my Redeemer lives,
>   and that at the last he will stand upon the earth;
> and after my skin has been thus destroyed,
>   then in my flesh I shall see God,
> whom I shall see on my side,
>   and my eyes shall behold, and not another...."

Job 19:21-27

The Wicked Flourish

THE THEOLOGY HELD BY JOB AND HIS FRIENDS taught that God
rewards the good and punishes the wicked in this life, which
was the only life they knew. It is a teaching we find often in the
Bible. But his own experience has opened Job's eyes to the
reality that the wicked tend to do very well for themselves.

Job has lived virtuously, yet all his children have been
killed. His suffering is intensified by the thought of wicked
people he knows who live to a contented old age, surrounded by children as happy as Job's once were.

Job's theology is collapsing under the weight of his experience and observation of others' experience. Nothing makes
sense to him.

Listen as Job struggles with the injustice of life.

> "Why do the wicked live on,
>   reach old age, and grow mighty in power?
> Their children are established in their presence,
>   and their offspring before their eyes.
> Their houses are safe from fear,
>   and no rod of God is upon them....
> They send out their little ones like a flock,
>   and their children dance around.
> They sing to the tambourine and the lyre,
>   and rejoice to the sound of the pipe...."
>
> *Job 21:7-9; 11-12*

Yearning for God

IN SPITE OF EVERYTHING, Job continues to struggle with his relationship with God. He is like most of us when in the throes
of suffering that is more than we can handle: He does not
make much sense. He believes that God's heavy hand has
caused all his woes. Yet he yearns to see God, to lay his case
before God. It is like calling on a criminal to pass judgment
on himself.

269

Job has been a civic leader often called upon to act as judge at the city gates. He has always tried to be fair and to have special concern for the weak and helpless. So he imagines God as such a just judge. Yet his anguish is unabated because he has no access to this just judge.

Job makes us think of Jesus dying on the cross. According to Mark, his last words were, "My God, my God, why have you abandoned me?" (Mark 15:34). It is a great mystery that even people like Jesus and Job can feel abandoned by God. It is also a comfort to us all at the times when we feel that way. As God was really not far from Jesus or from Job, God is not far from us, despite our feelings to the contrary.

Listen to Job's anguished longing for his God.

Then Job answered:

"Today also my complaint is bitter;
his hand is heavy despite my groaning.
Oh, that I knew where I might find him,
    that I might come even to his dwelling!
I would lay my case before him,
    and fill my mouth with arguments.
I would learn what he would answer me,
    and understand what he would say to me.
Would he contend with me in the greatness
    of his power?
    No; but he would give heed to me.
There an upright person could reason with him,
    and I should be acquitted forever by my judge.
If I go forward, he is not there;
    or backward, I cannot perceive him;
on the left he hides, and I cannot behold him;
    I turn to the right, but I cannot see him...."

Job 23:1-9

Reminiscences

THE TONE OF JOB'S LAMENTS CHANGES in Chapter 29 to one of nostalgia. As he sits on his ash heap, he remembers the times when his life was very different. Sometimes we can learn more about a parent or loved one than we ever knew by listening to the memories that come back amidst their most painful times. This is the case with Job. This chapter gives us our most vivid picture of the kind of life Job lived before God allowed Satan to test him.

Job looks back nostalgically to the time when he felt very close to God. He remembers with pathos his children, now all dead. He remembers the respect with which he was greeted at the city gates, the place where business, political and judicial activity centered. He was not only respected by the powerful of his world, but also loved by the poor, the disabled and immigrants, who were liable to be taken advantage of by established citizens. He was known for both justice and charity. It is the memory of his good works that seems to give him the greatest pleasure, though it also gives pain by contrast with his present situation where he can help no one and he himself badly needs the kindly help he once gave to others.

Perhaps the saddest of his memories is that of his plans for his old age. Health and success in life made him expect the best. He imagined he would live as long as the phoenix, a legendary bird which renewed its life every hundred years. And he expected all of this to be in his nest, the home where he was surrounded by love, respect and wealth. It is a common expectation for those whose lives are blessed with success.

It is kind of a relief for Job, in the midst of pain and turmoil, to remember better days. All the pouring out of bitterness and the railing against the injustice of his fate have led him to a very different mood from that in which he started out, cursing the day he was born.

Perhaps Job here is a model for the review of life that is such an important part of our later years. We need to revisit the experiences of our earlier stages in order to find the meaning in our life as a whole. The review should lead us, as it will Job, into a new kind of wisdom.

Listen as Job reviews his life.

Job again took up his discourse and said:

> "Oh, that I were as in the months of old,
>> as in the days when God watched over me;
> when his lamp shone over my head,
>> and by his light I walked through darkness;
> when I was in my prime,
>> when the friendship of God was upon my tent;
> when the Almighty was still with me,
>> when my children were around me;
> when my steps were washed with milk,
>> and the rock poured out for me streams of oil!
> When I went out to the gate of the city,
>> when I took my seat in the square,
> the young men saw me and withdrew,
>> and the aged rose up and stood;
> the nobles refrained from talking,
>> and laid their hands on their mouths;
> the voices of princes were hushed,
>> and their tongues stuck to the roof of
>> their mouths.
> When the ear heard, it commended me,
>> and when the eye saw, it approved;
> because I delivered the poor who cried,
>> and the orphan who had no helper.
> The blessing of the wretched came upon me,
>> and I caused the widow's heart to sing for joy.
> I put on righteousness, and it clothed me;
>> my justice was like a robe and a turban.
> I was eyes to the blind,
>> and feet to the lame.
> I was a father to the needy,
>> and I championed the cause of the stranger.
> I broke the fangs of the unrighteous,
>> and made them drop their prey from their teeth.
> Then I thought, 'I shall die in my nest,
>> and I shall multiply my days like the
>> phoenix....'"

Job 29:1-18

Elihu

DURING THESE THIRTY CHAPTERS OF LAMENT from Job and advice from his friends, a young man whom we have not noticed has been standing by, Elihu. This was a culture in which wisdom was expected to come only with age, so no one expected the young man to enter the discussion.

This young man was not comfortable with the silence which custom imposed on him. Now he bursts forth with an abundance of words which more than compensate for his long, enforced silence.

The author introduces Elihu by telling us four times in four verses that he was angry. He was angry with Job because Job insisted on his innocence. He was angry at the three friends because they had not succeeded in refuting Job's arguments. He is the prototypical angry young man.

Elihu describes himself well as like a wineskin which is about to burst from the gases emitted by fermenting wine. His compulsion to set everyone straight is arrogant and presumptuous. He is almost a bit of comic relief between the long dialogue and the climax which is coming.

Job has demanded a hearing for his case before God. Elihu picks up on this idea and proclaims himself God's defender. He makes a fool of himself and provides a warning for those of us who are inclined to appoint ourselves defenders of God.

Elihu goes on for six chapters, repeating many of the arguments already made by the friends. In spite of his bravado, he has nothing much to add to the discussion. Job does not even bother to answer him, and in the conclusion which begins in the next chapter he is simply ignored.

Meet the angry young man, Elihu.

So these three men ceased to answer Job, because he was righteous in his own eyes. Then Elihu son of Barachel the Buzite, of the family of Ram, became angry. He was angry at Job because he justified himself rather than God; he was angry also at Job's three friends because they had found no answer, though they had declared Job to be in the wrong. Now Elihu had waited to speak to Job, because they were older than he. But when Elihu saw that there was no answer in the mouths of these three men, he became angry.

Elihu son of Barachel the Buzite answered:

"I am young in years,
    and you are aged;
therefore I was timid and afraid
    to declare my opinion to you.
I said, 'Let days speak,
    and many years teach wisdom.'
But truly it is the spirit in a mortal,
    the breath of the Almighty,
        that makes for understanding.
It is not the old that are wise,
    nor the aged that understand what is right.
Therefore I say, 'Listen to me;
    let me also declare my opinion.'
"See, I waited for your words,
    I listened for your wise sayings,
while you searched out what to say.
    I gave you my attention,
but there was in fact no one that confuted Job,
    no one among you that answered his words....
"They are dismayed, they answer no more;
    they have not a word to say.
And am I to wait, because they do not speak,
    because they stand there, and answer no more?
I also will give my answer;
    I also will declare my opinion.
For I am full of words;
    the spirit within me constrains me.
My heart is indeed like wine that has no vent;
    like new wineskins, it is ready to burst.
I must speak, so that I may find relief;
    I must open my lips and answer...."

Job 32:1-20

Questions for Reflection

1. Give examples of people who behave like Job's friends.

2. Do you think Job's complaint that God has treated him unjustly is valid?

3. When have you felt, as Job did after listening to his friends, that both God and people were against you?

—⁓—

4. Do you agree with Job that the wicked prosper?

5. Do you think remembering how good things used to be, as Job does, is helpful in hard times? In ordinary times, what value do you see in reflecting back on the experiences of your life?

6. Do you know a young person as eager to make an impression as Elihu was?

7. When have you felt, as Elihu did, that you would burst if you did not speak your mind?

Suggestions for Further Reading
Job 16 — 37

Prayer

Thank you, Lord Jesus, that by your death and resurrection you brought us eternal life.

We need your help to see the difference between adding to others' pain and comforting them. Help us not to burden others with our pain and suffering, and let us not add to the pain of others who look to us for help. Amen.

Pat Haggerty, 71, Denver, Colorado

CHAPTER TWENTY-FOUR

God Speaks to Job

God's Questions

IN THE PREVIOUS CHAPTERS, Job has been vehemently complaining that God has treated him unjustly and demanding that God appear as defendant in a court trial in which Job is sure he can prove God unjust. Job laments that of course God will not appear.

In chapter 38, God does appear, and things turn out very differently from what Job imagined. Job has been demanding that God answer many questions. Now the tables are turned; God is demanding that Job answer questions. They are strange questions indeed. "Where were you when I laid the foundations of the earth?" (Job 38:4). "Have you commanded the morning...and caused the dawn to know its place?" (Job 38:12).

The scene is not a courtroom, but a schoolroom. God, the great teacher, is using the Socratic method: asking questions whose purpose is not to get answers but to expand Job's mental horizons. Job's problem is that his world of thought is too small, too centered on his own limited experience. God the teacher is trying to force Job to think more broadly, and by doing so to recognize his own limitations.

What is even more important than God's questions is the fact that at last Job *sees* God face to face. The content of the whole conversation is less important than this experience of God's presence. Job's perception of his situation is going to be different simply because he has met God personally. This also happens in human relationships. A person with strong views on divorce or homosexuality or alcoholism often changes those views dramatically when a family member or close friend is connected with one of these words. Things are going to look different to Job now that he knows God personally.

God appears in a whirlwind. It is common in the Old Testament for God to appear in a setting of some violent upheaval of nature. In the Book of Job, the nature imagery is particularly apt because most of God's speech will use nature as vehicle for the message.

God bypasses all of Job's questions and demands. Job had been asking the wrong questions, expecting a kind of intellectual clarity that is not possible for humans. God's questions aim to make Job aware of the limits of human knowledge. When Job sees that he does not know even basic things about the world around him, he will begin to realize how presumptuous he was to demand to understand God's governing of the world.

God continues with a description of the creation of the world quite different from the familiar accounts in Genesis. Creation here is described as like the building of a house, with God, the master builder, laying a secure foundation and carefully measuring every wall.

This is followed by yet another description of creation. To understand this one, we have to remember that the Israelites were not seafarers, nor did they visit Mediterranean beaches for recreation. They knew about the Mediterranean, but they did not live in the port towns. What they heard of the sea was that it was terrible and great monsters lived in it. It represented chaos. One of the great works of the Creator was to separate the sea from the dry land. If God had not set limits to the sea, it would have covered the whole earth.

Here this terrifying chaos-monster is described whimsically as a newborn baby. God acts as midwife, dressing the infant and setting safe limits for it. What a vivid picture of the power and gentleness of God! This reminds us of God's conversation with Satan at the beginning of the book. God allowed Satan to reduce Job's well-ordered life to chaos, but God set limits to the chaos. In the same way, God allows the chaotic sea to be part of creation, but sets limits to it. God has ultimate control but, like a wise ruler, allows much freedom to each part of creation.

Listen as God questions Job.

> Then the Lord answered Job out of the whirlwind:
>
> "Who is this that darkens counsel by words
>   without knowledge?
> Gird up your loins like a man,
>   I will question you, and you shall declare to me.
> Where were you when I laid the foundation of
>   the earth?
>   Tell me, if you have understanding.
> Who determined its measurements—surely
>   you know!
>   Or who stretched the line upon it?
> On what were its bases sunk,
>   or who laid its cornerstone
> when the morning stars sang together
>   and all the heavenly beings shouted for joy?
> Or who shut in the sea with doors
>   when it burst out from the womb?—
> when I made the clouds its garment,
>   and thick darkness its swaddling band,
> and prescribed bounds for it,
>   and set bars and doors, and said,
> 'Thus far shall you come, and no farther,
>   and here shall your proud waves be stopped'?..."

Job 38:1-11

The Mysteries of Animal Life

GOD'S QUESTIONS NOW TURN TO THE ANIMAL WORLD. Probably the most beautiful nature poetry in Scripture occurs here, showing God's care for the wild creatures, about which humans know so little. From these creatures we can get a sense of the scope of God's concern. So far, Job and the friends have spoken as if humans were the center of the universe and the measure of all things. God the teacher is using the animal world to open Job's mind to a larger world.

The popularity of nature programs on TV and whale-watching expeditions show how fascinated we are by the lives of wild animals, usually so hidden from us and so totally out of our control. The poet who wrote these chapters clearly felt the same fascination.

God is present when the mountain goats and the deer give birth. It is also God who lets the wild ass go free and provides a dwelling place for it so that it can laugh at its domesticated relatives, tied down to serve humans. God seems to get a special delight from these creatures who have escaped the human compulsion to dominate them.

The only domesticated animal described is the horse. For the Israelites, the horse was not a work or pleasure animal; it was used almost exclusively for war. An ordinary person in time of peace would know of horses only from stories of battle. The horse is described as a high-spirited charger, terrifying to humans. God gives the war horse its strength; Job does not.

The questions then move to the world of the wild bird. "Is it by your wisdom that the hawk soars...and the eagle mounts up?" (Job 39:26, 27). Job has a lesson to learn from all these creatures.

Read God's words about the animals.

> "Do you know when the mountain goats
>   give birth?
>   Do you observe the calving of the deer?
> Can you number the months that they fulfill,
>   and do you know the time when they give birth,
> when they crouch to give birth to their offspring,
>   and are delivered of their young?
> Their young ones become strong, they grow
>   up in the open;
>   they go forth, and do not return to them.
> Who has let the wild ass go free?
>   Who has loosed the bonds of the swift ass,
> to which I have given the steppe for its home,
>   the salt land for its dwelling place?
> It scorns the tumult of the city;
>   it does not hear the shouts of the driver.

It ranges the mountains as its pasture,
and it searches after every green thing....
"Do you give the horse its might?
Do you clothe its neck with mane?
Do you make it leap like the locust?
Its majestic snorting is terrible.
It paws violently, exults mightily;
it goes out to meet the weapons.
It laughs at fear, and is not dismayed;
it does not turn back from the sword.
Upon it rattle the quiver,
the flashing spear, and the javelin.
With fierceness and rage it swallows the ground;
it cannot stand still at the sound of the trumpet.
When the trumpet sounds, it says 'Aha!'
From a distance it smells the battle,
the thunder of the captains, and the shouting.
Is it by your wisdom that the hawk soars,
and spreads its wings toward the south?
Is it at your command that the eagle mounts up
and makes its nest on high?
It lives on the rock and makes its home
in the fastness of the rocky crag...."

Job 39:1-8; 19-28

Job Is Silenced

AFTER THIS LONG DISCOURSE ON THE WONDERS of creation, the great teacher gently insists that the student Job respond. Job, as we can well understand, is overwhelmed. He puts his hand over his mouth to acknowledge that he has no response to God's arguments.

God is not satisfied with having squashed the opposition but is looking for something more. With magnificent irony, God will continue to question Job, who has imagined that he was on a level that entitled him to challenge God to legal combat.

God is putting Job in his place and showing him the inadequacy of his theology. Job's theology said that God's

281

justice required punishing the wicked and rewarding the just. In view of Job's sufferings, either he must be guilty or God must be unjust. Job was right to cling to his innocence, but he was wrong in deducing that God was unjust.

Job's image of God was of a powerful patriarch who by sheer power controlled every detail of creation, overriding the wills of creatures. This was almost a puppeteer God. Perhaps this was the only kind of authority figure Job had known. But the real God is more like a human leader who loves to see others free and does not force everything into a preset pattern. So not everything in life can be explained by a simple theory such as the just are rewarded and the wicked are punished.

Job's error, like that of so many of us, was in demanding that God play by Job's rules. The reality is that Job, like us, is simply not competent to pass judgment on God's way of governing the universe.

Read about Job's conversation with God.

> And the LORD said to Job:
>
> > "Shall a faultfinder contend with the Almighty?
> > Anyone who argues with God must respond."
>
> Then Job answered the Lord:
> "See, I am of small account; what shall I
> > answer you?
> > I lay my hand on my mouth...."
>
> *Job 40:1-4*

Behemoth

THE DIVINE TEACHER IS ENDLESSLY PATIENT. God let Job pour out his pain at great length. God will not scrimp words in response to Job. Two chapters of magnificent nature poetry have not fully convinced Job, so God pulls out of the divine teaching materials a teaching aid no student can resist, Behemoth, the hippopotamus!

I do not know if the poet had ever actually seen a hippopotamus, or merely heard tales that combined that animal with a mythical beast. He produces a picture of a magnificent animal, larger than life, perhaps a personification of the chaos every human fears. If he intended Behemoth to represent chaos, we find the same message here as in God's dealings with Satan and with the sea. God does not eliminate these frightening realities from creation, but keeps them in a set place, under control.

This is a being frightening to humans, but not to other animals who, knowing its vegetarian habits, play freely around the huge creature. God, far from being frightened, seems to delight in the ugly monster.

Meet Behemoth, the hippopotamus.

> "Look at Behemoth,
>> which I made just as I made you;
>> it eats grass like an ox.
> Its strength is in its loins,
>> and its power in the muscles of its belly.
> It makes its tail stiff like a cedar;
>> the sinews of its thighs are knit together.
> Its bones are tubes of bronze,
>> its limbs like bars of iron.
> It is the first of the great acts of God—
>> only its Maker can approach it with the sword.
> For the mountains yield food for it
>> where all the wild animals play.
> Under the lotus plants it lies,
>> in the covert of the reeds and in the marsh.
> The lotus trees cover it for shade;
>> the willows of the wadi surround it.
> Even if the river is turbulent, it is not frightened;
>> it is confident though Jordan rushes against
>> its mouth.
> Can one take it with hooks
>> or pierce its nose with a snare?..."

Job 40:15-24

—᠆᠆᠆᠆᠆—

Job's Final Word

GOD'S LONG, PATIENT EDUCATIONAL PROCESS is working. We now come to the climax of the Book of Job, where Job acknowledges that he has spoken of what he did not understand. This realization began when he put his hand on his mouth in silence, but a deeper level of assent now enables him to articulate his changed view.

It is not so much an argument that has changed Job's position as a new experience of God. The friends had expressed some of God's arguments, though not in such fine poetry. But conviction came not from a message to the head but from one to the heart, the experience of God. Like so many of us, Job did not think his way into an answer, but lived his way into an answer.

Job ends up, apparently, just where the friends wanted him, repenting in dust and ashes. But "repent" here has nothing to do with sin. It might be better translated "change my mind." We often find it harder to admit that some long held conviction is wrong than that we have committed some sin. The conviction seems more part of us.

Read Job's final word.

> Then Job answered the LORD:
>
> "I know that you can do all things,
> and that no purpose of yours can be thwarted.
> 'Who is this that hides counsel without
>   knowledge?'...
> Therefore I have uttered what I did not
> understand,
>   things too wonderful for me, which I did
>   not know."...
> I had heard of you by the hearing of the ear,
>   but now my eye sees you;

> therefore I despise myself,
>   and repent in dust and ashes."

Job 42:1-3; 5-6

The Friends Again

AFTER ADDRESSING JOB IN MAGNIFICENT POETRY, God turns to the friends in rather curt prose, saying clearly that Job has spoken well and they badly. This is surprising, since Job has just repented of what he said. God praises Job because he spoke truly about his own experience even though his theology was incorrect. The friends are condemned because they refused to acknowledge Job's experience, which threatened their inadequate theology.

The friends are a warning to pastoral counselors and those who try to support the sick and suffering by giving reasons for the trials. Their explanations are not completely wrong, but they are wrong in trying to force their explanations of the mystery of suffering on another person. Scripture and tradition offer many ways of coping with pain. None is perfect, but some are helpful to one person, others to another. The sufferer must seek what fits the situation. Others can only support that process, not control it.

The story now takes a surprising twist. God will forgive the friends their folly only if Job prays for them. Job is still on his ash heap. His fortunes have not yet been restored. Yet his prayers alone are powerful enough to win forgiveness for his friends. What a challenge to Job after all he has suffered from these men! He has become a new person through his experience of God, and praying for enemies is part of what is now expected of him. He is a reminder to us of the special power of the prayer of those who suffer.

God is clearly happy with the outcome of the testing of Job. God four times calls Job "my servant," the same title used in the heavenly scene that started the story. God is prouder than ever of Job.

Read God's word to the friends.

> After the LORD had spoken these words to Job, the LORD said to Eliphaz the Temanite: "My wrath is kindled against you and against your two friends; for you have not spoken of me what is right, as my servant Job has. Now therefore take seven bulls and seven rams, and go to my servant Job, and offer up for yourselves a burnt offering; and my servant Job shall pray for you, for I will accept his prayer not to deal with you according to your folly; for you have not spoken of me what is right, as my servant Job has done." So Eliphaz the Temanite and Bildad the Shuhite and Zophar the Naamathite went and did what the LORD had told them; and the LORD accepted Job's prayer.

Job 42:7-9

Conclusion

AFTER JOB HAS PRAYED FOR THE FRIENDS, God restores everything to him—seven more sons, three more daughters, double all his other riches, and one hundred and forty more years in which to enjoy them! Job's story began in his mature years, and the pattern was one of loss upon loss, and a life of inner struggle trying to cope with the losses. The ending brings totally unexpected grace.

We often read stories of young heroes like Tobias who pass through ordeals and come to a happy ending. But I have known older adults who struggled for years with the losses of aging, but arrived, purified as Job was, at a long final period of peace and joy. While on the surface the story is a fantasy, it speaks of a real human experience.

Job had a great deal more time to reminisce. He must have reflected on the long dark night during which everything seemed lost, even his relationship with God. For a while, excess of pain had caused him to deny meaning in life. Like many today, when his old understanding of life collapsed, he thrashed around a long time trying to integrate his old theology with his new experience. In retrospect, he could see that it was only through the breakdown of his old religious ideas that God had transformed and enlightened him.

But he did not spend all his time in reminiscence. He had ten new children to occupy his attention. He must have taken a special delight in the three beautiful daughters, because, in contrast to the culture of the times, they were given an inheritance like their brothers', and their names are mentioned, though their brothers' are not.

The famous prints of William Blake on the Book of Job show a rather stiff abundance of good things in Job's life at the beginning, but, after many pictures of Job's sufferings and of the whirlwind, show an exhilaration and joyousness in the final scene far beyond the beginning.

Read the happy ending of the story of Job.

> And the LORD restored the fortunes of Job when he had prayed for his friends; and the LORD gave Job twice as much as he had before. Then there came to him all his brothers and sisters and all who had known him before, and they ate bread with him in his house; they showed him sympathy and comforted him for all the evil that the LORD had brought upon him; and each of them gave him a piece of money and a gold ring. The LORD blessed the latter days of Job more than his beginning; and he had fourteen thousand sheep, six thousand camels, a thousand yoke of oxen, and a thousand donkeys. He also had seven sons and three daughters. He named the first Jemimah, the second Keziah, and the third Keren-happuch. In all the land there were no women so beautiful as Job's daughters; and their father gave them an inheritance along with their brothers. After this Job lived one hundred and forty years, and saw his children, and his children's children, four generations. And Job died, old and full of days.
>
> *Job 42:10-17*

Questions for Reflection

1. Why do you think God chose to answer Job out of a whirlwind?

2. God uses nature to teach Job. How have you learned about God from nature?

3. If the natural world is one way in which God speaks to us, what ought we as Christians do to show respect for the natural world?

4. If you were writing the Book of Job, what animal would you choose as an example of God's marvelous creation?

—∾∾—

5. God called Job to pray for the three friends. For whom do you think God is calling you to pray?

6. Job's experience of God speaking from the whirlwind changed Job's view drastically. What experience has changed your view drastically?

7. Do you think the happy ending increases or decreases the value of the Book of Job?

Suggestions for Further Reading
Job 38—42

Prayer

O Lord, our God of wisdom and of patience, may we, your children, be open to your earth's classroom of knowledge. May we, like Job, mature in this knowledge, realizing that you are the creator of *all.*

Our suffering is only a minute challenge of fidelity. Lord, instruct us to be more humble and forgiving; to be open to the vast amount of education yet to come. Assist us to see your judgment and mercy in our suffering; cause us to accept once again our new life which you have given us by unending wisdom and patience. Instill in our hearts not only a willingness, but a determination to be faithful to you, God, to ourselves and to others. May we acknowledge your supremacy over our lives and be always forgiving to others so that we may be worthy members of your family.

We give you praise and thanksgiving for your blessings and the challenges of life. In your most holy and precious name we pray. Amen.

Donna M. Zacher, 53, Denver, Colorado

Suggestions for Further Reading

Books on the Bible

The Catholic Study Bible. Oxford University Press, 1990. The New American Bible with a Reading Guide for each book of the Bible.

Brown, Raymond E. *Reading the Gospels With the Church From Christmas through Easter.* St. Anthony Messenger Press, 1996. An introduction to a Catholic approach to Scripture, with reflections on the Gospels for the principal parts of the Church year. This is very simply put by an outstanding scholar.

The Denver Catholic Biblical School Program. Paulist Press. This is a serious four-volume study program covering every book of the Bible. It can be used in a group or alone, but requires substantial study time in either case.

Rohr, Richard, and Joseph Martos. *The Great Themes of Scripture: Old Testament* and *The Great Themes of Scripture: New Testament.* St. Anthony Messenger Press, 1987 and 1988. Classic introduction to the spiritual themes of the Bible.

Weber, Gerard P. and Robert Miller. *Breaking Open the Gospel of Matthew; Breaking Open the Gospel of Mark; Breaking Open the Gospel of Luke; Breaking Open the Gospel of John.* St. Anthony Messenger Press, 1998, 1994, 1990, 1995. These four volumes include discussion questions and are ideal for personal reflection on the Gospels or small-group discussion.

Books on the Spirituality of Aging

Fischer, Kathleen. *Winter Grace: Spirituality and Aging.* Upper Room Books, 1998. This classic was previously published by Paulist Press. If you are going to read only one book on the subject, read this.

Leder, Drew. *Spiritual Passages: Embracing Life's Sacred Journey.* Jeremy P. Tarcher/Putnam, 1997. This study of insights on aging from the great religious traditions of the world shows how much wisdom we all have to share.

Schachter-Shalomi, Zalman and Ronald S. Miller. *From Age-ing to Sage-ing: A Profound New Vision of Growing Older.* Warner Books, 1995. New and exciting insights on the challenge of eldering today. A ground-breaking book by a rabbi, suitable for Christians and Jews.

Tournier, Paul. *Learn to Grow Old.* Westminster/John Knox Press, 1972. This classic was originally published under the title "Learning to Grow Old." Deep practical wisdom from a Christian psychotherapist.

Subscription

Scripture From Scratch. An excellent four-page article each month, with suggestions for praying with Scripture, living the Scriptures, discussing the Scriptures. A painless way to continue to grow in your understanding of the Bible. Bulk rates are available; very suitable for group discussion. Published by St. Anthony Messenger Press.